Ralph Storer is an Englishman now living ~~and~~ working in Edinburgh, and totally converted to the Scottish Highlands! He currently lectures in computer studies at Napier College, but his mountaineering, walking and caving interests have been pursued to a high level of expertise. He is a well respected walker, writing frequently for mountaineering magazines.

100 BEST ROUTES ON SCOTTISH MOUNTAINS

Ralph Storer

WARNER BOOKS

A WARNER BOOK

First published in Great Britain by David & Charles 1987

Published by Sphere Books Ltd 1990
Reprinted 1990, 1991 (twice)
Reprinted by Warner Books 1992 (twice)

Printed in England by Clays Ltd, St Ives plc

ISBN 0 7515 0300 2

Warner
A Division of
Little, Brown and Company (UK) Ltd
165 Great Dover Street, London SE1 4YA

TO MY MOTHER AND FATHER
WHO ALSO LOVED THE MOUNTAINS

Contents

THE WESTERN HIGHLANDS

THE NORTHERN HIGHLANDS

THE CAIRNGORMS

THE ISLANDS

Introduction

The mountain walker in Scotland is spoilt for choice. In the Highlands there are 277 Munros (separate mountains over 3,000 ft/914 m), a further 239 Tops over 3,000 ft/914 m, 221 Corbetts (separate mountains over 2,500 ft/762 m) and an uncounted number of hills over 2,000 ft/600 m—enough to last a lifetime and more. This book contains a personal choice of the 100 best walking and scrambling routes in this mountain playground; from short afternoon rambles to day-long expeditions; from roadside summits to remote mountain sanctuaries; from gentle paths to kneebreakingly-steep hillsides; from hands-in-pockets-whistle-while-you-walk strolls to thrilling scrambles.

Any book of this nature begs the question 'What constitutes *best*?', for beauty lies in the eye of the beholder. Some walkers may prefer the vast windswept plateaux of the Cairngorms in winter, others the sharp peaks of Skye on a long summer gloaming. For the purposes of this book the 100 routes chosen are the ones I have found to be most enjoyable, would most want to repeat and would most recommend to newcomers, given the following constraints:

1. A route must ascend a mountain over 2,000 ft/600 m. The fascination with Munros has for too long led to the neglect of some superb smaller mountains; of the 100 routes in this book 22 are on mountains under 3,000 ft/914 m.

2. A route must contain no rock climbing (ie on which a rope would normally be required). This does not exclude some scrambles on which nervous walkers would never venture even with a safety net.

3. A route must start from a place that can be reached by motorised transport (plus a ferry if necessary), and end at the same place. There are too many guidebooks whose routes begin in the middle of nowhere and end somewhere else in the middle of nowhere.

4. A route must be able to be completed by walkers of reasonable fitness in a single day. This does not exclude some routes whose completion may be impracticable in daylight in winter.

5. The overall list of routes must represent a cross-section of all Highland regions. One hundred routes in Skye, no matter how attractive, would be unsuitable for a guidebook to the best of Scotland.

The list that appears in this book has already provoked many hours of

11

Routes

The 100 routes are divided into six regions in accordance with accepted geographical divisions and common usage:

heated debate among colleagues, and may it continue to do so among readers. Yet the amount of agreement is surprising, so much so that I would venture to say that most experienced Scottish walkers would agree with the vast majority of mountains chosen (if not with the exact routes). May the following pages while away many an hour in planning, anticipation and reflection.

Sketch Maps

Sketch maps show each route's major features but are not intended for use on the hill. They are hand-drawn to the same orientation and mostly the same scale as Ordnance Survey 1:50,000 maps. Some routes are too long to be shown at 1:50,000 scale so, routes 26, 42, 49, 65, 76, 79, 81, 82, 83 and 84 are shown at half scale (ie 1:100,000). The 1:50,000 scale is suitable for most Scottish mountain walking, but the OS 1:25,000 Outdoor Leisure maps to the Cuillin and Torridon Hills and the High Tops of the Cairngorms are recommended.

Beside each sketch map is indicated the number of the OS 1:50,000 map on which the route appears and the grid reference of the route's starting point (eg route 67—OS: 19, GR: 114850). Some routes overlap two OS maps (eg route 60—OS: 19/25) and others appear on either of two maps (eg route 100—OS: 13 or 14).

The classification of mountains as Munros or Tops is based on the 1984 edition of Munro's Tables, incorporating Brown and Donaldson's revisions. Many walkers (including the author) regret any tampering with Sir Hugh Munro's list, but the 1984 edition is now the *de facto* arbiter of the Tables; may future editions revert to the original list. There are no clear criteria of what makes a mountain a Munro, a Top or neither, beyond the definition of a Munro as a separate mountain over 3,000 ft/ 914 m and a Top as a subsidiary summit over 3,000 ft/914 m.

Map Symbols:

▲	Munro
△	Top (in Munro's Tables)
●	Other summit over 3,000 ft/914 m
○	Summit over 2,500 ft/762 m
■	Summit over 2,000 ft/600 m
□	Summit under 2,000 ft/600 m
≈	Road (public or accessible to public)
- - - -	Route
....	Other paths/cart tracks/forest roads etc
++++++++	Railway
+++●+++	Station
■	Building

13

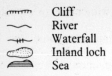

~~~~~   Cliff
~~~   River
~~~   Waterfall
   Inland loch
   Sea

Measurements

Route distances are specified in both miles (to the nearest half-mile) and kilometres (to the nearest kilometre); short distances in the text are specified in metres (an approximate imperial measurement is yards).

Mountain heights are specified in metres and feet. Metric heights have been obtained from OS 2nd Series 1:50,000 maps. Equivalent heights in feet have been obtained by multiplying the height in metres by 3.28 (rounded down); these may not tally with heights on old OS one-inch-to-the-mile maps, which were obtained from an earlier survey.

The total amount of ascent for the whole route is specified to the nearest 10 m (50 ft). This is an approximation based on OS map heights and contours, which are shown at 10 m intervals and are in many instances omitted because of cartographic complexity.

Route times (to the nearest half-hour) are based on the time it should take a person of reasonable fitness to complete the route in good summer conditions. They take into account length of route, amount of ascent, technical difficulty, type of terrain and short stoppages, but do not make allowances for long stoppages and adverse weather. They are roughly standard between routes for comparison purposes and can be adjusted where necessary by a factor appropriate to the individual.

In winter routes will normally take much longer, depending on conditions. A pre-dawn start is often necessary and some of the longer routes are best tackled as two-day expeditions, camping en route or making use of a bothy (useful bothies are noted in the text).

Mountain names

Most Highland names are Gaelic in origin and the ability to pronounce and understand Gaelic names can add much to the pleasure of walking in Scotland. To this end each route is provided with a guide to the pronunciation and meaning of all mountain names and (where space allows) most other physical features named in the text.

The production of such a guide is made difficult by a number of factors. OS maps, despite their otherwise excellence, appear to have been named by Sassenachs, for they abound in Gaelic misspellings, misunderstandings, misuses and misplacements. With some misgivings the OS spelling has been retained for purposes of standardisation, except in the case of Rum, whose OS 'h' (Rhum) was added out of Victorian prudishness and should no longer be tolerated. Names annotated with an asterisk do not appear on OS maps.

Some OS misspellings make pronunciation impossible. Stob Diamh (route 13), for instance, is a misspelling of either Damh (stag) or Daimh (the genitive of Damh); any attempt at a direct pronunciation would be ludicrous. In addition some names have become anglicised to such an extent that it would be pedantic to enforce a purist pronunciation on a non-Gaelic speaker; eg the correct pronunciation of Ben is something akin to Pane, with a soft *n* as in the first syllable of *onion*. Moreover, pronunciation differs, sometimes markedly, throughout the Highlands and Islands.

Despite these problems the phonetic guide given in this book should enable a good attempt at a pronunciation that would be intelligible to a Gaelic speaker. In connection with the guide the following points should be noted:

Y before a vowel pronounced as in *you*

OW pronounced as in *town*

CH pronounced as in Scottish *loch* or German *noch*

TCH pronounced as *ch* in *church*

OE pronounced as in French *oeuf* or the *u* in *turn*

Toponymy (the study of place name meanings) is complicated by OS misspellings, changes in spelling and word usage over the centuries, words with more than one meaning and unknown origin of names (Gaelic, Norse, Irish etc). For example, consider the origin of the names Ben Nevis (see route 24) and Cuillin (see route 95). Meanings given in this book are the most commonly accepted, even if disputed; when the meaning is doubtful it is annotated with *poss* (ie possible); some names are too obscure to be given any meaning.

Assessment and Seasonal Notes
The assessment is intended as a brief overview of the nature of the route during summer conditions. Under snow, Scottish mountains become much more serious propositions. Paths are obliterated, grassy hillsides become treacherous slopes, ridges become corniced, stone shoots become snow gullies, walking becomes more difficult and tiring, terrain becomes featureless in adverse weather, white-outs and spindrift reduce visibility to zero.

Winter conditions vary from British to Alpine to Arctic from November through to April, though sometimes earlier and later and varying from locality to locality—it is possible to encounter hard snow and ice even in October and May. No one should venture into the Scottish mountains in winter without adequate clothing, an ice-axe and experience (or the company of an experienced person). In hard winter conditions crampons will also be required. The number of accidents, many of them fatal, which have occurred in Scotland over the last few winters, should leave no one in doubt as to the need for caution.

Many of the routes in this book become roped mountaineering expeditions in winter and should not be attempted by walkers; such routes are indicated by a Seasonal Note of 'A major mountaineering expedition'. The feasibility of other routes in winter depends on grade and conditions; in general the higher the summer grade the higher the winter grade. Note, however, that even a normally straightforward winter route like the ascent of Ben Wyvis (route 66) may be subject to avalanche or hard ice, and there has been at least one fatality there.

The Scottish mountains in winter have an Alpine attraction and reward the prepared walker with unforgettable experiences but, if in doubt, stay off the hill. Bearing these points in mind, seasonal notes for each route indicate any specific places where particular difficulties are normally likely to be encountered, thus enabling the walker to be better prepared. Where an easier escape route presents itself this also is noted.

Grid

An at-a-glance grid for each route indicates the route's overall difficulty, where difficulty consists not only of grade (ie technical difficulty) but also type of terrain, difficulty of navigation in adverse weather and seriousness (ie difficulty of escape in case of curtailment of route for one reason or another). These factors vary over the duration of the route and should not be taken as absolute, but they provide a useful general guide and enable comparisons to be made between routes. Each category is graded 1 (easiest) to 5 (hardest).

Grade (ie technical difficulty):
    1 Mostly not too steep
    2 Appreciable steep sections
    3 Some handwork required
    4 Easy scramble
    5 Hard scramble

Terrain (irrespective of grade):
    1 Excellent, often on paths
    2 Good
    3 Reasonable

4 Rough
5 Tough

Navigation (ie difficulty of navigation with a compass in adverse weather):
1 Straightforward
2 Reasonably straightforward
3 Appreciable accuracy required
4 Hard
5 Extremely hard

Seriousness (ie difficulty of escape, based on criteria of length and restricted line of escape):
1 Straightforward escape
2 Reasonably straightforward escape
3 Appreciable seriousness
4 Serious
5 Very serious

It will be apparent from this grading system that not all the routes in this book are for novices. Many accidents in the Scottish hills are caused by walkers attempting routes outside their capabilities, and the grading system is intended to enable a more realistic route appraisal. On the more technically difficult routes easier alternatives are noted in the text or in the seasonal notes where applicable.

Text
Any access restrictions are noted in the text, apart from stalking restrictions. Whatever one's ethical stance on deer stalking, the fact remains that most of the Scottish Highlands is privately owned, and non-compliance with stalking restrictions is likely to be counter-productive and lead to the imposition of further restrictions. Further, if estate revenue is lost because of interference with stalking activities, the alternative may be afforestation or worse, which would increase access problems.

The stalking season for stags runs normally from mid-August to mid-October, but varies from locality to locality. Access notices dot the roadside and information on stalking activities can be obtained from estate offices and head stalkers. For a complete list of access restrictions and estate addresses see *Access for Mountaineers and Hillwalkers* (published jointly by the Mountaineering Council of Scotland and the Scottish Landowners' Federation). Land shown on the OS map as belonging to public bodies such as the National Trust for Scotland and the Nature Conservancy Council is normally not subject to access restrictions.

Note that river directions, left bank and right bank, in accordance with common usage, refer to the direction when facing downstream.

Acknowledgements

A book of this nature could not have been written without many years of experience on Scottish mountains and without the companionship of those who have accompanied me on the hill during those years. It would take too long and perhaps be inappropriate to thank all the companions who have climbed with me and aided, wittingly or unwittingly, in the writing of this book, for climbing forges bonds that need never be stated and that can never be broken. I am grateful to all of them for the hours spent in their company.

There are others without whose specific help this book could not have reached fruition. Donald MacDonald's advice on Gaelic was invaluable, although the phonetic interpretation of Gaelic pronunciation is my sole responsibility. Hazel Crompton provided the fine map lettering. Mandy Millar's literary expertise helped correct many a grammatical error. Jo Crompton and Wendy Gibson provided transport and support during a hectic climbing season. I thank them all.

100 BEST ROUTES
ON SCOTTISH
MOUNTAINS

Route 1: **THE COBBLER**

OS MAP: 56
GR: 295054
Distance: 5½ miles (9 km)
Ascent: 900 m (2,950 ft)
Time: 6 hr

	1	2	3	4	5
Grade					●
Terrain			●		
Navigation		●			
Seriousness		●			

Assessment: a route of sharp scrambles and surprises on a remarkable Southern Highland peak.

Seasonal notes: in winter conditions, the slopes to the summit ridge require care, and the ascent of the summit rocks of the south and central peaks, beautiful when iced, may be impracticable.

The Cobbler (884 m, 2,900 ft)

Allt Sugach
   Owlt *Sooc*ach, Cheerful Stream
Allt a' Bhalachain
   Owlt a *Val*achin, Stream of the Boy (also known as the Buttermilk Burn)

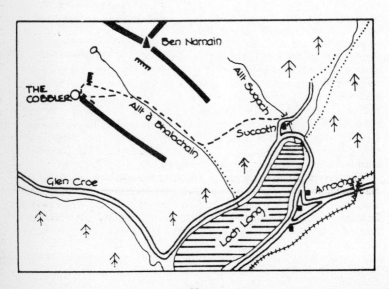

'There must be something magnetic about The Cobbler. Many times I have gone to Arrochar alone, meaning to climb Ben Vane, the Brack or one of the other tops, but early afternoon would find me nearing the summit of The Cobbler.'

BEN HUMBLE (*On Scottish Hills*, 1946)

The great rock peak of The Cobbler, looking like a cobbler bent over his last, dominates the approach to Arrochar from Loch Lomond. It is the most striking mountain in the Southern Highlands, its folds of mica schist erupting into three bold and rocky tops that have long been the haunt of Glasgow walkers and climbers. It is by far the most spectacular of all the Arrochar Alps yet, because it fails to reach the magic 3,000 ft (914 m) mark, it is often ignored in favour of neighbouring Munros of less character. In such ways does the Munro bagger miss the best of the Highlands, for the ascent of the three tops involves some exhilarating scrambling, and the main summit has a surprising sting in the tail.

Begin at Succoth on the south side of the bridge over the Allt Sugach, taking the path that climbs up the hillside and around the forest to reach the Allt a' Bhalachain. Beyond a dam, the path follows the left bank of the burn to the Narnain Boulders, two large rocks that have yielded climbs and a howff. A few hundred metres further on the path crosses the burn and heads up into the corrie beneath the three peaks. The centre peak is the highest; the south (left-hand) peak is known as The Cobbler's Wife, the north (right-hand) peak is known as The Cobbler's Last. The north peak has impressive overhangs, which look daunting, but it is the easiest of the three peaks to ascend.

Climb to the bealach between the centre and north peaks, making a detour, if so inclined, to search for The Cobbler Cave at the foot of the obvious Ramshead Ridge beneath the north peak. Once onto the plateau, turn right to follow the broad ridge to the north summit rocks. The view over the edge is not recommended to those who suffer from vertigo. Return to the bealach and walk up to the main peak. The summit block is a short, exposed, scramble that has turned back many a walker. It involves crawling through a rock window ('Argyll's Eyeglass') and climbing a couple of airy sloping ledges to the flat roof. In legend every Campbell chief had to prove his manhood by gaining the top.

The traverse to the south peak is a good scramble, which some walkers may prefer to omit; remember that you must reverse the ascent of the south peak in order to regain the bealach between it and the centre peak. Descend from this bealach to regain the corrie and the path back to Succoth.

Route 2: **BEN LOMOND**

OS MAP: 56
GR: 360986
Distance: 7 miles (11 km)
Ascent: 1,010 m (3,300 ft)
Time: 5½ hr

	1	2	3	4	5
Grade	●				
Terrain	●				
Navigation		●			
Seriousness	●				

Assessment: a long and easy ascent above probably the most beautiful of Scottish lochs.

Seasonal notes: most of the route remains easy under normal snow conditions, but the final section around the rim of the north-east corrie may require care.

Ben Lomond (974 m, 3,195 ft)
   Beacon Mountain (derived from the practice of lighting fires on the summit to summon local men to arms)

Ptarmigan (931 m, 2,398 ft)
   Note for masochists: the Ben Lomond race record (up and down) stands at just over 1 hr.

'What would the world be, once bereft
Of wet and wilderness?
Let them be left,
O let them be left, wildness and wet;
Long live the weeds and wilderness yet.'

GERARD MANLEY HOPKINS (*Inversnaid*)

Ben Lomond, the most southerly Munro in Scotland, stands sentinel over that most beautiful of lochs, Loch Lomond. It is easily accessible from the lowlands and its ascent from the lochside is probably the most popular in the Highlands, apart from Ben Nevis. An early traveller wrote of the ascent that 'it is very irksome and in some places so steep that we were obliged to crawl on hands and knees', but be assured that today there is a well trodden path all the way to the top.

   Begin at the car park just beyond Rowardennan Hotel, at the end of the minor road along the eastern shore of Loch Lomond. The path goes through the trees and climbs grass slopes to reach the gentle south ridge, which it follows to the foot of the summit pyramid. Here the route steepens, the path zigzagging up stony slopes and around the rim of the fine north-east corrie to the summit.

   To vary the return route, descend westwards via the subsidiary top of Ptarmigan for more intimate views of the island-studded loch. Continue

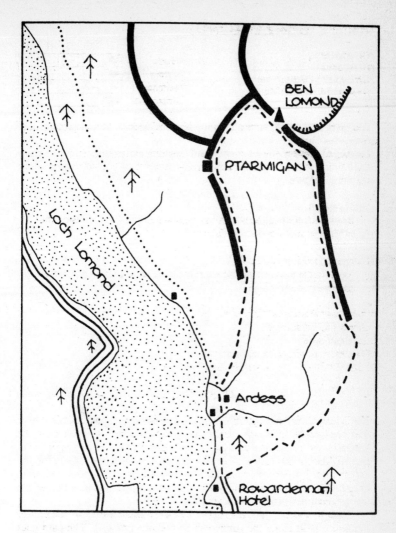

down Ptarmigan's south ridge to reach the private road at Ardess and so
return to your starting point.

Ben Lomond is almost constantly under threat from HEP schemes;
farm roads scar the hillsides, and there are plans to 'improve' amenities
for visitors; may it resist these threats and continue to inspire future
generations as it did Gerard Manley Hopkins (see above).

Route 3: **BEN VENUE**

OS MAP: 57
GR: 503064
Distance: 5½ miles (9 km)
Ascent: 670 m (2,200 ft)
Time: 4½ hr

	1	2	3	4	5
Grade	●				
Terrain	●				
Navigation	●				
Seriousness	●				

Assessment: a short and pleasant route amidst rugged and picturesque scenery on the edge of the Highlands.
Seasonal notes: at its most colourful in spring and autumn.

Ben Venue (729 m, 2,391 ft)
    Ben Ven*ew*, Mountain of the Caves (poss)
Gleann Riabhach
    Glen R*ee*-ach, Brindled Glen
Bealach nam Bo
    *Byal*ach nam *Boe*, Pass of the Cattle
Corrie na Urisgean
    Corra na *Oo*rish-can, Goblin's Cave

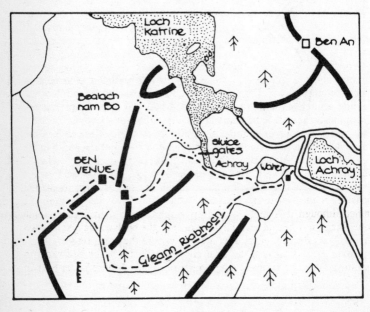

'High on the south, huge Benvenue
Down on the lake in masses threw
Crags, knolls and mounds, confusedly hurled,
The fragments of an earlier world;'

SIR WALTER SCOTT (*The Lady of the Lake*, 1810)

Despite its modest height Ben Venue merits inclusion in this book on account of its rugged mountain character. Its craggy wooded slopes enclose the island-studded eastern reaches of Loch Katrine in The Trossachs and give the engaging impression of a miniature Highland scene. It was here that Sir Walter Scott, Coleridge and the Wordsworths found inspiration, and today The Trossachs has a thriving tourist industry feeding on the legends of *The Lady of the Lake* and *Rob Roy*.

The view of Ben Venue across Loch Achray to the east is one of the most photographed in The Trossachs, and the most pleasant ascent is also from this side, providing one of the shortest and easiest routes in this book. Begin at Loch Achray Hotel on the west side of the loch. Behind the hotel a forestry road signposted 'Forest Walks' leads off the trees. This eventually becomes a path leading up Gleann Riabhach, tunnelling through the trees on a carpet of pine needles. The route through the maze of forestry tracks is waymarked by blue posts and easily followed. Once out of the trees, the path turns right into the craggy upper glen, bypassing a waterfall and climbing to a large cairn on Ben Venue's south-west ridge. Turn right for the summit, a grand viewpoint from where the main peaks of the Southern Highlands can be picked out one by one across Loch Katrine.

To descend, cross to the lower eastern top of Ben Venue's twin summits and continue to the wide grass gully just beyond it. A steep path goes down the gully on the right of the river, the islands of Loch Katrine nestling attractively beneath your feet. Should you lose this path lower down, much fun will be had among the tree-girt crags above the lochside. The path joins another running along the south shore of the loch at the sluice gates. This path comes from the Bealach nam Bo, the rocky defile on Ben Venue's north ridge, whose name derives from the days when it was used by Rob Roy to smuggle cattle from the lowlands back to his home in Glen Gyle. Just below the bealach, among the crags above the lochside, is the Corrie na Urisgean, which may give the mountain its name, although it is more of a deep amphitheatre than a cave; some amusement may be had searching for it. *NB*: the bealach may be reached directly from the summit by a pathless descent of the north ridge.

From the sluice gates, the Bealach nam Bo path heads eastwards to become a forestry road leading pleasantly beside the Achray Water back to your starting point.

Route 4: **BEN LUI**

OS MAP: 50
GR: 343291
Distance: 11¹/₂ miles (18 km)
Ascent: 950 m (3,100 ft)
Time: 7¹/₂ hr

	1	2	3	4	5
Grade			●		
Terrain				●	
Navigation			●		
Seriousness			●		

Assessment: a classic skyline circuit on one of Scotland's most shapely mountains.
Seasonal notes: the steep bounding ribs of Coire Gaothaich may be impracticable under snow or when iced, but the scenery is magnificent.

Ben Lui (1,130 m, 3,707 ft)
    in Gaelic Beinn Laoigh (Loe-y), Calf Mountain, or poss from Gaelic
    Luaidhe (*Loo*-iya), Lead, after the Tyndrum lead mines
Coire Gaothaich*
    Corra *Gœ*-ich, Corrie of Wind

Scottish winter climbing was pioneered in Coire Gaothaich in the 1890s by the newly formed Scottish Mountaineering Club, at a time when Tyndrum's two railway stations made it a major mountaineering centre. Central gully (Grade 1) was first climbed in 1891.

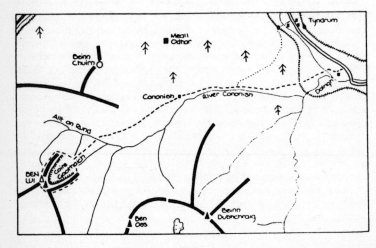

'Light cloud was low, but suddenly, just before we reached Cononish farm, it was blown clear from the Ben, and there soared the mountain, all dazzling white snow and blue shadow, with the azure sky behind, a glorious and unforgettable vision.'

W. KERSLEY HOLMES on his favourite mountain (*Tramping Scottish Hills*, 1946)

Ben Lui is regarded by many as the most beautiful mountain in Scotland. Its twin summits frame the perfect horseshoe of Coire Gaothaich, whose central gully is one of the great classics of Scottish winter mountaineering. Under snow, Lui looks truly Alpine, especially when viewed up the glen of the River Cononish from the A82 between Crianlarich and Tyndrum, and it is from here that the circuit of the corrie is best approached.

Begin at Dalrigh, 1 mile (2 km) south-east of Tyndrum, and take the Land Rover track past Cononish Farm to its end near the Allt an Rund; it may be possible to obtain permission to drive to Cononish, but the track is extremely rough. Cross the river and climb up steep grass slopes beside a tumbling burn into Coire Gaothaich. In the bowl of the corrie in springtime you may have to pick your way across avalanche debris from the huge cornice that forms above the central gully.

 Climb out to the south (left-hand) rim of the corrie and scramble up the steepening rib to the summit. Care is required as the ground is steep and loose, but it is always possible to traverse left to the easier south-east ridge. The short summit ridge slung between the two tops is a grand place from which to admire the extensive view and the architecture of the corrie. To complete the circuit, walk round the corrie edge to the north-west top and descend the northern rim.

Route 5: **THE GLEN FALLOCH GROUP**

OS MAP: 50 or 56
GR: 352219
Distance: 10½ miles (17 km)
Ascent: 1,250 m (4,100 ft)
Time: 8 hr

	1	2	3	4	5
Grade		●			
Terrain				●	
Navigation					●
Seriousness	●				

Assessment: a grassy ridge walk over complex and fascinating terrain.
Seasonal notes: a fine, if lengthy, winter's tramp.

An Caisteal (995 m, 3,264 ft)
  An *Cash*-tyal, The Castle
Beinn a' Chroin (946 m, 3,103 ft)
  Ben a *Chraw*-in, Mountain of Danger (poss)
Beinn Chabhair (933 m, 3,060 ft)
  Ben *Chav*ir, Antler Mountain
Sron Gharbh (708 m, 2,322 ft)
  Srawn *Gharra*v, Rough Nose
Stob Creag an Fhithich (c685 m, c2,250 ft)
  Stop Craik an *Ee*-ich, Peak of the Raven's Crag

In the heart of the Southern Highlands south of Crianlarich lie a group of
popular mountains that rise directly from the roadside. They are characterised by long twisting ridges and broad bealachs, mainly grassy but
studded with rock outcrops, and they make good, high, tramping country.
This book recommends three routes in the area (routes 5–7), beginning
with the traverse of the trio of peaks above Glen Falloch, which includes

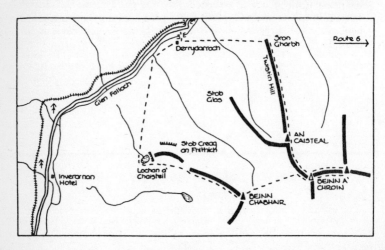

some of the most interesting physical features in the Southern Highlands.

Begin at Derrydarroch in Glen Falloch, 3 miles (5 km) south-west of Crianlarich on the A82. Cross the River Falloch (bridge) and make directly across the rough moor for the summit of Sron Gharbh at the end of Twistin Hill. Twistin Hill is the undulating grassy ridge that forms the attractive skyline ahead and provides the best approach to An Caisteal, the first of the three peaks. Near the summit of An Caisteal the ridge steepens and displays some curious features; on the left, a number of small caves burrow into the hillside and a large cleft almost cuts the ridge in two. Beyond lies the castellated knoll that probably gives the mountain its name, and then easier slopes lead to the flat summit.

Descend the grassy south-east ridge, and follow a path winding down among outcrops to the bealach below Beinn a'Chroin, the second of the trio. Thread your way up Beinn a'Chroin's steep craggy west face to the west top, then follow the summit ridge eastwards across a dip to the higher east top. Return to the bealach and descend the grassy gully on the south side for about 50 m (150 ft), until a traverse can be made below outcrops across the undulating hillside to the lochan at the foot of the north-east ridge of Beinn Chabhair, the third of the three peaks. A stiff 300 m (1,000 ft) pull on steep grass among outcrops is required to gain the summit.

The north-west ridge leading back down to Glen Falloch is the most interesting of the day. Quite narrow near the top, it soon broadens and requires the negotiation of some steep drops. Further down, the terrain becomes extraordinarily complex, and at times it seems difficult to make any progress at all in the labyrinth of grassy knolls that obstruct the way. If possible, steer left of Stob Creag an Fhithich and reach the delightful hidden spot of Lochan a' Chaisteil in a crag-girt hollow; the crags fall straight into the water and give the fanciful appearance of a castle. From here aim northwards to join the path along the River Falloch back to Derrydarroch.

Route 6: **CRUACH ARDRAIN**

OS MAP: 50/51
GR: 392249
Distance: 7 miles (11 km)
Ascent: 1,010 m (3,300 ft)
Time: 5½ hr

	1	2	3	4	5
Grade		●			
Terrain		●			
Navigation		●			
Seriousness		●			

Assessment: a pleasant skyline walk around an extensive corrie, which includes an interesting traverse of the highest peak.

Seasonal notes: the descent from Cruach Ardrain towards Stob Garbh is steep and difficult in winter; it can be turned by a descent into the south-east corrie, but care is required in finding a line back to the bealach below Stob Garbh.

Cruach Ardrain (1,046 m, 3,431 ft)
    Cru-ach *Ard*ran, High Mound
Grey Height (685 m, 2,247 ft)
Meall Dhamh (814 m, 2,670 ft)
    Myowl Ghaff, Stag Hill
Stob Garbh (960 m, 3,149 ft)
    Stop *Garr*av, Rough Peak
Stob Coire Bhuidhe (855 m, 2,805 ft)
    Stop Corra *Voo*-ya, Peak of the Yellow Corrie
Creag na h-Iolaire
    Craik na *Hyill*era, Eagle's Crag

The fine wedge-shaped peak of Cruach Ardrain rises prominently above the forests of Coire Ardrain, its north face cut by a conspicuous Y-shaped gully. The round of the undulating corrie skyline makes a very pleasant stravaig.

Begin at Inverardran 800 m east of Crianlarich. Go directly up the hillside behind the cottage to a stone wall, then turn right to follow a line of pylons for ½ mile (1 km), until a bridge over the railway south of Crianlarich is reached. From here, bear left on an obvious path that goes up a wide clearing to reach a broken fence, then follow the fence uphill to emerge onto the north-west shoulder of the Grey Height.

A broad, grassy ridge leads onwards to Meall Dhamh, becoming steeper and more interesting as it climbs onto the flat roof of Cruach Ardrain (in mist note that the summit lies beyond the first two cairns reached). Continuing around Coire Ardrain a steep rocky descent (requiring care) leads to a bealach and onto the rocky peak of Stob Garbh, beyond which there is a pleasant descent along the eastern arm of Coire Ardrain to Creag na h-Iolaire.

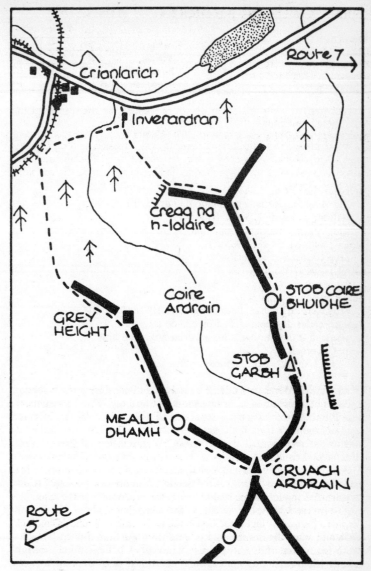

From here descend steep grass slopes on the right to an obvious fire-break leading down into the trees. At the end of the break a path tunnels through to the next descending break, which ends at a T-junction. Turn left, then keep right to reach the stone wall above Inverardran.

33

Route 7: **BEN MORE and STOB BINNEIN**

OS MAP: 51
GR: 457275
Distance: 10 miles (16 km)
Ascent: 1,500 m (4,900 ft)
Time: 8 hr

	1	2	3	4	5
Grade		●			
Terrain			●		
Navigation		●			
Seriousness	●				

Assessment: a long, mainly grassy ridge walk across the highest of the Crianlarich mountains.
Seasonal notes: care is required on the north-east ridge of Ben More in winter, but otherwise the route is a fine winter expedition with no especial difficulties.

Ben More (1,174 m, 3,851 ft)
 Big Mountain, usually pronounced as in English
Stob Binnein (1,165 m, 3,822 ft)
 usually pronounced and sometimes spelled Sto*bin*ian, Anvil Peak
Stob Creagach (904 m, 2,965 ft)
 Stop *Craik*ach, Craggy Peak
Meall na Dige (966 m, 3,169 ft)
 Myowl na *Jeek*a, Hill of the Dyke
Stob Coire an Lochain (1,066 m, 3,497 ft)
 Stop Corr an Lochan, Peak of the Corrie of the Lochan
Bealach-eadar-dha-beinn (c855 m, c2,800 ft)
 *Bya*lach-*aitar-gha*-ben, Pass between two mountains
Coire Chaorach★
 Corra *Chœr*ach, Corrie of Rowan Berries

Of all the Ben Mores in Scotland, Crianlarich's Ben More is the highest; it is the highest mountain in Britain south of Strathtay. With its neighbour, Stob Binnein, from which it is separated by a 300 m (1,000 ft) dip, it is a familiar landmark from both east and west; the unbroken lines of the two mountains' symmetrical cones convey an impression of great height, especially when dusted with snow. It was here that astronomers came in 1769 to observe the transit of Venus, and it was a winter ascent here that made Naismith, the 'father' of the Scottish Mountaineering Club, realise that Scottish mountains needed to be treated as seriously as the Alps.

 The normal route of ascent is the steep and tedious climb from Benmore Farm, but by far the best route is the circuit of Coire Chaorach, cradled between the eastern arms of Ben More and Stob Binnein. Begin at the bridge over the Allt Coire Chaorach, 5 miles (8 km) east of Crianlarich on the A85. Just east of the bridge a track leads into the forestry plantations. Keep right at all forks; the main track crosses the river after 15 min, turns left, then bears right away from the river up into Coire Chaorach.

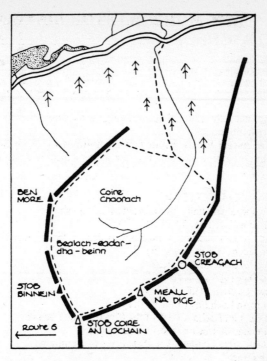

At the forest edge (note this point for later re-entry during the descent), cross the heathery corrie and climb the broad north-east ridge of Stob Creagach. Beyond the summit an undulating descent to a craggy knoll astride a bealach is followed by a steeper ascent to Meall na Dige, then after another long broad bealach the ridge sweeps up elegantly to Stob Coire an Lochain and the castellated summit of Stob Binnein. From Stob Binnein a uniform 300 m (1,000 ft) descent (a perfect ski run in winter) leads to the Bealach-eadar-dha-beinn, and a stiff reascent is required to gain Ben More's rocky summit. It is said that on a clear day you can see half of Scotland from here.

Descend via the interesting north-east ridge which is enlivened by one or two outcrops and steepenings, although there is no difficulty. The view before you encompasses the length of Loch Tay and, if it is late in the day, the sight of Ben More's monolithic shadow stealing across the moors can be mesmerising. Continue down the ridge until a fence is reached, then follow the fence right into Coire Chaorach to rejoin the ascent route at the forest edge. To be sure of finding the track through the forest, follow the fence onto the floor of the corrie, until you reach a gap where an old track doubles back to join the main track.

Route 8: **BEN VORLICH and STUC A' CHROIN**

OS MAP: 51/57
GR: 633233
Distance: 10½ miles (17 km)
Ascent: 1,310 m (4,300 ft)
Time: 8 hr

	1	2	3	4	5
Grade		●			
Terrain			●		
Navigation			●		
Seriousness		●			

Assessment: a popular circuit around the bold mountains of Lochearn-side.
Seasonal notes: the descent of the north-east buttress of Stùc a' Chroin may be awkward under snow, and care should be exercised on the initial descent from Ben Vorlich, where a slip on the convex slope has caused at least one fatality.

Ben Vorlich (985 m, 3,231 ft)
    Mountain of the Bay (poss)
Stùc a' Chroin (975 m, 3,198 ft)
    Stoochk a *Chraw*-in, Peak of Danger (poss)
Dubh Choirein
    Doo *Chorr*in, Black Corries
Coire Buidhe
    Corra *Boo*-ya, Yellow Corrie

The south side of Loch Earn is dominated by Ben Vorlich, an interesting X-shaped mountain whose south-west ridge abuts sharply against Stùc a'Chroin's north-east buttress to provide an entertaining traverse.

Begin at Ardvorlich House on the south Loch Earn road. Go through the east gate and take the cart track that heads up Glen Vorlich on the left bank of the river. One mile (1½ km) from the roadside, at a small burn, branch left on a grassy track that climbs to the head of the glen, an attractive, narrow defile hemmed in by cliffs. Go through the defile and continue down to the old shieling of Dubh Choirein, in a forlorn position at the foot of Ben Vorlich's south-east ridge.

Branch right on a path that climbs onto Stùc a' Chroin's south-east ridge, then turn right along the ridge to gain the summit. The descent of the north-east buttress towards Ben Vorlich requires care, especially in mist; the crest is a hard scramble, but a steep path (marked by a cairn) can be found to the left. The continuation across the Bealach an Dubh Choirein to Ben Vorlich is straightforward. Ben Vorlich's summit is a short ridge with a cairn at the south-east end and a trig point at the north-west end. Descend from the north-west end by a path that goes down the north-east ridge to Glen Vorlich.

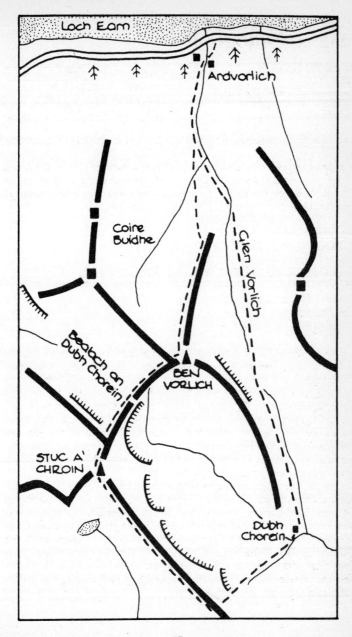

Route 9: **BEINN DORAIN and BEINN AN DÒTHAIDH**

OS MAP: 50
GR: 300395
Distance: 7¹/₂ miles (12 km)
Ascent: 1,270 m (4,150 ft)
Time: 6 hr

	1	2	3	4	5
Grade		●			
Terrain		●			
Navigation			●		
Seriousness		●			

Assessment: a straightforward ascent amidst fine scenery on the edge of Rannoch Moor.
Seasonal notes: the steep slopes to the bealach require care under snow.

Beinn Dorain (1,074 m, 3,523 ft)
    Ben *Doe*ran, Mountain of the Otter (from Gaelic dobhran) or
    Streamlet (from Gaelic dobhar)
Beinn an Dòthaidh (1,002 m, 3,287 ft)
    Ben an Daw-y, Mountain of the Scorching

''Twas health and strength, 'twas life and joy, to wander freely there,
To drink at the fresh mountain stream, to breathe the mountain air.'

On Beinn Dorain by DUNCAN BAN MACINTYRE, the famous Gaelic poet born at Inveroran in 1724.

The huge monolith of Beinn Dorain dominates the landscape between Tyndrum and Bridge of Orchy, its clean unbroken lines sweeping up dramatically to a steep summit cone, dwarfing the West Highland Railway line that contours around its foot and gives scale to the scene. Beinn Dorain is connected to Beinn an Dòthaidh by a bealach, which affords a pleasant approach route and enables the summit of Beinn an Dòthaidh to be taken in on the same expedition, to give a panoramic view of Rannoch Moor that is worth any effort.

Begin at Bridge of Orchy railway station. Go through the underpass and across a cart track, bear left on a path that climbs the left bank of the burn into the rough confines of Coire an Dòthaidh. From here, steep grass slopes lead to the bealach between the two mountains. Turn right to climb Beinn Dorain's broad north ridge to a large cairn; the true summit lies a short distance further along beyond a short dip.

Retrace your steps to the bealach and climb more steeply up to the west top of Beinn an Dòthaidh. The west top is the first of three on the broad summit plateau that abut the fine cliffs of the north-east corrie. Turn right to reach the central and highest top. Pause to admire the unforgettable view over the vast expanse of Rannoch Moor before returning to the bealach and so to Bridge of Orchy.

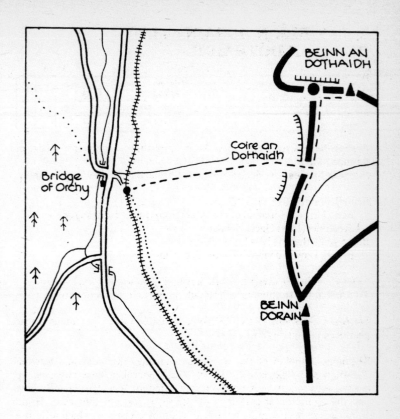

BEINN AN
DOTHAIDH

Coire an
Dothaidh

Bridge
of Orchy

BEINN
DORAIN

Route 10: **THE TARMACHAN RIDGE**

OS MAP: 51
GR: 606382
Distance: 7 miles (12 km)
Ascent: 820 m (2,700 ft)
Time: 5½ hr

	1	2	3	4	5
Grade			●		
Terrain		●			
Navigation		●			
Seriousness	●				

Assessment: an entertaining ridge walk easily reached from a high starting point.

Seasonal notes: one of the most sporting and enjoyable winter routes in the Southern Highlands; unavoidable difficulties are rare, although competence on snow is required and in hard conditions the windswept ridge may become icy.

Meall nan Tarmachan (1,043 m, 3,421 ft)
  Myowl nan *Tarr*amachan, Ptarmigan Hill
Meall Garbh (1,026 m, 3,366 ft)
  Myowl *Garr*av, Rough Hill
Beinn nan Eachan (995 m, 3,264 ft)
  Ben nan *Yech*an, Horse Mountain
Creag na Caillich (916 m, 3,005 ft)
  Craik na *Kyle*-yich, The Old Woman's Crag
Bealach Riadhailt* (should be Riaghailt)
  *Byal*ach *Ree*-a-ghiltch, Pass of the Rule
Coire Fionn Làirige
  Corra Fyoon *Lahr*ika, Corrie of the Fair Pass

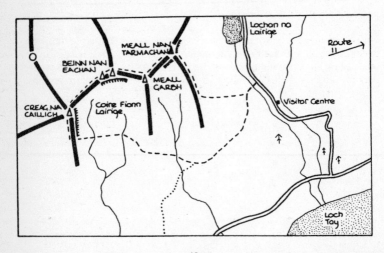

The undulating skyline of the Tarmachan Ridge presents an imposing backdrop to the Falls of Dochart at Killin. For 2 miles (3 km) it curves in an S-shape above the blue expanse of Loch Tay, at some points narrow and rocky, at others broad and grassy. The traverse of its four tops provides a pleasant ramble and scramble that is unfailingly entertaining.

The route begins on the minor road from Loch Tayside to Glen Lyon that leaves the A827 5 miles (8 km) east of Killin. Begin 400 m beyond the Ben Lawers visitor centre, taking the access track, which heads west across the moor to a disused quarry high up in Coire Fionn Làirige. When the track veers left round the south-east shoulder of Meall nan Tarmachan leave it, and climb directly onto the grassy shoulder, which becomes increasingly well defined as height is gained. At 914 m (3,000 ft) the ground falls away to a shallow bealach, and beyond that a steep 130 m (400 ft) climb leads up through broken craggy ground to the summit.

From the summit the main ridge beckons westwards to the more interesting lower tops. It is broad and knobbly at first and dotted with small knolls and lochans, but soon rears up more steeply to the sharp knob of rock that forms the castellated summit of Meall Garbh. The next section of ridge is the airiest of the day; a short rock step (of no difficulty) leads down to a narrow arete, which projects westwards for some 50 m before broadening and dropping down to the narrow defile of the Bealach Riadhailt. Beyond the bealach the best line is obscured by complex terrain, but the skyline is soon regained and the ridge curves upwards around Coire Fionn Làirige to the summit of Beinn nan Eachan. On the shoulder of Beinn nan Eachan a small cairn commemorates the inclusion of that point as a top in Munro's Tables, but it is an unremarkable spot.

Beyond Beinn nan Eachan, the ridge to Creag na Caillich, the fourth and final peak of the day, opens out into a broad, easy walk across a long bealach that provides a pleasant finish to the traverse. The Caillich has three tops that lie at a right angle to the main ridge and, as you wander out to the end, the other peaks of the Tarmachan Ridge come into fine perspective across Coire Fionn Làirige. From the Caillich a descent can be made to the quarry and back along the access track to your starting point, the only difficulty being a steep craggy section near the top, which is easily bypassed on the west.

Route 11: **BEN LAWERS**

OS MAP: 51
GR: 681399
Distance: 10 miles (16 km)
Ascent: 1,350 m (4,450 ft)
Time: 7 hr

	1	2	3	4	5
Grade		●			
Terrain		●			
Navigation			●		
Seriousness		●			

Assessment: a fine, high-level tramp around some hidden corners of the highest mountain in the Southern Highlands.
Seasonal notes: a fine winter walk. The negotiation of An Stùc may give problems, but normally all difficulties can be avoided by a long traverse on the north side.

Ben Lawers (1,214 m, 3,982 ft)
    Loud Mountain (from the sound of the Lawers Burn, Gaelic labhar) or
    Hoofshaped Mountain (from Gaelic ladhar)
Meall Garbh (1,118 m, 3,667 ft)
    Myowl *Garr*av, Rough Hill
An Stùc★ (1,118 m, 3,667 ft)
    An Stoochk, The Peak
Creag an Fhithich★ (1,047 m, 3,434 ft)
    Craik an *Ee*-ich, Raven Crag
Lochan nan Cat
    Cat Lochan

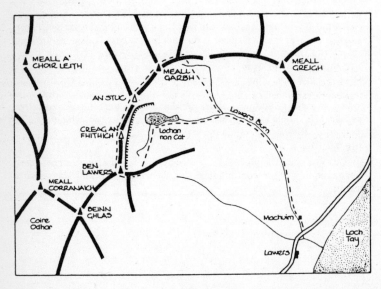

Upon approaching Killin from Lochearnhead via Glen Ogle, the mountains crowding the north side of Loch Tay burst suddenly into view, the huge mass of Ben Lawers sprawling behind the more intimate charms of Meall nan Tarmachan (route 10). Ben Lawers is the highest mountain in the Southern Highlands, its height estimated by early mapmakers to exceed 4,000 ft (1,220 m). Not until 1852 was it demoted to less than that magic figure, which so outraged one local that he had it topped up again with a 20 ft (6 m) summit cairn; this has long since collapsed.

If no longer one of the 'Scottish Fours', Ben Lawers remains a considerable attraction, not only for walkers but also for skiers and botanists. Coire Odhar was the first popular skiing area in Scotland and true mountain skiers still venture here today far from the mechanised crowds. Botanists are attracted by the rich Alpine flora that flourishes on Lawers' rich alkaline soil, prompting the National Trust for Scotland to buy the mountain in 1950, so easing access for walkers.

The complete traverse of the six Munros of the Lawers group is a considerable undertaking best done with transport at both ends; most walkers settle for the trade route to the summit, which begins at the NTS visitor centre (see route 10) and is a boring plod along an eroded path. A more interesting route starts from Lochtayside and takes in the narrowest section of the main ridge around the skyline above Lochan nan Cat.

Begin at the road to Machuim Farm at the bridge over the Lawers Burn just north of Lawers village on the A827. Walk past the farm, following a signposted path around the farm buildings and along the edge of the left embankment formed by the curiously deep-cutting river. The path crosses to the right bank and ends at a small dam, from where grass slopes lead up steeply to the north-east ridge of Meall Garbh and so to the summit.

From here the main ridge swings southwards to the summit of Ben Lawers around the corrie cradling Lochan nan Cat, one of the most beautiful lochans in the Southern Highlands; when viewed from the east its shape resembles a sitting cat. Between the two summits lies the most interesting of all the Lawers peaks: pointed An Stùc, whose slopes fall away steeply on all sides. Climb it on very steep grass (care when wet) and continue over the small hump of Creag an Fhithich to reach the summit of Lawers itself.

Descend the east ridge, making a way down to the secluded environs of Lochan nan Cat or continuing down the ridge to rejoin the route of ascent.

Route 12: **SCHIEHALLION**

OS MAP: 51
GR: 753557
Distance: 6 miles (10 km)
Ascent: 760 m (2,500 ft)
Time: 4½hr

	1	2	3	4	5
Grade	●				
Terrain		●			
Navigation	●				
Seriousness	●				

Assessment: a straightforward route up the backbone of the unusual Fairy Hill.
Seasonal notes: a normally easy introduction to the possibilities of winter walking in Scotland.

Schiehallion (1,083 m, 3,553 ft)
   Shee-*hal*yon, The Fairy Hill of the Caledonians

In 1774 Nevil Maskelyne, the Astronomer Royal, was attracted to Schiehallion by its regularity of shape, which he was able to utilise in his experiments on the estimation of the mass of the Earth. During this project Charles Hutton, one of the survey team, had the idea of drawing lines on the map to connect points of equal height, and thus contour lines were born.

Situated centrally between east and west coasts, and isolated by deep glens on all sides, Schiehallion is a familiar landmark in many views. From the west it shows up as a graceful symmetrical cone, which has a formidable appearance in white winter raiment, but its true character is revealed in views such as the Queen's View across Loch Tummel, when its long whaleback ridge can be seen sprawling over the moors. The very regularity, which makes Schiehallion attractive and photogenic, indicates

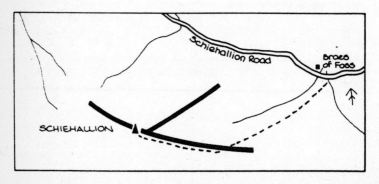

a lack of variety for the walker, but this is compensated for by the mountain's splendid isolation, its niche in mountaineering history and the ease of its ascent.

The recommended route is the *voie normale* from Schiehallion Road (the minor road that crosses Schiehallion's northern flank to link the B846 with Kinloch Rannoch). Begin at Braes of Foss car park just east of the farm of that name. A well trodden path, signposted Schiehallion, leads round the edge of forestry plantations and across the heathery moor to the foot of the broad east ridge. The cairned path climbs inexorably up the broad whaleback ridge, which becomes increasingly well defined and stony. A succession of false tops leads without incident to the rocky summit, an often exposed and windy spot commanding an extensive view to the north and west over a mosaic of loch and woodland scenery. A view indicator points out the salient features of the landscape. Descend by the same route.

Route 13: **BEN CRUACHAN**

OS MAP: 50
GR: 078268
Distance: 8 miles (13 km)
Ascent: 1,420 m (4,650 ft)
Time: 7 hr

	1	2	3	4	5
Grade			●		
Terrain			●		
Navigation				●	
Seriousness			●		

Assessment: Ben Cruachan's shattered skyline provides a narrow ridge walk that is one of the classic traverses of the Central Highlands.
Seasonal notes: in winter the traverse is a magnificent expedition for those competent on snow.

Ben Cruachan (1,126 m, 3,694 ft)
 Ben *Croo*-achan, Mountain of Mounds
Stob Garbh* (980 m, 3,215 ft)
 Stop *Garr*av, Rough Nose
Stob Diamh* (should be Damh) (998 m, 3,274 ft)
 Stop Daff, Stag Peak
Drochaid Ghlas* (1,009 m, 3,310 ft)
 *Droch*itch Ghlass, Grey Bridge
Stob Dearg* (1,104 m, 3,622 ft)
 Stop *Jerr*-ak, Red Peak
Meall Cuanail (918 m, 3,011 ft)
 Myowl *Coo*-anil, Hill of the Flocks
Lairig Torran*
 *Lahr*ik Torran, Pass of Mounds
Coire Caorach
 Corra *Cær*ach, Corrie of Rowan Berries
Coire Chat
 Corra Chat, Cat Corrie

Ben Cruachan is an impressive and beautiful mountain range in miniature which rises in splendid isolation between Loch Etive and Loch Awe, its jagged ridge supporting seven attractive peaks. The classic Cruachan traverse follows the skyline around Cruachan Reservoir, built in 1965 as part of an ambitious hydro-electric scheme. A massive cavern was excavated inside the mountain to house the machine room, and Cruachan is sometimes called the Hollow Mountain on account of this; it says much of human nature that the HEP scheme is now a greater tourist attraction than the mountain itself.

 Begin at Cruachan Power Station on the A85 by Lochaweside. Opposite the power station a road goes past the Falls of Cruachan up to the railway line, beyond which a path continues through a gate and doubles back to ascend the right bank of the Allt Cruachan. On reaching Cruachan Dam access road turn right, then turn left at a junction to

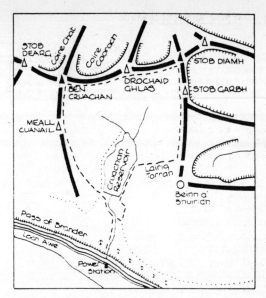

follow the road which ends on the east shore of the reservoir. Continue along the shore a short distance, then climb the grassy hillside to the Lairig Torran, an old pass formerly used for the movement of cattle from Dalmally to the grazing in the corrie now occupied by the reservoir.

From the lairig easy slopes lead on to the summit of Stob Garbh, then a steeper descent is followed by a gentle rise to Stob Diamh. Here the main ridge swings westwards around the rim of a craggy unnamed corrie to the steep bouldery slopes of Drochaid Ghlas. The narrow rocky top of Drochaid Ghlas is set back to the north of the main ridgeline (care in mist) and from it the north ridge drops steeply to remote Glen Noe to provide a fine scramble. The main ridge continues westwards, narrowing around the rim of Coire Caorach to the fine pointed summit of Ben Cruachan itself.

West of Ben Cruachan lies Stob Dearg, another pointed peak which, together with the main summit, forms the 'twin peaks of Cruachan'. If time and energy permit, it is worth continuing round the rim of Coire Chat to include this top. Like Drochaid Ghlas, both Ben Cruachan and Stob Dearg have narrow north ridges which provide entertaining scrambles.

The route of descent goes down Ben Cruachan's easy south ridge to the bealach before Meall Cuanail. It is possible to descend from here to the head of Cruachan Reservoir and to pick up a road along the west shore, but it is better to continue over Meall Cuanail and descend to the dam to prolong the view over island-studded Loch Awe. From the dam descend to the Allt Cruachan and rejoin the route of ascent.

Route 14: **BEN STARAV**

OS MAP: 50
GR: 136468
Distance: 8 miles (13 km)
Ascent: 1,100 m (3,600 ft)
Time: 6½ hr

	1	2	3	4	5
Grade				●	
Terrain			●		
Navigation		●			
Seriousness			●		

Assessment: a relentless ascent gives access to exhilarating high-level ridge walking.

Seasonal notes: a magnificent winter route for budding Alpinists. A rope is hardly required, although the upper section of the north ridge is usually quite exposed. The traverse to Stob Coire Dhéirg can be avoided if necessary by a descent into the south-east corrie followed by a traverse beneath the crest.

Ben Starav (1,078 m, 3,536 ft)
    Ben *Starr*av, Bold Mountain (poss)
Stob Coire Dhéirg* (1,020 m, 3,346 ft)
    Stop Corra *Yerr*ak, Peak of the Red Corrie
Glas Bheinn Mhór (997 m, 3,270 ft)
    Glas Ven Voar, Big Green Mountain
Allt Mheuran
    Owlt *Vai*-aran, River of Branches or Fingers

The bold peak of Ben Starav occupies a commanding position at the head of Glen Etive, that long and beautiful glen that leaves the A82 Glen Coe road at the western edge of Rannoch Moor and strikes south-west to Loch Etive. The mountain's striking symmetry and airy twin summits give it a classic appearance well reflected in its Gaelic name. The obvious route of ascent is via the north ridge that sweeps up steeply from the glen directly to the summit, providing a relentless approach but with ever expanding views and the promise of more exciting things to come.

Begin on the Glen Etive road 2½ miles (4 km) from the road end and take the track to Coleitir Farm. A path continues beyond the farm to the Allt Mheuran, which it crosses by a bridge 200 m upstream. Once across the stream, turn left and take the path up the left bank to a pine-studded gorge at the foot of the north ridge. Climb the ridge direct; it is steep and grassy at first, but narrows above fine cliffs towards the summit.

Continue round the rim of the summit plateau over the lower eastern top to the most interesting section of the route—the sharp arete leading to Stob Coire Dhéirg, which calls for some agreeable scrambling. Continuing eastwards, descend steeply to the bealach below Glas Bheinn Mhór and pick up a path on the left bank of the burn leading back to the Allt Mheuran.

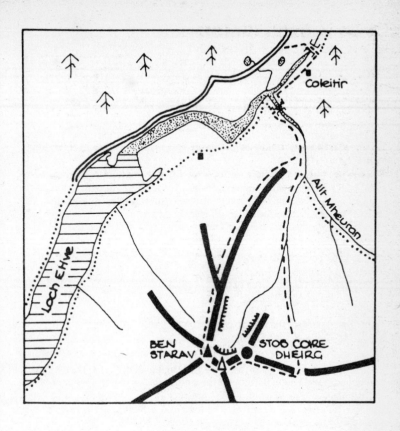

Route 15: **STOB GHABHAR**

OS MAP: 50
GR: 271423
Distance: 9½ miles (15 km)
Ascent: 970 m (3,200 ft)
Time: 6½ hr

	1	2	3	4	5
Grade				●	
Terrain		●			
Navigation		●			
Seriousness			●		

Assessment: a diverse circuit around one of the great corries of the Central Highlands, whose rim varies from broad plateau to narrow rocky ridge.

Seasonal notes: at its best under snow when the eastern corrie is heavily corniced and at its most impressive, but Aonach Eagach will require care under such conditions. To avoid Aonach Eagach bear south-eastwards down the western arm of the south-eastern corrie.

Stob Ghabhar (1,087 m, 3,566 ft)
    Stop *Ghoe*-ar, Goat Peak
Sron nan Guibhas (974 m, 3,195 ft)
    Srawn nan *Gew*as, Nose of the Pines
Aonach Eagach* (c991 m, c3,251 ft)
    *Oen*ach *Aik*ach, Notched Ridge
Allt Toaig (poss should be Taoig)
    Owlt *Toe*-ik, River of Passion

Stob Ghabhar is the finest mountain in the twisting Black Mount range which borders Rannoch Moor on the south-west, its pointed summit lying at the hub of a number of ridges that provide good walking above deep corries. The best route combines a round of the great eastern corrie with a descent of the attractive south-eastern corrie.

Begin at Forest Lodge 3½ miles (6 km) from Bridge of Orchy on the A8005. Follow a Land Rover track westwards to old Clashgour school-house, which is now Glasgow University Mountaineering Club's hut. Turn right, and follow the left bank of the Allt Toaig up to the entrance to the eastern corrie, using an excellent stalkers' track that peters out beside a series of waterfalls.

Descend into the corrie beneath cliffs that rise 400 m (1,300 ft) to the summit plateau, and gain the northern rim (Sron nan Guibhas) at the point of least resistance. The rim begins as a knobbly ridge, but soon broadens out onto the extensive summit plateau. The summit is perched close to the edge of the upper couloir, a classic ice route first climbed in 1897.

From the summit, continue along the southern rim of the corrie onto the most exciting section of the round—the narrow ridge of Aonach Eagach, whose airy crest calls for some simple scrambling. Descend into

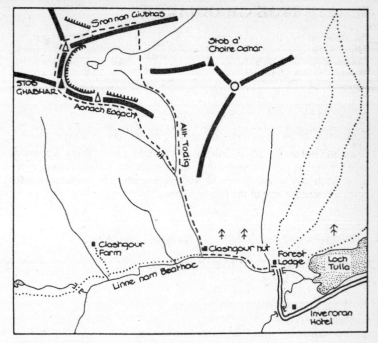

the south-eastern corrie when convenient and follow the burn down beside a fine waterfall to regain the track along the Allt Toaig.

Note: for strong walkers who can arrange transport at both ends, the complete traverse of the Black Mount, from White Corries (GR 266524) in the north to Forest Lodge in the south, is a classic high-level expedition in either direction. The route follows the spine of the range across the summits of Meall a'Bhuiridh, Clach Leathad, Aonach Mor and Stob Ghabhar, without once dropping below 730 m (2,400 ft). A north-to-south traverse enables the White Corries chairlift to be used to gain height.

Route 16: **BEINN A' BHEITHIR**

OS MAP: 41
GR: 081580
Distance: 10 miles (16 km)
Ascent: 1,340 m (4,400 ft)
Time: 7½ hr

	1	2	3	4	5
Grade				●	
Terrain			●		
Navigation			●		
Seriousness			●		

Assessment: a scramble of great character followed by a classic ridge walk.

Seasonal notes: an exhilarating winter traverse. The difficult north-east ridge of Sgorr Bhan can be avoided, if necessary, by an ascent of the easy north ridge.

Beinn a' Bheithir
   Ben a *Vai*-hir, Mountain of the Serpent
Sgorr Dhearg (1,024 m, 3,359 ft)
   Skorr *Yerr*ak, Red Peak
Sgorr Dhonuill (1,001 m, 3,284 ft) (should be Dhomhnuill)
   Skorr *Ghonn*ill, Donald's Peak
Sgorr Bhan* (947 m, 3106 ft)
   Skorr Vahn, White Peak
Sgorr a' Chaolais*
   Skorr a *Chœli*sh, Peak of the Narrows
Eas nam Meirlach*
   Ess nam *Mare*-lyach, The Robber's Waterfall

The entrance to Loch Leven west of Glen Coe is dominated by the craggy hump of Sgorr Dhonuill and its more graceful neighbour Sgorr Dhearg, which together form the Beinn a' Bheithir group. The beithir was a destructive serpent, but the mountain today shows no trace of his deeds and provides an attractive traverse with fine coastal views.

The approach to the summits is hampered by gross afforestation in the northern corries, and the normal Munro bagger's route from Gleann a' Chaolais requires precise route-finding if use of a machete is to be avoided. A much finer approach is that from Ballachulish village (West Laroch), which entails a ¾ hour road walk at the end of the day but more than compensates for this by the beauty and interest of the ascent route.

Begin at Ballachulish village 1 mile (2 km) west of Glen Coe village on the A82. Take the street signposted 'Public Footpath to Glen Creran' that runs up the left bank of the River Laroch to a farmyard. A Land Rover track continues to the foot of the north-east ridge of Sgorr Bhan, a magnificent ridge, which has a real mountaineering ambience about it. As it rises, it narrows to a rocky arete and breaks out into several short steep pitches that call for easy but invigorating scrambling (mostly avoidable if necessary).

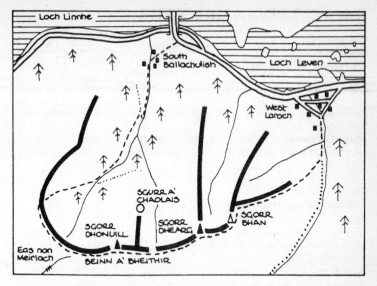

From Sgorr Bhan, the ridge curves round to Sgorr Dhearg in a perfect arc, which provides an exquisite aerial passage; when corniced, the symmetry of its unbroken line is breathtaking. Beyond Sgorr Dhearg a long easy-angled descent to a bealach is followed by a steeper climb up to Sgorr Dhonuill. Halfway up, a side ridge branches off to the rock tower of Sgorr a' Chaolais, which those with an excess of energy will find a sporting scramble well worth their attention. The final slopes of Sgorr Dhonuill provide further easy scrambling.

To complete the traverse of Beinn a' Bheithir, continue round the head of Gleann Chaolais, making a detour if time permits to view the Eas nam Meirlach. Beyond a subsidiary top, a wide grass gully enables easy access to the glen. Once into the glen, trend right through sparse tree cover to reach a path that follows the left bank of the Allt a' Chaolais to a forestry road. Still on the left bank of the river follow the road, which further down zigzags to a lower level and eventually reaches South Ballachulish. Branch right on a Land Rover track that crosses the river to reach the main road, and end the day with a pleasant stroll back to Ballachulish village along Loch Levenside.

Route 17: **BIDEAN NAM BIAN**

OS MAP: 41
GR: 175566
Distance: 6 miles (10 km)
Ascent: 1,150 m (3,750 ft)
Time: 6 hr

	1	2	3	4	5
Grade		●			
Terrain	●				
Navigation			●		
Seriousness		●			

Assessment: a route of great variety around the glens and ridges of a complex and beautiful mountain.

Seasonal notes: winter difficulties should not be underestimated; ridges may be corniced and the headwall of Coire Gabhail becomes a steep snow climb (in which case an ascent to the saddle between Bidean and Stob Coire nan Lochan may be easier).

Bidean nam Bian (1,150 m, 3,772 ft)
   *Beej*an nam *Bee*-an, Peak of the Mountains or Hides
Stob Coire nan Lochan (1,115 m, 3,658 ft)
   Stop Corra nan Lochan, Peak of the Corrie of the Lochan
Beinn Fhada (927 m, 3,041 ft)
   Ben *Att*a, Long Mountain
Stob Coire Sgreamhach (1,070 m, 3,510 ft)
   Stop Corra *Screv*ach, Peak of the Loathsome Corrie
Coire Gabhail*
   Corra *Ga*-hil, Corrie of the Bounty

Nothing, not even a glorious summer's day, can entirely disperse the air of solemnity that pervades that most famous (and infamous) of glens, Glen Coe—the 'glen of weeping'. This is due not only to memories of the Massacre, when in 1692 the Campbells fell upon the MacDonalds, butchering many and dispersing the rest into the raging blizzard, but also to the mountains, which shut in the glen dramatically to both north and south.

But if the depths of the glen can be dispiriting, the mountains are a complete contrast. To the north Aonach Eagach (route 20) provides the finest scramble outside Skye, while the south side of the glen is dominated by Bidean nam Bian, the highest mountain in Argyll, whose graceful summit lies at the hub of more than 12 miles (20 km) of ridges, mostly over 914 m (3,000 ft). As MacCulloch wrote in 1824, 'He who has time must be told that all the beauty of Glenco [sic] will not be found from the roadside.'

Bidean is a retiring mountain whose summit lies hidden behind three bold spurs known as the Three Sisters of Glen Coe, and it is one of the few mountains that is arguably best approached by its valleys rather than by its ridges, for the glens between the sisters are of exceptional interest.

Begin in Glen Coe at the car park 100 m west of Allt-na-reigh Cottage.

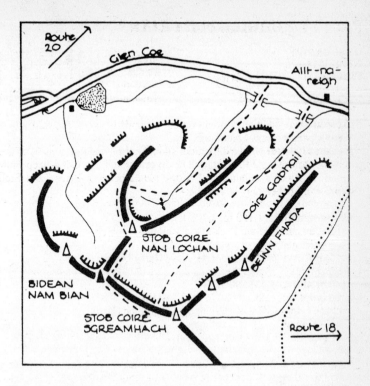

Take the path that crosses the River Coe below the cottage (footbridge) and that climbs up the rocky gorge of the Allt Coire Gabhail through chaotic boulder fields. At 370 m (1,200 ft) it debouches into the flat-bottomed Coire Gabhail (also known as The Lost Valley), a fascinating mountain sanctuary where the MacDonalds used to secrete their cattle (and anyone else's) in times of trouble. The steep surrounding walls give the corrie the appearance of an Alpine cirque; at the entrance, a warren of short caves up on the right is worth exploring; a huge boulder provides scrambling exercises.

Cross the corrie, where the river disappears underground, and take the path that ascends the left bank of a deep gorge to the corrie headwall. Turn right along the corrie rim for the short walk to the summit. To descend, cross the narrow north-east spur, taking great care in mist to hit off at the right point, to reach Stob Coire nan Lochan, a graceful summit perched high above crag-girt Coire nan Lochan. Descend the left (northern) arm of Coire nan Lochan around the cliffs to reach the lochans nestling below, and pick up the path that goes down the right bank of the tumbling river to your starting point.

Route 18: **BUACHAILLE ETIVE BEAG**

OS MAP: 41
GR: 171514
Distance: 5½ miles (9 km)
Ascent: 1,050 m (3,450 ft)
Time: 5½ hr

	1	2	3	4	5
Grade		●			
Terrain					●
Navigation	●				
Seriousness	●				

Assessment: a tough ascent, followed by an attractive ridge walk.
Seasonal notes: a good introduction to winter ridge walking. On the initial steep descent from the summit of Stob Dubh, a beautiful cornice forms and may give problems.

Buachaille Etive Beag
    Boo-a*chil*-ya Etive Bake, Little Shepherd of Etive
Stob Dubh (958 m, 3,143 ft)
    Stop Doo, Black Peak
Stob Coire Raineach (924 m, 3,031 ft)
    Stop Corra *Rahn*-yach, Peak of the Corrie of Ferns
Lairig Eilde
    *Lahr*ik *Ail*ja, Pass of the Hinds
Lairig Gartain
    *Lahr*ik *Garst*in, Pass of the Tics

At the junction of Glen Coe and Glen Etive the two shepherds of Etive stand watch over the wilderness of Rannoch Moor. The Buachaille Etive Beag is less grand than its big brother the Buachaille Etive Mór (route 19) but it is a fine mountain in its own right, rising in one bold swoop above Dalness in Glen Etive to a narrow summit ridge.

Begin at Dalness, aiming west up the hillside around the edge of a fence to reach the path through the Lairig Eilde. After a short distance, leave the main path and take a side path, which curves round above an obvious tiered waterfall, to reach the south-south-west ridge of the Buachaille. Climb the ridge direct, on steep grass at first, then through an awkward boulder field, to reach the level summit ridge of Stob Dubh. This is a delightful spot from which to view the Buachaille's second top, Stob Coire Raineach, across a deep bealach. The interesting intervening ridge is initially level for a few hundred metres then it narrows and descends steeply to an undulating section before the final drop to the bealach. From here climb the craggy knob of Stob Coire Raineach for the summit panorama of Central Highland peaks strung out north of the Blackwater Reservoir.

Returning to the bealach, descend easy grass slopes on the east to reach the Lairig Gartain path, which leads up over the lairig and down past a series of waterfalls to your starting point.

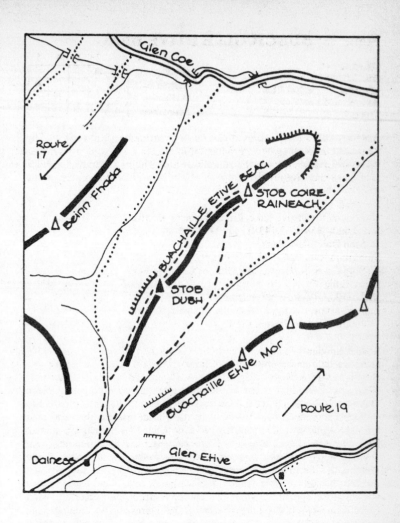

Glen Coe

Route 17

△ Beinn Fhada

BUACHAILLE ETIVE BEAG

△ STOB COIRE RAINEACH

△ STOB DUBH

△ Buachaille Etive Mor

Route 19

Dalness

Glen Etive

57

Route 19: **BUACHAILLE ETIVE MÓR**

OS MAP: 41
GR: 221563
Distance: 8½ miles (14 km)
Ascent: 1,080 m (3,550 ft)
Time: 6½ hr

	1	2	3	4	5
Grade			●		
Terrain					●
Navigation				●	
Seriousness			●		

Assessment: a steep ascent amidst magnificent rock scenery, followed by a pleasant walk along an undulating ridge.

Seasonal notes: an impressive mountain in winter; although the ridge contains no difficulties, the headwall of Coire na Tulaich becomes a steep snow climb, sometimes corniced at the exit.

Buachaille Etive Mór
    Boo-a*chil*-ya Etive Moar, Big Shepherd of Etive
Stob Dearg (1,022 m, 3,352 ft)
    Stop *Jerr*ak, Red Peak
Stob na Doire (1,011 m, 3,316 ft)
    Stop na Durra, Peak of the Grove
Stob Coire Altruim (939 m, 3,080 ft)
    Stop Corra *Alt*rim, Peak of the Corrie of Rearing
Stob na Bròige (955 m, 3,133 ft)
    Stop na *Braw*-ika, Peak of the Hoof
Coire na Tulaich
    Corra na *Tool*ich, Corrie of the Knoll

Buachaille Etive Mór is one of the finest mountains in Scotland. On the approach to Glen Coe from the east it rears up improbably above the flat expanse of Rannoch Moor like a huge arrowhead, bristling with rock and ice routes. Behind the summit, three further tops punctuate a long backbone, stretching above Glen Etive, offering a fine and often neglected ridge walk. For capable scramblers Curved Ridge (the left edge of the gully to the left of the obvious Crowberry Tower near the summit) is a magnificent ascent route slightly harder than Aonach Eagach and graded a Moderate rock climb. For walkers, however, the only feasible approach to the Buachaille is the climber's descent route via Coire na Tulaich.

Begin at Altnafeadh, on the Glen Coe road, and take the path over the River Coupall (bridge) past Lagangarbh climbers' hut. The well worn peaty path crosses the moor and scrambles up the right wall of the gorge of the burn that comes down from Coire na Tulaich. (*NB:* the path to the foot of Curved Ridge branches left beneath the cliffs.) Go straight up the scree gully at the head of the corrie (care required), then turn left and climb the summit rockpile of Stob Dearg for the stupendous view over Rannoch Moor.

A worthwhile diversion is a short descent over the top to view

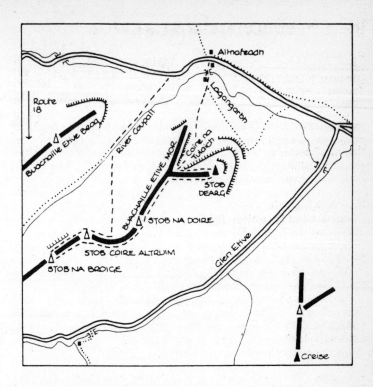

Crowberry Tower, whose ascent provides an exciting short scramble that is not as hard as it looks and gives a taste of north face exposure. Imagine Crowberry Ridge below the tower as it is in winter, 'a sensational arete arrayed in shark's fins of translucent ice' (as W.H. Murray described it on the first ascent).

From Stob Dearg, return to the head of Coire na Tulaich (great care required in mist) and follow the ridge, now grassy and with pools nestling in hollows, as it curves round to the foot of Stob na Doire. A steep, stony traverse of this peak leads to a narrow grassy bealach from where the final two peaks of Stob Coire Altruim and Stob na Bròige are soon reached. The stroll along the final section of ridge, level and narrow, provides a pleasant finish to the traverse, and ends on the tranquil dome of Stob na Bròige for a fine view of Loch Etive far from the busy summit of Stob Dearg.

From Stob na Bròige, return to the grassy bealach at the foot of Stob na Doire and descend grass slopes to the Lairig Gartain path that leads back through the broad trench between Buachaille Etive Mór and Buachaille Etive Beag to Altnafeadh.

Route 20: **AONACH EAGACH**

OS MAP: 41
GR: 174566
Distance: 6 miles (10 km)
Ascent: 1,000 m (3,300 ft)
Time: 7½ hr

	1	2	3	4	5
Grade					●
Terrain			●		
Navigation		●			
Seriousness					●

Assessment: the most sensational scramble on the Scottish mainland.
Seasonal notes: a major winter mountaineering expedition.

Aonach Eagach
    Oen-ach *Aik*ach, Notched Ridge
Am Bodach (943 m, 3,093 ft)
    Am *Bott*ach, The Old Man
Meall Dearg (953 m, 3,126 ft)
    Myowl *Jerr*ak, Red Hill
Stob Coire Leith (940 m, 3,083 ft)
    Stop Corra Lay, Peak of the Grey Corrie
Sgorr nam Fiannaidh (967 m, 3,172 ft)
    Skorr nam *Fee*-anny, Peak of the Fians

'On a certain day of snow and ice and sunshine I stayed at home while two friends made their first traverse of the ridge. Afterwards one of them told me he was disappointed because it was not as difficult as he had expected. He ought to have been almighty thankful.'

BEN HUMBLE (*On Scottish Hills*, 1946)

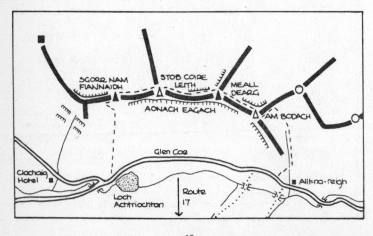

Aonach Eagach lays claim to being the finest ridge on the Scottish mainland. For almost 2 miles (3 km) its pinnacled crest lines the northern side of Glen Coe, providing exciting, sometimes daunting, scrambling in exposed situations. Its traverse comes close to being graded a rock climb in several sections, but those with a good head for heights, who take it slow and easy and savour its situations to the full, will find it an immensely satisfying route. Note that, unlike most scrambles in this book, there is no way of bypassing the awkward sections, and for most of the traverse there is no easy way off down to the glen.

Begin at the car park 100 m west of Allt-na-reigh cottage, where a path goes up to the south-east ridge of Am Bodach. It is possible to scramble directly up this ridge, but the easiest way to gain the summit is to follow the path across the ridge into a ravine on the far side and climb beside the burn to reach the main ridge at the saddle north-east of Am Bodach. From here easy slopes lead onto Am Bodach where the ridge proper begins. The first obstacle is encountered almost immediately in the form of an awkward descent on polished rock; if wearing a rucksack, parts of this section may be best tackled facing inwards. From the foot of the descent the ridge continues sharply but more easily to Meall Dearg, which has a unique place in Scottish mountaineering history as in 1901 it became the final Munro on the list of A.E. Robertson, the first person to complete all the Munros.

Beyond Meall Dearg, pinnacles bar the way to Stob Coire Leith. There is no way around them and, although the route has been well worn by generations of climbers, there are several places that will cause you to pause for inspiration and curse the author whose guidebook recommended this route. The last two pinnacles involve particularly spectacular scrambling before you can catch your breath on the easy walk to Stob Coire Leith. From here the now easy ridge continues to Sgorr nam Fiannaidh, a wonderful viewpoint overlooking Loch Leven.

The safest way back down to the glen from the summit of Sgorr nam Fiannaidh is to continue westwards along the ridge for a short distance then descend south-eastwards into a small corrie and to continue down rough quartzite slopes to reach the roadside near Loch Achtriochtan. The day ends with a 2½ mile (4 km) walk back up the glen to Allt-na-reigh. *NB:* the direct descent to Clachaig Inn is dangerous and should not be attempted.

Route 21: **MULLACH NAN COIREAN and STOB BÀN**

OS MAP: 41
GR: 143684
Distance: 8 miles (13 km)
Ascent: 1,150 m (3,750 ft)
Time: 6 hr

	1	2	3	4	5
Grade			●		
Terrain				●	
Navigation				●	
Seriousness			●		

Assessment: a circuit of two contrasting mountains, combining a pleasant plateau stroll with the steeper ridges of the White Peak (Stob Bàn).

Seasonal notes: under snow the route requires technical competence, especially the final section of the north-east ridge of Mullach nan Coirean and the descent of the east ridge of Stob Bàn, whose junction with the south-west ridge may be corniced.

The Mamores
    The Big Round Hills (literally Breasts)
Mullach nan Coirean (939 m, 3,080 ft)
    Mullach nan *Corr*an, Summit of the Corries
Stob Bàn (999 m, 3,277 ft)
    Stop Bahn, White Peak
Sgor an Iubhair* (1,001 m, 3,284 ft)
    Skorr an *Yoo*-ir, Yew Peak
Coire Deirg*
    Corra *Jerr*ak, Red Corrie
Coire a' Mhusgain*
    Corr a *Vush*kin, Corrie of the Shellfish

Glen Nevis is one of the most striking of all Scottish glens and around its upper reaches are clustered more fine peaks than are to be found in any other like-sized area of the Scottish mainland. Routes 24–6 describe the mountains on the north side of the glen while routes 21–3 explore the excellent walking of the shapely Mamores range, which contains over a dozen tops. All could be done in a very long day by following the twisting main ridge and bagging outliers but, as with the Cuillin of Skye, this would unjustly ignore some fine approaches and secondary ridges.

The most westerly Mamores are Mullach nan Coirean and Stob Bàn. The Mullach has an undistinguished plateau summit but throws out some interesting ridges towards Glen Nevis, whereas Stob Bàn is a contrasting shapely cone that makes a picturesque backdrop to the view up Glen Nevis; its quartzite top is often mistaken for a snowcap. The round of the two peaks makes a fine tramp best done from west to east in order to save the best until last.

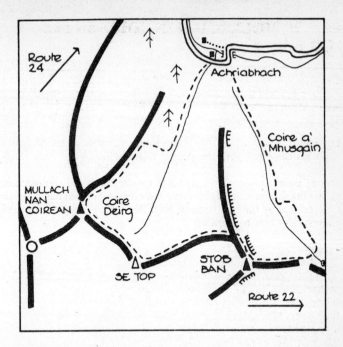

Begin at Achriabhach Farm in Glen Nevis just west of where the road crosses the river beside a waterfall. Take the forest road signposted 'A Forest Walk' into the woods. After 150 m take the obvious path on the left, to regain the road higher up, and follow it up Coire Deirg to its end. Climb the steep slopes on the right to the Mullach's north-east ridge, then follow a path along the narrowing crest to the broad summit.

From the summit follow the edge of the plateau around Coire Deirg to the south-east top, beyond which the plateau narrows to a ridge and a path scrambles over a rocky hump to the foot of Stob Bàn's west ridge. The ascent of this ridge is straightforward at first but, after its junction with the north ridge, steep and awkward quartzite slopes lead up to the summit.

To complete the round, descend the east ridge of Stob Bàn, which abuts sharply against the south-west ridge (easily missed in adverse weather). It leads down steeply at first before levelling off towards the bealach beneath Sgor an Iubhair. From the bealach descend left into Coire a' Mhusgain and pick up a good stalkers' path that clings to the right bank of the gorge of the Allt Coire a' Mhusgain, a delightful descent beneath the crags of Stob Bàn's east face and through an old stand of birch to the roadside near Achriabhach.

Route 22: **THE RING OF STEALL**

OS MAP: 41
GR: 168691
Distance: 8½ miles (14 km)
Ascent: 1,500 m (4,900 ft)
Time: 7½ hr

	1	2	3	4	5
Grade				●	
Terrain			●		
Navigation			●		
Seriousness			●		

Assessment: a ramble and scramble of unfailing interest along the narrowest ridges of the Mamores, with several airy sections and a magnificent approach walk.
Seasonal notes: a classic winter traverse, but not for beginners.

Sgurr a' Mhàim (1,099 m, 3,605 ft)
  Skoor a *Va*-im, Peak of the Breast (-shaped hill)
Stob Choire a' Mhail* (c980 m, c3,215 ft)
  Stop Chorr a *Va*-il, Peak of the Corrie of the Rent
Sgor an Iubhair* (1,001 m, 3,284 ft)
  Skorr an *Yoo*-ir, Yew Peak
Am Bodach (1,032 m, 3,385 ft)
  Am *Bott*ach, The Old Man
Stob Coire a' Chairn* (981 m, 3,218 ft)
  Stop Corr a Chairn, Peak of the Corrie of Cairns
An Garbhanach (975 m, 3,198 ft)
  An *Garr*avanach, The Rough Place
An Gearanach* (985 m, 3,231 ft)
  An *Gyerr*anach, The Sad or Querulous Place (or poss the Short Ridge, from Gaelic Gearr Aonach)
Coire nan Criamh*
  Corra nan *Cree*-av, Leek Corrie (poss, from Gaelic creamh)
Coire Dubh*
  Corra Doo, Black Corrie
Steall
  Shtyowl, Waterfall

The horseshoe of peaks around Coire a' Mhàil above Steall waterfall provides the best round in the Mamores, with seven tops over 914 m (3,000 ft) connected by entertainingly narrow ridges. Moreover, the approach to Steall is the most impressive of any mountain route in Scotland. It begins at the car park at the end of the Glen Nevis road where the mountains close in on the glen. Ahead lies the unique Nevis Gorge, where the Water of Nevis thunders over a tangle of enormous boulders and which has been described as being of Himalayan character. Its inundation by the HEP scheme, which was proposed in 1961, would have been an act of irredeemable vandalism.

A path penetrates the gorge high above the river, and clings to the

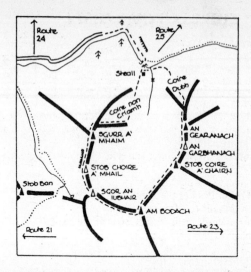

thickly wooded precipice; care is needed in places. It debouches unexpectedly into a hidden mountain sanctuary, an enclosed grassy plain onto the end of which plunges the 100 m (300 ft) Steall waterfall. Keep to the path until Steall climbers' hut can be seen across the river on the right, then cross the wire bridge below the hut. For many walkers this is the most heartstopping moment of the day, for the bridge consists of only three wires, one for the feet and one on each side for the hands, and the crossing of this swaying tightrope above the turbulent river is not for the fainthearted.

Beyond the hut, thread a way up right among the crags to the north-east ridge of Sgurr a' Mhàim. This leads to the summit without difficulty, but a more interesting scramble can be had by crossing Coire nan Criamh to the left and ascending the east ridge. Continuing south over the summit, the Devil's Ridge is encountered; this begins with an easy descent to a saddle before rising along an airy crest, with a few awkward moves, to Stob Choire a' Mhàil. The ridge then broadens across a dip to join the main spine of the Mamore range at Sgor an Iubhair.

Eastwards, easy grass slopes are followed over Am Bodach to Stob Coire a' Chairn, where the main ridge is left once more for a side ridge that strikes north to complete the horseshoe of Coire a' Mhàil. A sharp descent and reascent, with optional scrambling, leads to the rocky top of An Garbhanach, and here the ridge narrows briefly to an exposed arete before broadening to the last top of the day, An Gearanach. From here descend easy slopes onto the north-east spur, picking up a good path, which zigzags down Coire Dubh around the foot of Steall waterfall, to rejoin the path back through the Nevis Gorge.

Route 23: **BINNEIN MÓR and NA GRUAGAICHEAN**

OS MAP: 41
GR: 186630
Distance: 9 miles (15 km)
Ascent: 1,180 m (3,850 ft)
Time: 6¹/₂ hr

	1	2	3	4	5
Grade		●			
Terrain		●			
Navigation			●		
Seriousness		●			

Assessment: a pleasant approach on good paths leads to a typically fine Mamore ridge walk.

Seasonal notes: the easiest of the three Mamore routes in winter, yet one which still requires competence on narrow snow ridges and care on the negotiation of Na Gruagaichean's twin summits.

Binnein Mór (1,128 m, 3,700 ft)
  Been-yan Moar, Big Peak
Na Gruagaichean (1,055 m, 3,461 ft)
  Na *Groo*-agichan, The Maidens
Sgurr Eilde Beag★ (956 m, 3,136 ft)
  Skoor *Ail*ja Bake, Small Peak of the Hind
Coire na Gabhalach★
  Corra na *Gav*alach, Corrie of the Lease (poss, from Gaelic gabhail) or
  Fork (poss, from Gaelic gobhlach)
Coire na Bà★
  Corra na Bah, Cattle Corrie

The eastern peaks of the Mamores are most easily reached from Kinlochleven, enabling an exploration of the southern flanks of this fine range. Good stalkers' paths lead into the hills and ease the approach to the most interesting section of the eastern Mamore ridge, that connecting the twin peaks of Na Gruagaichean to the tapering summit crest of Binnein Mór.

Begin at Mamore Lodge, reached by a rough road from the B863 just east of Kinlochleven (small fee for car park), and take the Land Rover track that heads east across the hillside. Just before the high point of the track, branch left on a stalkers' path, which rises round the south-east shoulder of Sgurr Eilde Beag, then branch left again on a path that zigzags up the shoulder to the summit. From here cross a dip to the south top of Binnein Mór, then continue along the sharp bouldery summit ridge to the north top, the crowning point of the entire Mamore range.

Returning to the south top, follow the main ridge as it sweeps round Coire na Gabhalach to the summit of Na Gruagaichean. Beyond the summit a deep rocky defile requires a steep descent and reascent of 60 m (200 ft) to gain the nearby north-west top, from where easier slopes lead

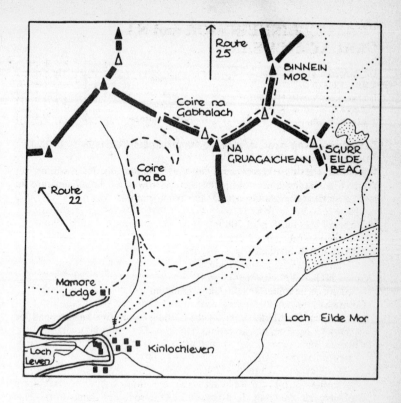

down to the wide bealach at the head of Coire na Bà. From here a stalkers' path heads down into the corrie to rejoin the Land Rover track near Mamore Lodge.

Route 24: BEN NEVIS and the CMD ARETE

OS MAP: 41
GR: 128718
Distance: 9$\frac{1}{2}$ miles (15 km)
Ascent: 1,660 m (5,450 ft)
Time: 8$\frac{1}{2}$ hr

	1	2	3	4	5
Grade				●	
Terrain		●			
Navigation				●	
Seriousness					●

Assessment: a classic ridge walk amidst spectacular rock scenery on Britain's highest mountain.

Seasonal notes: a spectacular winter route requiring technical competence on narrow snow ridges and iced rocks; the CMD arete requires great care and the summit slopes of the Ben are dangerous when iced. If in doubt, ascend by the descent route, but note that, when the tourist path is obliterated by snow, the route across the summit plateau requires extremely accurate navigation; there are more accidents here than anywhere else in Scotland.

Ben Nevis (1,344 m, 4,409 ft)
    obscure; possibilities include Ugly Mountain (from Gaelic nimhaise), Venomous Mountain (from Gaelic nimh), Heavenly Mountain (from Gaelic neamh), Mountain with Keen Atmosphere (from Gaelic neamh), Cloud-capped Mountain (from Gaelic neamh-bhathais), Terrible Mountain (from old Irish neamheis); may be named after the River Nevis.
Carn Mór Dearg (1,223 m, 4,012 ft)
    Carn Moar *Jerr*ak, Big Red Cairn
Carn Dearg Meadhonach (1,180 m, 3,871 ft)
    Carn *Jerr*ak *Mee*-anach, Middle Red Cairn
Meall an t-Suidhe (711 m, 2,322 ft)
    Myowl an *Tu*-ya, Hill of the Seat
Coire Leis
    Corra Laysh, Leeward Corrie
Allt a'Mhuilinn
    Owlt a' *Vool*in, Mill Stream

Ben Nevis, monarch of the British hills, is a mountain on the grand scale. Its summit lies only a few hundred feet below the permanent snow line and is in cloud for an average of 300 days of the year. To the south and west, its enormous bulk towers over the narrow confines of Glen Nevis, while to the north-east it rims Coire Leis with a 1 mile (2 km) face of 600 m (2,000 ft) cliffs. The normal route of ascent is the tiresome 'tourist' path up the western slopes, but the Ben deserves better, and the true mountain lover will forsake the normal route for the skyline of Coire Leis, a classic ridge walk in a spectacular situation.

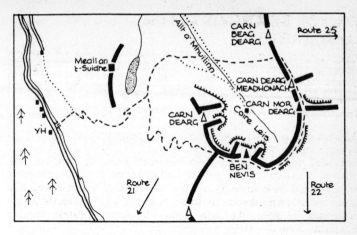

Begin at the youth hostel in Glen Nevis and take the engineered tourist path up the badly eroded hillside. This path joins the old track from Achintree Farm and climbs steadily onto the plateau between Meall an t-Suidhe and Carn Dearg. At a sharp right fork alongside Lochan Meall an t-Suidhe, take the path that continues straight on towards the Allt a'Mhuilinn. When the path descends right towards Coire Leis, leave it and pick a route across the Allt a' Mhuilinn and up the steep, grass slopes of Carn Dearg Meadhonach. The ascent is relentless but the views into Coire Leis and westwards over Loch Eil more than compensate. From the summit a short scramble to the first top on the pinnacled east ridge makes a pleasant diversion.

From Carn Dearg Meadhonach continue across a short dip to the summit of Carn Mór Dearg, beyond which the ridge narrows to form the famous 'CMD arete'—the sharp rocky crest that rims the head of Coire Leis. Those with a head for heights will revel in boulder-hopping along the crest, while a well worn path among the boulders provides easier going for the less balletic. All the while the spectacular north face of the Ben is close at hand, giving the route a real mountaineering flavour. Beyond a small top, the arete veers right and provides easier walking until it abuts against the south-east slopes of the Ben, where a sting in the tail provides an interesting scramble. A final stiff 300 m (1,000 ft) climb up stony slopes is required to reach the roof of Britain. The view is considerable, and there is much of interest on the summit plateau besides, including the forlorn ruins of the Observatory.

Descend via the tourist path, taking great navigational care across the plateau in adverse weather. As you descend the seemingly interminable zigzags you will thank the author of the guidebook who suggested that you avoided their ascent.

Route 25: **THE AONACHS**

OS MAP: 41
GR: 184778
Distance: 11½ miles (18 km)
Ascent: 1,530 m (5,000 ft)
Time: 8 hr

	1	2	3	4	5
Grade			●		
Terrain			●		
Navigation					●
Seriousness					●

Assessment: a wild walk at 4,000 ft (1,220 m) amidst rock scenery of Alpine grandeur.

Seasonal notes: spectacular in winter; the ascent of the spur to Aonach Mór may be impracticable, and the final slopes to Aonach Beag require care when iced.

Aonach Beag (1,236 m, 4,055 ft)
    *Oen*ach Bake, Little Ridge
Aonach Mór (1,219 m, 3,999 ft)
    *Oen*ach Moar, Big Ridge
Tom na Sròine (918 m, 3,011 ft)
    Towm na *Scrawn*a, Knoll of the Nose
Stob Coire an Fhir Dhuibh* (983 m, 3,225 ft)
    Stop Corr an Eer *Ghoo*-y, Peak of the Corrie of the Black Man
Stob an Cul Choire* (1,097 m, 3,599 ft)
    Stop an Cool Chorra, Peak of the Back Corrie
Coire an Lochain*
    Corr an Lochan, Corrie of the Lochan
Coire an t-Sneachda*
    Corr an *Drech*ka, Corrie of Snow
Allt Choille-rais
    Owlt *Chull*-ya Rash, Stream of the Shrubwood

East of Ben Nevis lie the two fascinating high peaks of Aonach Mór and Aonach Beag. Aonach Beag is the sixth highest mountain in Britain and is, in fact, higher than Aonach Mór, whose name derives from its bulk rather than its height. They are wild and lonely mountains, especially so in the fastness of their huge eastern corries, where the remote setting seems to add to the grandeur of the rock architecture.

The best approach is from the north-west, where a minor road leaves Torlundy on the A82 north of Fort William and goes through a lime quarry to end close to the forest boundary. Begin here, bearing right on a forest road at the forest fence. Keep left at the first two forks to follow the line of the British Aluminium Company Railway eastwards. At the next fork, just before a pile of sleepers, bear right on a branch road which ends at a dam over the Allt Choille-rais. Cross the dam and follow traces of a path through birches on the right bank of the turbulent river to reach the forest fence, then climb relentless grass slopes to the summit of Tom na Sròine.

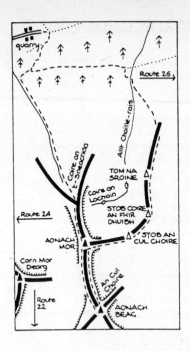

Interest now increases as the well defined ridge is followed over Stob Coire an Fhir Dhuibh to Stob an Cul Choire. Initially the Grey Corries (route 26) and the perfect bowl of Aonach Mór's Coire an Lochain command the attention, but increasingly glimpses of Aonach Beag's stupendous north-east corrie (An Cul Choire) spur you onwards. From the summit of Stob an Cul Choire this corrie is revealed in all its glory; the prominent rock ridge is the classic north-east ridge first climbed by Naismith in 1895. In spring huge cornices rim the corrie and the scale is Alpine.

From Stob an Cul Choire descend the fine rocky ridge which abuts against Aonach Mór and climb a steep spur up to the summit plateau, bypassing a rock bluff on the right. From the flat mossy summit, gentle slopes lead down around the rim of An Cul Choire (great care in mist) to the steeper climb onto the dome of Aonach Beag. The views left into the corrie and right over the CMD arete to Ben Nevis are spectacular.

To descend, return to Aonach Mór and cross the length of the summit plateau to the easy slopes of Coire an t-Sneachda. This corrie often holds snow throughout the year and plans for a downhill ski development here are well advanced. Further down, a short firebreak leads to a forest road which rejoins the approach route.

71

Route 26: **THE GREY CORRIES**

OS MAP: 41
GR: 252807
Distance: 17½ miles (28 km)
Ascent: 1,620 m (5,300 ft)
Time: 10½ hr

	1	2	3	4	5
Grade				●	
Terrain				●	
Navigation		●			
Seriousness					●

Assessment: one of the longest and most entertaining ridge walks on the mainland.

Seasonal notes: in winter, sections of the ridge narrow to snow aretes, which provide a classic traverse for competent winter walkers. If time is short, the route can be curtailed by a descent northwards from Stob Coire Easain over Beinn na Socaich.

Stob Coire na Ceannain (1,121 m, 3,677 ft)
    Stop Corra na *Kyown*an, Peak of the Corrie of the Little Head
Stob Choire Claurigh (1,177 m, 3,861 ft)
    Stop Chorra Clowry, obscure
Stob a' Choire Leith★ (1,105 m, 3,625 ft)
    Stop a Chorra Lay, Peak of the Grey Corrie
Stob Coire Cath na Sine★ (1,080 m, 3,543 ft)
    Stop Corra Ca na Sheena, Peak of the Corrie of the Battle of the Elements
Caisteal★ (1,104 m, 3,622 ft)
    Cash-tyal, Castle
Stob Coire an Laoigh★ (1,115 m, 3,658 ft)
    Stop Corr an *Loe*-y, Peak of the Calf Corrie
Stob Coire Easain (1,080 m, 3,543 ft)
    Stop Corr *Ess*an, Peak of the Waterfall Corrie
Sgurr Choinnich Mór (1,095 m, 3,592 ft)
    Skoor *Choan*-yich Moar, Big Peak of the Moss
Sgurr Choinnich Beag (966 m, 3,169 ft)
    Skoor *Choan*-yich Bake, Little Peak of the Moss
Allt Choimhlidh
    Owlt Chawly, Stream of Meeting (poss)

The peaks east of the Aonachs are less massive and more graceful, forming a group of a dozen tops linked by a high, sometimes sharp, ridge. They are collectively known as the Grey Corries, after the colour of their quartzite summits, and their traverse makes a magnificent ridge walk rivalling that of the Mamores to the south. As for the Aonachs, the best approach is from the north where subsidiary ridges jut out between deep corries that hold snow late into the year.

Begin at Corriechoille Farm at the end of the minor road from Spean Bridge along the beautifully wooded south bank of the River Spean. Take

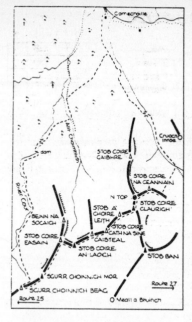

the Land Rover track south past the farm and past a right fork; continue straight on over the British Aluminium Company Railway line along the old drove road through the forest to the Lairig Leacach. Leave the track just before the foot of the craggy northeast spur of Stob Coire na Ceannain and scramble up beside a burn on the right to reach a shallow corrie. Bear right, up stony slopes, then left along a more well defined ridge to the summit.

The ridge proper now begins with the best scramble of the day along the narrow connecting ridge to Stob Coire Claurigh, the highest of the Grey Corries. The scrambling is nowhere hard and is easily avoided if necessary. From the summit the tortuous twistings of the Grey Corries ridge are spread out before you, with Ben Nevis providing a soaring backdrop. The narrow ridge twists and turns and undulates over a succession of tops, never dipping below 1,020 m (3,350 ft) and providing a glorious stravaig, of great interest.

At Stob Coire Easain the ridge does a 90° turn left, narrows to a deeply-fissured quartzite pavement and descends to a 940 m (3,100 ft) bealach before rising once more to the shapely summit of Sgurr Choinnich Mór. Beyond lies the last top on the ridge, the grassy hump of Sgurr Choinnich Beag; though hardly a 'grey corrie' there is no excuse for not climbing it.

Return to the bealach between Sgurr Choinnich Mór and Sgurr Choinnich Beag, descend into the remote upper valley of the River Cour and follow the right bank down beside inviting pools and cascades. Lower down cross the river at a dam to pick up a forest road that recrosses the river at the forest boundary. Follow the road to the bridge over the Allt Choimhlidh, turn left at a T-junction, then keep right at the next fork to emerge from the trees and rejoin the track to Corriechoille.

Route 27: **THE EASAINS**

OS MAP: 41
GR: 350782
Distance: 10 miles (16 km)
Ascent: 1,040 m (3,400 ft)
Time: 6½ hr

	1	2	3	4	5
Grade			●		
Terrain				●	
Navigation		●			
Seriousness		●			

Assessment: a pleasant circuit of the twin Easains enlivened by the interest of their approaches.

Seasonal notes: in winter, the steepness of the ascent and descent of Stob Coire Easain should not be underestimated, especially as the summit slopes are often iced.

Stob Coire Easain (1,116 m, 3,661 ft)
    Stop Corr *Ess*an, Peak of the Waterfall Corrie
Stob a' Choire Mheadhoin (1,106 m, 3,628 ft)
    Stop a Chorra *Vee*-an, Peak of the Middle Corrie
Creag Fhiaclach
    Craik *Ee*-aclach, Toothed Crag
Meall Cian Dearg
    Myowl *Kee*-an *Jerr*ak, Redheaded Hill
Coire Làire
    Corra *Lah*ra, Low Corrie
Lairig Leacach
    *Lah*rik *Lyechk*ach, Slabby Pass
Coire Easain Beag*
    Corr *Ess*an Bake, Little Waterfall Corrie

The twin Munros of Stob Coire Easain and Stob a' Choire Mheadhoin, known collectively as the Easains, stand in splendid isolation between Loch Treig to the east and the Lairig Leacach to the west. The ridge connecting the two peaks rims the slabby Coire Easain Beag and provides a fine circuit whose approaches hold much interest besides.

Begin at Fersit on the River Treig, at the end of the minor road that leaves the A86 Loch Laggan road 5 miles (8 km) east of Roybridge. Take the path on the right up to the line of the British Aluminium Company Railway and climb onto the ridge left of Creag Fhiaclach. Relatively level going leads to the foot of the craggy nose of Meall Cian Dearg, with Loch Treig stretching away to the left, and the West Highland Railway line incongruously hugging its shore. Pick a route straight up the nose and continue along the fine high-level ridge leading to Stob a' Choire Mheadhoin's stony summit.

The route onwards descends around the rim of Coire Easain Beag, whose folding is impressive, to a sharp dip before the ascent of Stob Coire Easain. Continue over the summit down steep, stony slopes around the

74

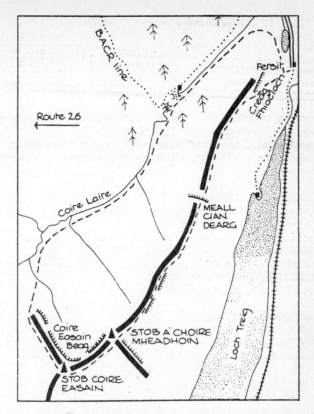

cliff edge to reach Coire Làire and pick up a path along the right bank of the river. This path eventually meets the British Aluminium Company Railway line, which takes you past some interesting old pipeline workings and along a delightfully easy track all the way back to Fersit.

The course of the British Aluminium Company Railway line is a familiar sight on all approaches to the mountains south of Glen Spean. The nineteen-mile line was built in the 1920s to aid construction of a pipeline carrying water from Loch Treig to the aluminium works at Fort William. The Coire Laire intake, which captures the waters of the Allt Laire, was famous for its hairpin bend (GR 324774) and its still, which kept construction workers happy at their task. The line was gradually replaced by forestry roads and formally closed in 1971. There have been schemes to reopen the line for tourist purposes, but so far nothing has been implemented.

Route 28: **THE GEAL CHARN GROUP**

OS MAP: 42
GR: 547787
Distance: 15½ miles (25 km)
Ascent: 1,750 m (5,750 ft)
Time: 10½ hr

	1	2	3	4	5
Grade				●	
Terrain			●		
Navigation					●
Seriousness					●

Assessment: a testing traverse of the narrow ridges that surround one of the most remote plateau summits in the Highlands.

Seasonal notes: The Lancet Edge under snow, and the summit plateau of Geal Charn in foul winter weather, should be avoided by the inexperienced.

Sgor Iutharn* (1,014 m, 3,326 ft)
  Skoor *Yoo*-arn, Hell Peak
Geal Charn* (1,132 m, 3,713 ft)
  Gyal Charn, White Cairn
Aonach Beag (1,114 m, 3,654 ft)
  *Oen*ach Bake, Little Ridge
Beinn Eibhinn (1,100 m, 3,608 ft)
  Ben *Aiv*in, Odd or Happy Peak
Diollaid a' Chairn (922 m, 3,256 ft)
  *Jull*itch a Chairn, Saddle of the Cairn
Carn Dearg (1,034 m, 3,392 ft)
  Carn *Jerr*ak, Red Cairn
Bealach Dubh
  *Byal*ach Doo, Black Pass
Loch an Sgoir
  Loch an *Skaw*-ir, Loch of the Peak
Loch Coire Cheap
  Loch Corra Chyepp, Loch of the Carp Corrie
Allt a' Chaoil-reidhe
  Owlt a Chœl *Rai*-ya, Stream of the Level Narrows

It is difficult to believe that any mountains in the Central Highlands could be as remote as 8 miles (13 km) from the nearest public road as the eagle flies, yet such is the case with the high peaks of Ben Alder Forest. The approach is eased, however, by the enlightened policy of the Ben Alder estate, which permits ready access for climbers to the private road along Loch Ericht from Dalwhinnie to Ben Alder Lodge (ring Dalwhinnie 224 to obtain a key for the locked gate). This is magnificent walking and backpacking country, wild and rugged, crisscrossed by ancient tracks and endowed with well placed bothies.

The private road from Dalwhinnie crosses the railway line south of the station, holds to the west shore of Loch Ericht as far as Ben Alder Lodge

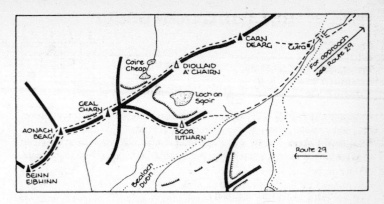

and then veers west towards Loch Pattack. The path into the hills begins at a shed ½ mile (1 km) before Loch Pattack and heads south-west along the right bank of the Allt a' Chaoil-reidhe. The mountains are naturally divided into two groups by the deep gash of the Bealach Dubh; to the left is Ben Alder (route 29) and to the right is the Geal Charn group (described here). The summit of Geal Charn itself lies well back at the end of an extensive plateau; what immediately catches the eye is Sgor Iutharn and its north-west ridge (The Lancet Edge), which drops to meet the path.

To reach the Geal Charn group, leave the right-bank path just before Culra Lodge and bothy and cross the river (bridge) to a parallel path that runs along the left bank past Culra into the jaws of the Bealach Dubh. Leave this path after crossing the burn coming down from Loch an Sgoir and climb The Lancet Edge direct. As height is gained, the ridge narrows to a rocky crest, which provides pleasant scrambling in a fine situation above the moors of the approach route. Beyond The Lancet Edge lie Sgor Iutharn and the grassy plateau of Geal Charn, where great care is required in mist. The summit cairn is at the north-west edge of the plateau and beyond it is a fine walk along a narrowing ridge, reminiscent of the Mamores, which undulates across Aonach Beag and curves round grace-fully to the summit of Beinn Eibhinn.

Return along the ridge as far as Geal Charn, then keep going north-east down the sharp ridge (difficult to locate in mist) that separates Loch Coire Cheap from Loch an Sgoir. Continue over Diollaid a' Chairn to reach Carn Dearg, then descend directly to Culra to rejoin the approach route.

Route 29: **BEN ALDER**

OS MAP: 42
GR: 547787
Distance: 11½ miles (19 km)
Ascent: 730 m (2,400 ft)
Time: 7½ hr

	1	2	3	4	5
Grade				●	
Terrain			●		
Navigation					●
Seriousness					●

Assessment: a fine scrambling route with a real mountaineering flavour on an exceptional mountain.

Seasonal notes: both the Long and Short Leachas are considerable undertakings under snow, and the featureless summit plateau of Ben Alder is best avoided in foul winter weather. In case of difficulty, the easiest descent route from the summit is to go west for 1 mile (1½ km), then north to reach the Bealach Dubh (incorrectly placed on OS map—see sketch map for route 28).

Ben Alder (1,048 m, 3,766 ft)
    Rock Water Mountain (poss, named after the Alder Burn)
Coire na Leith-chais
    Corra na *Lyeh*-chas, Corrie of the Half-foot or Half-twist
Loch a' Bhealaich Bheithe
    Loch a *Vyal*ich *Vay*-ha, Loch of the Birch Pass

Ben Alder is a mountain that attracts the devotion of all those who love the wild places of Scotland. It is unique among Central Highland peaks for its remoteness and its vast summit plateau, almost 400 acres (4 sq km) in extent, which dominates the marvellous walking country west of Loch Ericht. On its eastern flank, the huge Garbh (Rough) Coire provides majestic snow and ice routes for winter-hard men, but it is the two narrow ridges to the north-east, the Long Leachas and the Short Leachas, which provide the most exciting circuit for the mountain walker.

Use the same approach route as for route 28, following the path along the right bank of the Allt a' Chaoil-reidhe to Culra. Instead of crossing the river to Culra, hold to the path on the right bank as far as the burn coming down from Loch a' Bhealaich Bheithe, then make directly for the foot of the Long Leachas that bounds Coire na Leith-chais on the right. The ridge narrows to provide an exhilarating scramble up to the stony summit plateau. The summit lies 1 mile (2 km) south around the plateau rim above the cliffs of Garbh Coire, and may be difficult to locate in mist.

From the summit, retrace your steps to the head of Coire na Leith-chais and descend the other rim, the Short Leachas, which provides another good scramble down to rejoin the approach path.

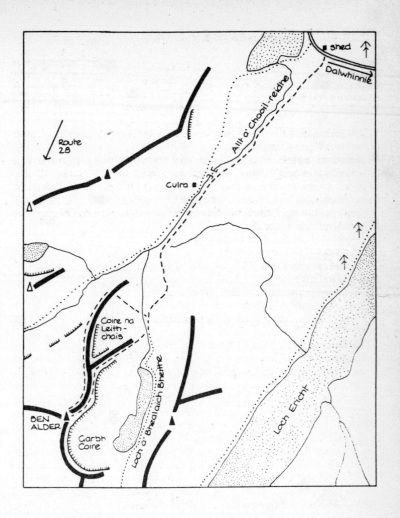

Route 30: **CREAG MEAGAIDH**

OS MAP: 42
GR: 483873
Distance: 10 miles (16 km)
Ascent: 910 m (3,000 ft)
Time: 6½ hr

	1	2	3	4	5
Grade		●			
Terrain		●			
Navigation					●
Seriousness				●	

Assessment: a walk amidst impressive cliff and corrie scenery in the hidden recesses of a complex and majestic mountain.

Seasonal notes: the summit plateau and the environs of Coire Ardair demand great respect in winter and spring.

Creag Meaghaidh (1,128 m, 3,700 ft)
    Craik Meggy, Bogland Crag (poss)
Puist Coire Ardair* (1,095 m, 3,592 ft)
    Poosht Corr *Ard*ar, Post of the High Corrie
Creag Mhór* (1,066 m, 3,497 ft)
    Craik Voar, Big Crag
Sron a' Choire*
    Srawn a Chorra, Nose of the Corrie
Coire Choille-rais*
    Corra *Cull*-ya-rash, Corrie of the Shrubwood
Lochan Uaine
    Lochan Oo-*an*-ya, Green Lochan
Coill a' Choire
    Cull-ya Chorra, Wood of the Corrie

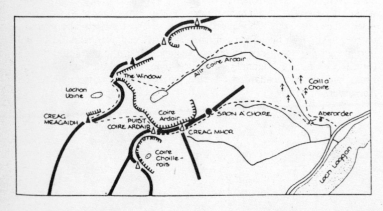

The complex topography of Creag Meagaidh, as seen from afar, does not prepare one for the scale and grandeur of its secluded corries. Coire Ardair, especially, is one of the hidden gems of the Scottish Highlands and a supreme winter climbing area, with towering buttresses split by great ice gullies (posts), which provide testing ascents. Yet, despite its splendour and its designation as a Site of Special Scientific Interest, Creag Meagaidh has been saved from the ravages of commercial afforestation only by the purchase of the Coire Ardair approach route by the Nature Conservancy Council in 1985. The whole sorry affair was unfortunately only one example of the crying need for a land policy that will preserve the wild land of Scotland for the future. For the moment Creag Meagaidh is safe, however, and its delightful recesses await those who are prepared to leave the roadside.

Begin at the NCC car park at Aberarder Farm on the A86 Loch Laggan road. Follow the track past the farm and up the right-hand side of the gracefully curving glen and pass through the birch woods of Coill a' Choire. The great cliffs of Coire Ardair soon appear and loom ever more impressively as the path approaches the lochan-filled hollow at the heart of the corrie.

The cliffs are 1½ miles (2 km) long and up to 450 m (1,500 ft) high, and the route to the summit plateau traverses right beneath them up to the curious nick in the skyline known as The Window. Note that Coire Ardair holds snow late into the year and this section of the route is prone to avalanche. At The Window, turn left to climb up onto the extensive summit plateau. A large cairn is reached, and the true summit lies a short distance beyond at the edge of cliffs above Lochan Uaine.

The most interesting descent route is via the southern of Coire Ardair's two protecting arms. To reach it, head back across the plateau to the corrie rim (great care required in mist) and continue round the cliff edge; there are spectacular views of the lochan far below. A well defined ridge leads over Puist Coire Ardair to the fine viewpoint of Creag Mhór, from where it is worth descending southwards for a short distance to view the perfect bowl of Coire Choille-rais with its cliff-girt lochan, the perfect partner to Coire Ardair. To reach Aberarder, descend over Sron a' Choire into the shallow south-eastern corrie, keeping left of the burn, and make for a fence running diagonally across the moor to the Allt Coire Ardair. From here a path leads down beside the river to a bridge and so to Aberarder.

Route 31: **GARBH BHEINN**

OS MAP: 40/49
GR: 929597
Distance: 7½ miles (12 km)
Ascent: 1,310 m (4,300 ft)
Time: 7½ hr

	1	2	3	4	5
Grade			●		
Terrain					●
Navigation					●
Seriousness			●		

Assessment: a Grand Tour of an impressive rock peak.
Seasonal notes: in winter, steep snow slopes on either side of the Bealach Feith an Amean may be impracticable, and it may be best to ascend via the descent route. The descent from the summit to the southeast summit demands extreme caution in adverse weather.

Garbh Bheinn (885 m, 2,903 ft)
   *Gara*v Ven, Rough Mountain
Druim an Iubhair
   Drum an *Yoo*-ir, Yew Ridge
Sgor Mhic Eacharna (c640 m, c2,100 ft)
   Skorr Veechk *Ech*arna, MacEcharn's Peak
Beinn Bheag (c730 m, c2,400 ft)
   Ben Vake, Little Mountain
Bealach Feith an Amean*
   *Byal*ach Fay an?, Pass of the Bog of the ? (obscure)
Sron a' Gharbh Choire Bhig
   Srawn a *Gara*v Chorra Veek, Nose of the Little Rough Corrie
Leac Mhór*
   Lyechk Voar, Big Slab

The mountainous district of Ardgour is cut off from the popular playgrounds of Glen Coe and Glen Nevis by the long sea inlet of Loch Linnhe. The Corran ferry crosses the loch but, as there are no Munros to be climbed, the area remains relatively quiet. Its long, lonely glens and rugged mountains are well worth exploring, however, and none more so than Garbh Bheinn, the great rock peak that is prominent in the view across Loch Linnhe. The rock buttresses of Garbh Bheinn's north-east face dominate the upper reaches of Coire an Iubhair and make the round of the corrie skyline the best route in Ardgour, with plenty of opportunities for scrambling amidst the impressive rock scenery.

    Begin at the car park on the east side of the bridge over the Abhain Coire an Iubhair, in Glen Tarbert, on the A861. Climb steep, tussocky grass slopes to gain Druim an Iubhair, the broad and complex ridge that swings gradually left around the corrie to the summit of Sgor Mhic Eacharna. Across the corrie, the north-east face of Garbh Bheinn becomes ever more impressive. Dropping 300 m (1,000 ft) directly from the summit to the corrie floor is The Great Ridge, first climbed in 1897. To its

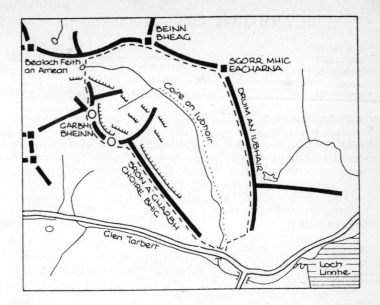

immediate north is The Great Gully, at one time a notorious 'last great problem', not climbed until 1946. Further right is the four-tiered north-east buttress, whose third tier contains the Leac Mhór, a huge slab, said to be the biggest in Scotland, measuring approximately 150 m (500 ft) by 90 m (300 ft).

Beyond Sgor Mhic Eacharna the terrain becomes increasingly rocky. A steep descent and reascent is required to gain Beinn Bheag, and then the ridge narrows attractively above wild glens to both north and south. Continue along the ridge until it swings right at a rocky knoll and from here descend steep grass rakes among outcrops to the Bealach Feith an Amean, at the head of Coire an Iubhair.

Garbh Bheinn rises directly above. From the lochan in the jaws of the bealach go straight up a steep grass gully, which cuts through the cliffs, to reach the rim of the fine north-west corrie, whose slabby walls have an almost Cuillin grandeur. Clamber up the left-hand skyline, with ample opportunity for scrambling on the excellent gneiss, to reach the summit.

Descend around the cliff edge to the south-east top; there are traces of a path, but take great care in mist not to cut left too soon. Continue south-eastwards down the long rocky ridge of Sron a'Gharbh Choire Bhig, with stunning views over Loch Linnhe, to complete the circuit of Coire an Iubhair.

Route 32: **THE ROIS-BHEINN RIDGE**

OS MAP: 40
GR: 765816
Distance: 11½ miles (18 km)
Ascent: 1,640 m (5,400 ft)
Time: 9 hr

	1	2	3	4	5
Grade			●		
Terrain				●	
Navigation					●
Seriousness		●			

Assessment: a long and lonely ridge walk across craggy terrain with views that will be long remembered.

Seasonal notes: a fine winter tramp of testing length; steep snow slopes may be encountered.

Rois-Bheinn (882 m, 2,893 ft)
   Ross Ven, Mountain of Horses (from Norse hross) or Showers (from Gaelic Fras)
Beinn Coire nan Gall
   Ben Corra nan Gall, Mountain of the Corrie of the Strangers
Druim Fiaclach (869 m, 2,851 ft)
   Drum *Fee*-aclach, Toothed Ridge
An t-Slat-bheinn (823 m, 2,700 ft)
   An Tlat Ven, The Wand Mountain
Sgurr na Ba Glaise (874 m, 2,867 ft)
   Skoor na *Bah Glash*a, Peak of the Grey Cow
An Stac (814 m, 2,670 ft)
   An Stachk, The Stack
Bealach an Fhiona
   *Byal*ach an *Fyoon*a, Pass of the Wine
Coire a'Bhuiridh
   Corr a Voory, Corrie of Bellowing (of stags)

The district of Moidart, which stretches from Loch Shiel to the Sound of Arisaig, is surrounded by green loch-filled glens and rendered easily accessible by the West Highland·Railway and the 'Road to the Isles' from Fort William to Mallaig. Yet the interior is wild and remote, and the traverse of Rois-Bheinn and its satellites, though never reaching Munro height, is one of the finest ridge walks in the Western Highlands. Large amounts of bare rock enliven the traverse of the ridge, which is winding, undulating, complex and constantly interesting.

Take the minor road, signposted Glenshian, 700 m south of the junction of the A830 and A861 at Lochailort. Do not follow the road to Glenshian but bear immediately right to the cottages at Inverailort. The route begins here, following a grassy cart track left through fields in front of the cottages. When the track turns left at an old wartime building, take the path that goes straight on up the defile right of Tom Odhar onto the open moor. When the path ends, cross the Allt a' Bhuiridh and make a

84

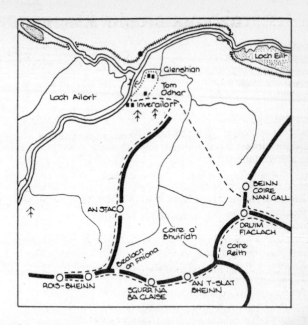

fairly steep rising traverse across the tussocky slopes of Beinn Coire nan Gall to the lochan at the bealach below Druim Fiaclach. Steep grass slopes then lead up among outcrops to this first top on the main ridge.

The route to Rois-Bheinn goes south-west, but first wander out to the end of the east ridge, which gives Druim Fiaclach its name, where sharp folds of rock thrust out of the ground like sharks' fins and provide pleasant scrambling. From the summit follow the south-west ridge as it snakes around the edge of the craggy headwall of Coire Reith (Ram) and turns south to descend steeply to a bealach; a path meanders among the outcrops. Beyond the bealach, the ridge twists westwards once more, over rocky terrain dotted with lochans (confusing in mist), to reach the grassy top of An t-Slat-bheinn. Outcrops now give way to boulders as the ridge leads over Sgurr na Ba Glaise and down to the Bealach an Fhiona for the final climb up to Rois-Bheinn.

Rois-Bheinn's east and higher top is reached first, but the short stroll out to the west top is a must for the magnificent view of the western seascape, of which you have been afforded only tantalising glimpses during the course of the traverse. Return to the Bealach an Fhiona and descend northwards to a lower bealach below the rocky hump of An Stac. To complete the round of Coire a' Bhuiridh and prolong the westward view, traverse An Stac to regain the path beside Tom Odhar back to your starting point.

Route 33: **THE CORRYHULLY HORSESHOE**

OS MAP: 40
GR: 906808
Distance: 13 miles (21 km)
Ascent: 1,400 m (4,600 ft)
Time: 8 hr

	1	2	3	4	5
Grade			●		
Terrain			●		
Navigation			●		
Seriousness				●	

Assessment: an entertaining horseshoe ridge that gains in interest as it progresses.
Seasonal notes: a rewarding winter traverse, but of testing length and one that requires care on narrow and steep sections.

Sgurr Thuilm (963 m, 3,159 ft)
  Skoor *Hool*am, Peak of the Knoll or Holm
Sgurr nan Coireachan (956 m, 3,136 ft)
  Skoor nan *Corr*achan, Peak of the Corries
Druim Coire a'Bheithe
  Drum Corr a *Vay*-ha, Ridge of the Birch Corrie
Beinn Gharbh (825 m, 2,706 ft)
  Ben *Gharr*av, Rough Mountain
Meall an Tarmachan (826 m, 2,709 ft)
  Myowl an *Tarr*amachan, Ptarmigan Hill
Sgurr a' Choire Riabhaich (852 m, 2,795 ft)
  Skoor a Chorra *Ree*-ach, Peak of the Brindled Corrie
Coire Thollaidh
  Corra Hully, Corrie of the Hollow

In the district of Locheil, north-west of Fort William, lies a fine group of mountains well hidden from the A830 Mallaig road but rendered easily accessible by deep glens carrying good tracks. The two finest routes in the area are the south-west ridge of Streap (route 34) and the horseshoe circuit of Sgurr Thuilm and Sgurr nan Coireachan above Coir Thollaidh.

Begin on the A830 at Glenfinnan, where Prince Charlie raised his standard at the start of his 1745 adventure. The area has many associations with Charlie; following his defeat at Culloden he crossed the Locheil hills no less than three times while escaping from his pursuers. Take the private road signposted 'Glenfinnan Lodge' on the west side of the bridge over the River Finnan. The road goes under the railway viaduct (built in 1899 and said to contain the remains of a horse and cart that fell into one of the hollow pillars during construction), and continues along the right bank of the river beside forestry plantations.

After 2½ miles (4 km) a Land Rover track signposted 'Public Footpath to Loch Arkaig' branches right past Corryhully bothy, which is

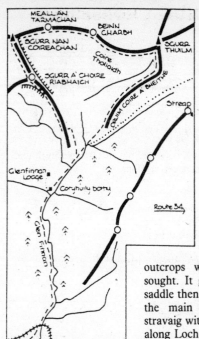

well maintained by Glenfinnan estate in exemplary fashion. Follow the track to the foot of Druim Coire a'Bheithe, the south-west ridge of Sgurr Thuilm that dominates the view ahead. Strike up the ridge on easy grass slopes and continue over a subsidiary top to reach the main summit. Charlie and his followers waited here all day while redcoats scoured the glens, then escaped northwards under cover of darkness.

The ridge of Sgurr nan Coireachan twists and undulates westwards for $2^{1}/_{2}$ miles (4 km); it is mainly broad and grassy, though with some rock outcrops where mild scrambling can be sought. It goes over a subsidiary top to a saddle then rises over a succession of tops to the main summit, providing a pleasant stravaig with ever-widening views westwards along Loch Morar to the glistening sea. Old fence posts mark most of the route.

Sgurr nan Coireachan marks the end point of the main ridge, but the most interesting section of the route is still to come. The south-east ridge of Sgurr nan Coireachan, which completes the horseshoe, narrows along the edge of impressive cliffs to the summit of Sgurr a'Choire Riabhaich, then steepens and narrows once more before finally opening out. It makes a fitting finish to a fine round. Near the foot of the ridge, just before the last short rise, descend left to pick up an excellent stalkers' path that leads gently around the nose of the ridge to rejoin the Land Rover track to Corryhully.

Route 34: **STREAP**

OS MAP: 40
GR: 931799
Distance: 10 miles (16 km)
Ascent: 1,070 m (3,500 ft)
Time: 6¹/₂ hr

	1	2	3	4	5
Grade			●		
Terrain			●		
Navigation			●		
Seriousness		●			

Assessment: a good introduction to the pleasures of walking narrow ridges.

Seasonal notes: snow transforms the summit ridge of Streap into snow aretes, which are beautiful, but which should be left well alone by the inexperienced.

Streap (909 m, 2,982 ft)
    Strape, Climbing
Streap Comhlaidh (898 m, 2,946 ft)
    Strape Cawly, Climbing Adjoining
Stob Coire nan Cearc (887 m, 2,910 ft)
    Stop Corra nan Kyairk, Peak of the Corrie of the Hens (ie grouse)
Coire Chuirn*
    Corra Choorn, Corrie of Cairns
Gleann Dubh Lighe
    Glen Doo *Lee*-ya, Glen of the Black Flood

The wonderfully-named Streap is the high point of a long ridge stretching from Glenfinnan to Loch Arkaig, the south-west section of which provides the most interesting ascent in the Locheil district. Begin at the bridge over the Dubh Lighe on the A830, 2 miles (3 km) east of Glenfinnan, taking the forestry road up the right bank of the river. Keep right at a fork after 15 min, and when Gleann Dubh Lighe bothy comes into view take the side track down to the river and cross to a path that continues up the glen past the bothy to a ruined shieling in Coire Chuirn. From here climb directly to the Bealach Coire nan Cearc, keeping close to the burn to avoid slabs.

At the bealach, the ridge proper begins with an ascent among outcrops to the summit of Stob Coire nan Cearc. From here the final section of Streap's south-west ridge looks exceedingly sharp, and the pleasant stroll to its foot gains from anticipation. On closer inspection, however, the ascent turns out to be easier than it looks, having some fine situations but requiring only elementary handwork. From the summit, a short steep descent south-eastwards leads to another narrow section, bypassed by a path on the left, although again of no difficulty. The descent continues interestingly to a dip before a steep reascent to the grassy dome of Streap Comhlaidh. Regain the ruined shieling in Coire Chuirn by descending the south ridge.

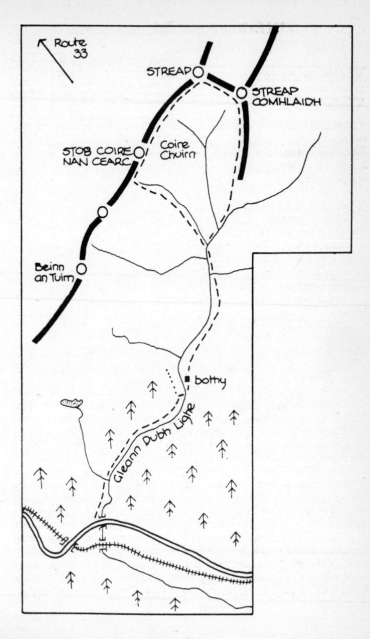

Route 35: **SGURR NA CICHE and GARBH CHIOCH MHÓR**

OS MAP: 33
GR: 981915
Distance: 13 miles (21 km)
Ascent: 1,180 m (3,850 ft)
Time: 8½ hr

	1	2	3	4	5
Grade			●		
Terrain					●
Navigation					●
Seriousness					●

Assessment: an archetypal West Highland ridge walk on a classic peak.
Seasonal notes: a classic winter traverse full of entertaining problems and not for the inexperienced. Note that late snow in the gully below the Feadan may cause unexpected difficulties.

Sgurr na Ciche (1,040 m, 3,412 ft)
    Skoor na *Keech*a, Breast (-shaped) Peak
Garbh Chioch Bheag* (968 m, 3,175 ft)
    *Garr*av *Chee*-och Vake, Little Rough Breast (-shaped peak)
Garbh Chioch Mhór (1,013 m, 3,323 ft)
    *Garr*av *Chee*-och Voar, Big Rough Breast (-shaped peak)
Feadan na Ciche*
    *Fai*tan na *Keech*a, Whistle of the Breast (-shaped peak)
Allt Coire nan Uth
    Owlt Corra nan Oo, River of the Udder Corrie

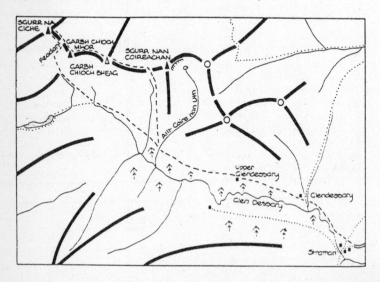

Few peaks in the Highlands excite the imagination as much as Sgurr na Ciche, whose steep symmetrical summit cone, soaring skywards like a miniature Matterhorn, gives the mountain a classical appearance from most angles. The ascent of Sgurr na Ciche and its rocky neighbour Garbh Chioch Mhór shows the Western Highlands at their best, combining the sharpness of the ridges of Kintail with the remoteness and ruggedness of the peaks of Knoydart.

The route begins at Strathan at the western end of Loch Arkaig, reached by the long winding road from Spean Bridge that is rough and private in its latter stages but whose use is not restricted. A Land Rover track continues to Upper Glendessary, but is very rough, and it is best to park near the fork just before Strathan. The small building on the left just beyond the fork is the barracks, where redcoats stood watch for Prince Charlie during his wanderings.

Take the right branch at the fork and follow the track up Glen Dessary to the house at Upper Glendessary. This beautiful glen, once wild and rugged, has been vandalised by the planting of regiments of conifers. Behind the house, a path goes up the hillside and continues along the glen above the plantations. Follow it as far as the Allt Coire nan Uth, then take a direct line up the hillside to the Bealach nan Gall below Garbh Chioch Bheag's eastern end.

The terrain now becomes rougher as the ridge to Sgurr na Ciche is followed westwards over a succession of rocky bumps to Garbh Chioch Bheag and Garbh Chioch Mhór. This is a fine ridge walk, with an impressive drystone wall to mark the way. Between Garbh Chioch Mhór and Sgurr na Ciche is the gap known as the Feadan na Ciche, whose name is best appreciated on a windy day. The descent into the Feadan is straightforward, but the direct line from here up to the summit of Sgurr na Ciche is beset by crags which are best skirted on the left. The superb panorama from the rooftop summit includes a unique view along the fjordlike confines of Loch Nevis.

In foul weather note the route up, in order to avoid difficulties on the way down, for the descent begins by a return to the Feadan. From here go down the bouldery gully on the south side until below the crags of Garbh Chioch Mhór, where a curious, level, grassy terrace can be found leading south-east around the crags. From the end of the terrace, easy grass slopes lead down to Glen Dessary and to the path to Upper Glendessary and Strathan.

Route 36: **LADHAR BHEINN**

OS MAP: 33
GR: 949066
Distance: 20 miles (33 km)
Ascent: 1,830 m (6,050 ft)
Time: 12 hr

	1	2	3	4	5
Grade				●	
Terrain			●		
Navigation				●	
Seriousness					●

Barrisdale approach (each way):
    6 miles (10 km), 300 m (1,000 ft), 3 hr
Ascent from Barrisdale
    8 miles (13 km), 1,230 m (4,050 ft), 6 hr

Assessment: a route of great stature; both the approach and the ascent demand superlatives.
Seasonal notes: the route is best done on a long, hot, summer's day. From Barrisdale, the ascent of Stob a' Chearcaill and the traverse of Stob a' Choire Odhair under snow are best left to experts.

Ladhar Bheinn (1,020 m, 3,346 ft)
    usually pronounced *Lar*ven, Hoofshaped Mountain
Stob a' Chearcaill
    Stop a *Hyair*cil, Circle Peak
Aonach Sgoilte (849 m, 2,785 ft)
    *Oen*ach Scul-tya, Cleft Ridge
Stob a' Choire Odhair (957 m, 3,139 ft)
    Stop a Chorr *Oa*-ir, Peak of the Dun Corrie
Coire Dhorrcail
    Corra *Ghor*cil, Torquil's Corrie
Creag Bheithe
    Craik *Vay*-ha, Birch Crag
Stob na Muicraidh
    Stop na Moocry, Peak of the Herd of Pigs

Lahdar Bheinn, the most westerly Munro on the mainland, is regarded by many people (including the author) as the most beautiful mountain in the British Isles. It is a mountain of soaring ridges, spectacular corries, testing remoteness and stunning panoramic views. Moreover, with its neighbours Luinne Bheinn and Meall Buidhe (route 37), it stands in one of the most rugged, beautiful and inaccessible parts of the country—the Knoydart peninsula. The peninsula is demarcated by Loch Hourn to the north and Loch Nevis to the south; two sea lochs that, in form and character if not in scale, have the appearance of Norwegian fjords. Upper Loch Hourn, in particular, is so hemmed in by craggy hillsides that no sun reaches its southern shore for some months during the winter.

    As befitting a mountain of its stature, Ladhar Bheinn is not easy to

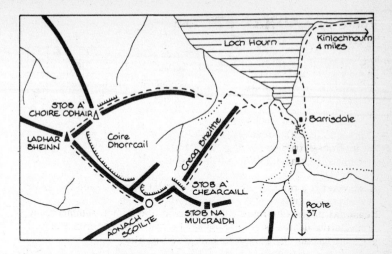

reach. The nearest starting point is Kinloch Hourn, at the end of the minor road along Loch Garry from the A87. From the road end, an obvious path continues past the jetty and along the south shore of Loch Hourn for 6 miles (10 km) to Barrisdale Cottage at the foot of Ladhar Bheinn. This is one of the finest coastal walks in Scotland; the path winds around the bays and promontories of the loch, sometimes clinging to the shoreline, sometimes climbing up and down through the bracken. As an approach route it is rivalled only by the Coruisk coastal walk (see route 97).

When the path rounds the last corner before Barrisdale Bay, Ladhar Bheinn bursts stunningly into view with the cliffs of Coire Dhorrcail towering over the waters of the loch. Cross the bridge over the River Barrisdale and take the stalkers' path that goes right into Coire Dhorrcail across the shoulder of Creag Bheithe. Once onto the shoulder, leave the path and climb up to the imposing rock face of Stob a'Chearcaill, which bars the way ahead abruptly. On closer inspection, the Stob becomes a thought-provoking but relatively straightforward scramble, though greasy when wet (if you wish to avoid this, ascend Stob a' Chearcaill from Barrisdale via Stob na Muicraidh).

The route onwards rims the rocky headwall of Coire Dhorrcail, and is of unfailing interest, as it leads to the summit 100 m beyond the junction with the ridge to Stob a' Choire Odhair. A descent via this ridge enables a fine circuit to be made. The ridge is narrow and the sharp summit of Stob a' Choire Odhair is an idyllic viewpoint, with mountain upon mountain crowding the confines of Loch Hourn. It is with reluctance that you will descend into Coire Dhorrcail to pick up the path back to Barrisdale.

Route 37: **LUINNE BHEINN and MEALL BUIDHE**

OS MAP: 33
GR: 949066
Distance: 23½ miles (38 km)
Ascent: 1,900 m (6,300 ft)
Time: 14 hr

	1	2	3	4	5
Grade			●		
Terrain				●	
Navigation					●
Seriousness					●

Barrisdale approach (each way):
   6 miles (10 km), 300 m (1,000 ft), 3 hr
Ascent from Barrisdale:
   11½ miles (18 km), 1,300 m (4,300 ft), 8 hr

Assessment: a magnificent route across the roughest mountains in Knoydart.
Seasonal notes: the route is best done on a long, hot, summer's day. From Barrisdale its many steep sections make it a demanding winter expedition outside the capabilities of the inexperienced.

Luinne Bheinn (939 m, 3,080 ft)
   Loon-ya Ven, Mountain of Melody (poss. from Gaelic luinneag)
Meall Buidhe (946 m, 3,103 ft)
   Myowl *Boo*-ya, Yellow Hill
Druim Leac a'Shith
   Drum Lyechk a Hee, Ridge of the Fairy Slab
Coire Odhar*
   Corr *Oa*-ar, Dun Corrie
Màm Unndalain*
   obscure
Màm Barrisdale
   Barri's dale (poss. from Norse)

Although not as majestic as their neighbour, Ladhar Bheinn (route 36), the extremely rough and remote mountains of Luinne Bheinn and Meall Buidhe in the Knoydart peninsula are fine mountains in their own right and are a rich prize for walkers. Begin at Kinloch Hourn and take the path to Barrisdale (as for route 36). Once across the River Barrisdale keep left on the main track for a short distance, then take a path on the right that soon forks. Take the left branch to the Màm Unndalain and climb Luinne Bheinn's narrowing north-east ridge to its twin tops, of which the western one is the higher.

The route onwards, across the complex, connecting ridge to Meall Buidhe, is barred initially by steep, craggy ground and it is best to go west for a short distance until a grassy gully gives access to an obvious grassy

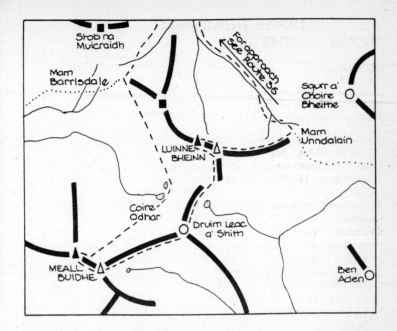

terrace leading back to the ridge. Continue round the rim of magnificent glaciated Coire Odhar, perhaps the roughest of all Knoydart corries, and climb the north-east ridge of Meall Buidhe. As on Luinne Bheinn there are two tops of which the western one is the higher.

To complete a fine round, descend the gully between the two tops into Coire Odhar and aim for the two lochans cupped in its craggy recesses. From the lochans contour across steep ground beneath Luinne Bheinn to the Màm Barrisdale, from where a path leads back to Barrisdale.

Route 38: **GLEOURAICH and SPIDEAN MIALACH**

OS MAP: 33
GR: 029030
Distance: 7 miles (11 km)
Ascent: 1,130 m (3,700 ft)
Time: 5½ hr

	1	2	3	4	5
Grade		●			
Terrain		●			
Navigation			●		
Seriousness	●				

Assessment: a pleasant ridge walk reached by the best mountain path in the Western Highlands.

Seasonal notes: normally no especial problems in winter, although the paths may be obliterated by snow.

Gleouraich (1,035 m, 3,395 ft)
    *Glyaw*rich, Mountain of Uproar (poss)
Craig Coire na Fiar Bhealaich* (1,006 m, 3,300 ft)
    Craik Corra na *Fee*-ar *Vyali*ch, Crag of the Corrie of the Slanting Pass
Spidean Mialach (996 m, 3,267 ft)
    *Speej*an *Mee*-alach, Peak of Lice
Coire Mhèil
    Corra Vale, Mill Corrie
Loch Quoich
    Cuckoo Loch (from Gaelic Cuaich)
Loch Fearna
    Loch *Fair*na, Alder Loch
Allt Coire Peitireach (poss should be Peithireachd)
    Owlt Corra *Peh*irachk, Stream of the Corrie of Errands

To the north of Loch Quoich rise some of the most easily climbed mountains in the Western Highlands, characterised by grassy hillsides to the south and rocky corries to the north. The ascent of Gleouraich uses perhaps the finest stalkers' path in the country, giving access to an undulating ridge walk, which leads pleasantly along the rim of the northern corries to Spidean Mialach.

Begin 1 mile (2 km) east of the bridge over the northern arm of Loch Quoich, just west of the Allt Coire Peitireach. A roadside cairn marks the start of the Gleouraich path, built to serve Glenquoich Lodge which is now inundated beneath the waters of the enlarged loch; the overgrown rhododendrons here are all that remain of the former lodge gardens. The excellent path climbs onto the south-west ridge of Gleouraich, with airy views down into Glen Quoich, and ends a short distance from the summit.

The route onwards to Spidean Mialach goes south-eastwards from the summit around the finest of the northern corries to Craig Coire na Fiar

Ben Dorain from near Auch *(Route 9)*

Cruach Ardrain (centre) from near Crianlarich *(Route 6)*

The Tarmachan Ridge from Loch Tay *(Route 10)*

Ben Starav from Invercharnan, Glen Etive *(Route 14)*

Buachaille Etive Beag from near Altnafeadh *(Route 18)*

The Easains from the Grey Corries *(Route 27)*

The south-west ridge of Streap *(Route 34)*

On the north ridge of Aonach air Chrith *(Route 41)*

Ciste Dhubh from An Caorann Mor *(Route 44)*

The summit of Creag Ghorm a' Bhealaich *(Route 53)*

Beinn Eighe from near Kinlochewe *(Route 61)*

Ben Hope from the north *(Route 77)*

Am Basteir, Sgurr nan Gillean and Sgurr a' Fhionn Choire from the east ridge of Bruach na Frithe *(Route 92)*

Gars-bheinn from Sgurr a' Choire Bhig *(Route 94)*

Bla Bheinn from Loch Slapin *(Route 97)*

In The Sanctuary of The Storr *(Route 98)*

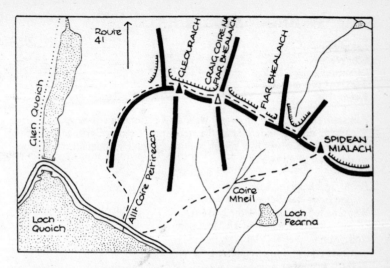

Bhealaich, then zigzags down another stalkers' path to the Fiar Bhealaich. Beyond here, a stony ascent undulates around the edge of three more rocky corries to the summit of Spidean Mialach. To descend, go down easy slopes towards Loch Fearna, bear right into Coire Mhèil to pick up yet another stalkers' path that deposits you at the roadside 400 m east of your starting point.

Route 39: **BEINN SGRITHEALL**

OS MAP: 33
GR: 843105
Distance: 6 miles (10 km)
Ascent: 1,070 m (3,500 ft)
Time: 5 hr

	1	2	3	4	5
Grade		●			
Terrain				●	
Navigation		●			
Seriousness			●		

Assessment: a top-of-the-world walk above stunning seascapes.
Seasonal notes: under snow, the steepness of Beinn Sgritheall's slopes and the consequences of a slip should not be underestimated; the narrow section may be awkward.

Beinn Sgritheall (974 m, 3,195 ft)
   Ben *Scree*-hal, Scree Mountain
Beinn na h-Eaglaise (804 m, 2,637 ft)
   Ben na *Heck*lisha, Church Mountain
Coire Min
   Corra Meen, Smooth Corrie
Bealach Arnasdail
   Arni's dale (from Norse)

'The view remains in my mind as perhaps the most beautiful I have seen in Scotland.'

SIR HUGH MUNRO

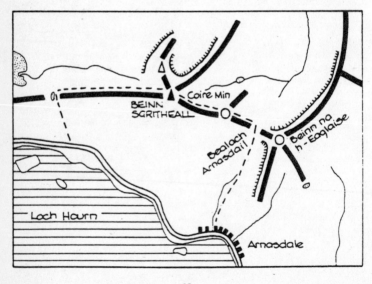

Beinn Sgritheall is a mountain apart. Isolated from the tangle of peaks in the neighbouring districts of Knoydart and Kintail it rises in one great sweep from the north shore of Loch Hourn, like an enormous tent whose roof consists of a ½ mile (1 km) ridge. The lochside slopes steepen from grass and wood to scree, hardly inviting an ascent in an area of outstanding peaks. Yet this gives a misleading impression of the mountain, for its northern flank has some fine corries and the traverse of the east and west ridges makes a wonderful walk, quite exposed in one section, on a mountain whose summit seems detached from the Earth.

Begin at the beautiful village of Arnisdale at the end of the long minor road that leaves the A87 at Shiel Bridge. From the bridge over the river, which comes down from the Bealach Arnasdail, go straight up the left bank behind the row of cottages that front the bay. Open hillside is soon reached, and a path of sorts climbs beside an old fence past some fine waterfalls. There is no respite from the remorseless steepness, but height is gained fast. Follow the line of the fence when it crosses the river and continues to a lochan in the jaws of the bealach beneath the craggy north-west face of Beinn na h-Eaglaise. From here, climb the steepening cone, which forms the east top of Beinn Sgritheall, and with any luck you will find a path left of the crest to ease the ascent of the final stony slopes leading to the flat summit.

The broad grassy ridge, which continues round the rim of Coire Min to the main summit, provides one of the most pleasant walks to be found on any Scottish mountain. The slopes down to Loch Hourn and the open sea are hidden by their steepness, and the sensation is one of being isolated from the Earth. The view of the Knoydart mountains and across the mouth of Loch Hourn to the island of Rum is stunning. Just before the summit the ridge narrows appreciably around the narrow corrie headwall; there is some exposure but no difficulty.

Descend to the foot of the rocky west ridge on a good path, reaching a lochan that completes Beinn Sgritheall's symmetry. Just before the lochan a cairn on a boulder marks the start of a cairned path that meanders down steep grass and craggy wooded slopes to the roadside. The path is difficult to follow lower down, and the author has yet to discover exactly where it reaches the road. The day ends with a lochside stroll back to Arnisdale.

Route 40: **THE SADDLE**

OS MAP: 33
GR: 968143
Distance: 7 miles (11 km)
Ascent: 1,040 m (3,400 ft)
Time: 6 hr

	1	2	3	4	5
Grade	•				●
Terrain		●			
Navigation			●		
Seriousness					●

Assessment: the most sensational ridge scramble in the Western Highlands, but with no unavoidable difficulties.

Seasonal notes: a major winter mountaineering expedition.

The Saddle (1,010 m, 3,313 ft)
Sgurr nan Forcan* (958 m, 3,143 ft)
    Skoor nan *Forr*acan
Spidean Dhomhuill Bhric (940 m, 3,083 ft) (should be Dhomhnuill)
    *Speej*an *Ghonn*-il Vreechk, Spotty Donald's Peak
Sgurr Leac nan Each (919 m, 3,015 ft)
    Skoor Lyechk nan Yech, Peak of the Horse's Slab
Meallan Odhar (c610 m, c2,000 ft)
    *Myowl*an *Oa*-ar, Dun Hill
Biod an Fhithich (c630 m, c2,070 ft)
    Beet an *Ee*ich, Raven's Point
Bealach Coire Mhàlagain
    *Byal*ach Corra *Val*agin, obscure
Coire Uaine*
    Corra Oo-*an*-ya, Green Corrie

From Loch Cluanie to Loch Duich, the deep narrow confines of Glen Shiel carry the A87 north to Kyle of Lochalsh and Skye, and no other glen makes so many fine mountains so easily accessible. With nine Munros to the south of the road, eleven to the north and many other tops besides, there is enough here to repay many a visit. This book recommends eight routes in the area (routes 40–7) and begins with the ascent of what is universally acknowledged to be the finest mountain in Glen Shiel—The Saddle, a complex peak of craggy corries, long tapering ridges and graceful summits. The finest ridge of all is the east ridge over Sgurr nan Forcan; if taken direct it ranks alongside Aonach Eagach (route 20) and the Torridon ridges as one of the most sensational on the mainland, and it is certainly the classic scramble of the Western Highlands.

    Begin in Glen Shiel 300 m north of the bridge over the Allt Mhàlagain. Look for an excellent stalkers' path that leaves the roadside, meanders up the east ridge of Meallan Odhar and cuts right to the bealach below Biod an Fhithich. From here a path goes left to the foot of the Forcan Ridge and takes a grassy route up the first steep rise, with one or two pieces of handwork to give you a foretaste of what is to come. On breasting the rise

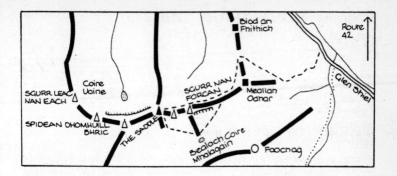

the rocky summit of Sgurr nan Forcan bursts into view, buttressed by great slabs of rock, and here the excitement really begins.

The arete leading up to the summit is extremely sharp in places and a few sections provide hard scrambling, but on closer inspection the route onwards is usually easier than it looks, and a summer path below the crest on the right avoids all difficulties if necessary. Beyond the summit, the excitement continues; an initial steep descent requires care and further on, towards the east top of The Saddle, a knife edge provides some particularly interesting scrambling; a path again avoids all difficulties.

From The Saddle's main top, the ridge continues quite narrowly over the west top and around the head of Coire Uaine to Spidean Dhomhuill Bhric and Sgurr Leac nan Each, both of which are worthy objectives if you wish to extend the route. From the main summit descend a steep grass and boulder slope to the south and bear left towards the Bealach Coire Mhàlagain, aiming for two small lochans just above the bealach to the left. A few metres further down, a wall contours beneath Sgurr nan Forcan to rejoin the ascent route at the foot of the ridge.

Route 41: **AONACH AIR CHRITH and MAOL CHINN-DEARG**

OS MAP: 33
GR: 044114
Distance: 6 miles (10 km)
Ascent: 900 m (2,950 ft)
Time: 5½ hr

	1	2	3	4	5
Grade				●	
Terrain		●			
Navigation	●				
Seriousness		●			

Assessment: one of the most sporting, yet most ignored ridges in Glen Shiel.

Seasonal notes: in winter, narrow snow aretes and iced rocks may greatly increase the difficulty of the traverse of Aonach air Chrith, and the descent towards Maol Chinn-dearg may also require extra care.

Aonach air Chrith (1,021 m, 3,349 ft)
    *Oen*ach air Chri, Trembling Ridge
Maol Chinn-dearg (981 m, 3,231 ft)
    Mœl Cheen *Jerr*ak, Bare Redheaded Hill
Druim Thollaidh
    Drum Hully, Ridge of the Hollow
Druim Coire nan Eirecheanach
    obscure

The South Glen Shiel Ridge contains no less than seven Munros, which can easily be ticked off in a day if transport can be arranged at both ends, but the best route on this side of the glen is a combination of the narrowest section of the main ridge with the 'trembling' north ridge of Aonach air Chrith.

Begin 2 miles (3 km) west of Cluanie Inn on the A87, just beyond a right-hand bend where a road sign warns of rockfall danger. A stalkers' path leaves the roadside and forks to climb Druim Thollaidh and Druim Coire nan Eirecheanach. From the fork go left across the moor and climb the steep grassy hump that marks the end of Anoach air Chrith's north-east ridge. Continue up bouldery slopes and scramble along the sharp crest leading to the north top. After a short dip, two rock bluffs which stand astride the connecting ridge to the main summit go direct, although all the fun can be bypassed on the right if necessary.

From Aoanach air Chrith follow the path along the main ridge to Maol Chinn-dearg. The initial descent around the cliff edge calls for some elementary handwork but, beyond a saddle, the path becomes a staircase in the grass. To complete the round, descend Druim Coire nan Eirecheanach (Maol Chinn-dearg's well defined north-east ridge), and follow the well engineered stalkers' path, mentioned above, for an effortless descent to the roadside.

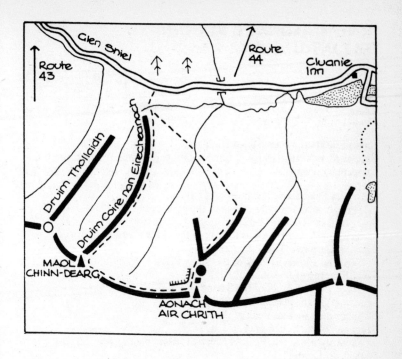

Route 42: **THE FIVE SISTERS OF KINTAIL**

OS MAP: 33
GR: 966210
Distance: 12 miles (19 km)
Ascent: 1,590 m (5,200 ft)
Time: 8¹/₂ hr

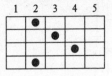

	1	2	3	4	5
Grade		●			
Terrain			●		
Navigation				●	
Seriousness		●			

Assessment: the classic West Highland ridge walk.
Seasonal notes: a lengthy, but exceptional, winter traverse for those competent on snow.

Sgurr nan Spainteach* (990 m, 3,247 ft)
    Skoor nan *Spahn*-tyach, Peak of the Spaniards
Sgurr na Ciste Duibhe (1,027 m, 3,369 ft)
    Skoor na *Keesh*-tya *Doo*ya, Peak of the Black Chest or Coffin
Sgurr na Carnach (1,002 m, 3,287 ft)
    Skoor na *Carn*ach, Peak of the Stony Place
Sgurr Fhuaran (1,068 m, 3,503 ft)
    Skoor *Oo*-ran, Peak of the Spring
Sgurr nan Saighead (929 m, 3,047 ft)
    Skoor nan *Sigh*-at, Peak of the Arrows
Sgurr na Mòraich (876 m, 2,873 ft)
    Skoor na *Maw*rich, Peak of Morvich (ie sea-plain)
Bealach an Lapain*
    *Bya*lach an *Lah*-pin, The Easy Pass (poss)
Coire Domdain* (should be Domhain)
    Corra *Doe*-in, Deep Corrie
Gleann Lichd
    Glen Licht, Slabby Glen (from Gaelic Leac)

The mountains bordering the north side of Glen Shiel are fine-looking hills with a more complex topography than on the south side, and to appreciate their separate characters to the full four routes (routes 42–5) are recommended. The most westerly group of mountains is known as the Five Sisters of Kintail. The view of them from the Glenelg road across Loch Duich is one of the most famous in the Western Highlands, their grassy southern slopes falling steeply into Glen Shiel at an average angle of more than 30°, giving an impression of tremendous height. According to legend there were originally seven sisters, daughters of a local farmer. Two were taken as brides by visiting brothers, who promised to send back their five other brothers for the remaining five sisters. But no one came, and to preserve their beauty while they waited, the sisters agreed to let the local wizard transform them into the peaks whose beauty has bewitched travellers ever since.

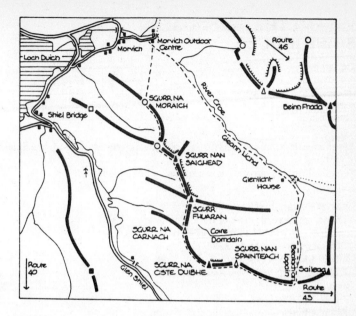

Without transport at both ends the traverse of the Five Sisters is best approached from the north. Begin at Morvich Outdoor Centre in Strath Croe, reached by a minor road that leaves the A87 at the head of Loch Duich. Take the Land Rover track that branches right along the narrow confines of Gleann Lichd, and becomes a path continuing past Glenlicht House to the foot of Coire Domdain. From here climb directly up to the Bealach an Lapain and turn right to ascend the narrow grassy east ridge of Sgurr nan Spainteach.

The route onwards is a magnificent high-level walk along the main ridge of the Five Sisters around the head of wild Coire Domdain, firstly reaching Sgurr na Ciste Duibhe (note the curious hollow on the intervening bealach, which may be confusing in mist), then turning north and broadening over the stony top of Sgurr na Carnach to the steep summit slopes of Sgurr Fhuaran, the highest peak of the group. From here go down the north-west ridge a short distance, to avoid steep ground, then cut back right to continue along the main ridge around impressive slabs to the summit pyramid of Sgurr nan Saighead. Still to come is the most interesting section of the route, a narrow crest that leads enjoyably to the north-west top of Sgurr nan Siaghead, beyond which broader slopes lead onward to Sgurr na Mòraich, the fifth and lowest sister, with magnificent views over Loch Duich. The day ends with a steep descent back to Morvich.

Route 43: **THE NORTH GLEN SHIEL RIDGE**

OS MAP: 33
GR: 054115
Distance: 8 miles (13 km)
Ascent: 1,360 m (4,450 ft)
Time: 6½ hr

	1	2	3	4	5
Grade		●			
Terrain		●			
Navigation				●	
Seriousness		●			

Assessment: a narrow undulating ridge walk typical of the Glen Shiel mountains.
Seasonal notes: narrow snow aretes may be encountered.

Sgurr an Fhuarail (988 m, 3,241 ft)
  Skoor an *Oo*-aril, Peak of the Cold Place
Aonach Meadhoin* (1,003 m, 3,290 ft)
  *Oen*ach *Mee*-an, Middle Ridge
Sgurr a' Bhealaich Dheirg (1,038 m, 3,405 ft)
  Skoor a *Vyali*ch *Yerr*ak, Peak of the Red Pass
Saileag (959 m, 3,146 ft)
  *Sahl*ak, Little Heel
Meall a' Charra
  Myowl a Charra, Uneven Hill (poss)
Coire na Cadha
  Corra na *Ca*ha, Corrie of the Pass
Coire Tholl Bhruach*
  Corra Howl *Vroo*-ach, Corrie of the Hollow of the Slope

The peaks east of the Five Sisters of Kintail (route 42) have much in common with their more famous neighbours. Their traverse exhibits the same character of fine, high-level walking along narrow ridges, with wild corries to the north and plunging grass slopes to the south. Unlike the Five Sisters, however, their ascent from Glen Shiel is eased by two subsidiary ridges, which enable a fine circuit to be made.

  Begin at the bridge over the Allt Coire Tholl Bhruach 1½ miles (2 km) west of Cluanie Inn on the A87 and take the path up the left bank of the river to the foot of Coire na Cadha. From here climb steep grass slopes to the bump on the skyline that marks the top of the south-east ridge of Sgurr an Fhuarail, then turn left to follow the narrowing ridge across the sharp summit of the Sgurr to Aonach Meadhoin. Continuing westwards, the well defined ridge next reaches the broad level top of Sgurr a' Bhealaich Dheirg, whose summit cairn lies some 70 m out along the rocky north-east ridge, and then the ridge descends narrowly before rising once more over grass slopes to Saileag.

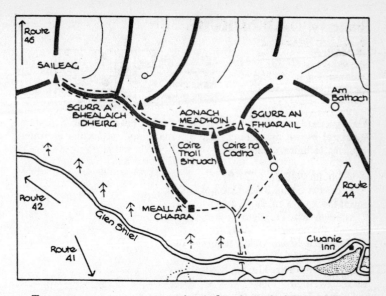

To return, retrace your steps to just before the bealach beyond Sgurr a'
Bhealach Dheirg and branch right down the broad south ridge leading out
to Meall a' Charra. From the last top on the ridge descend left around the
forestry plantations to rejoin the path beside the Allt Coire Tholl Bhruach.

Route 44: **CISTE DHUBH**

OS MAP: 33
GR: 090121
Distance: 8 miles (13 km)
Ascent: 1,000 m (3,300 ft)
Time: 6 hr

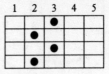

	1	2	3	4	5
Grade			●		
Terrain		●			
Navigation			●		
Seriousness		●			

Assessment: a narrow ridge walk on a retiring, but attractive, mountain.
Seasonal notes: the summit ridge is corniced and spectacular in winter, requiring technical competence.

Ciste Dhubh (982 m, 3,221 ft)
    Keesh-tya Ghoo, Black Chest or Coffin
Am Bàthach (798 m, 2,618 ft)
    Am *Bah*-ach, The Byre
Bealach a' Chòinich
    *Byal*ach a *Choan*-yich, Pass of the Bog
An Caorann Mór
    An *Cœr*an Moar, The Big Rowan
Allt a' Chaorainn Mhóir
    Owlt a *Chœr*in *Voe*-ir, River of the Big Rowan

Of the many fine mountains enclosing Glen Shiel, Ciste Dhubh is the most retiring. It lies to the north of the glen half hidden behind the grassy lump of Am Bàthach, yet anyone who catches a glimpse of its soaring summit will be drawn to it. And who could resist the lure of its name?

Begin at the bridge over the Allt a' Chaorainn Mhóir 1 mile (1½ km) east of Cluanie Inn on the A87. Keeping right of the forestry plantation, climb directly up the steep grass slopes of Am Bàthach to the unique summit, a narrow grass ridge that seems totally out of place among the rocky Glen Shiel hills. Descend to the boggy Bealach a' Chòinich and continue up the south ridge of Ciste Dhubh. The ascent is on steep grass as far as a rocky top, then becomes much more narrow and interesting. A path clings to the crest of the ridge and leads sharply to the summit of the mountain above the cliffs of the east face. Under normal conditions there is no difficulty, but care is required in high winds or in winter conditions.

Descend the steep grassy east ridge, veering right into the eastern corrie when beyond the craggy upper section, and aim directly for the Allt a' Chaorainn Mhóir. Pick up a path on the left bank which becomes a Land Rover track, descending An Caorann Mór to reach the roadside 200 km from your starting point.

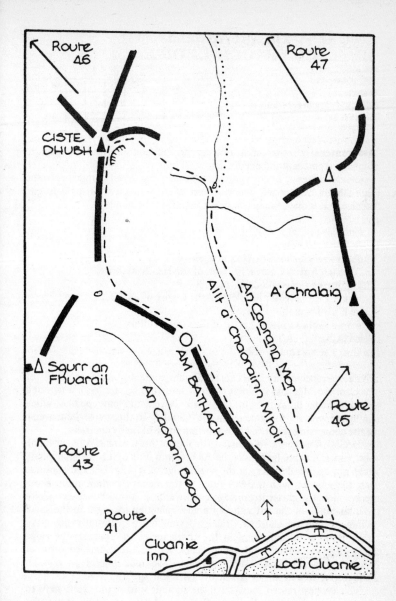

Route
46

Route
47

CISTE
DHUBH

A' Chralaig

An Caorann Mor

Allt a' Chaorainn Mhoir

Sgurr an
Fhuarail

AM BATHACH

An Caorann Beag

Route
45

Route
43

Route
41

Cluanie
Inn

Loch Cluanie

Route 45: A' CHRALAIG and MULLACH FRAOCH-CHOIRE

OS MAP: 33
GR: 092121
Distance: 8 miles (13 km)
Ascent: 1,110 m (3,650 ft)
Time: 6 hr

	1	2	3	4	5
Grade				●	
Terrain		●			
Navigation		●			
Seriousness		●			

Assessment: a route across two contrasting mountains, which includes the best scramble in the north Glen Shiel hills.

Seasonal notes: a major winter mountaineering expedition; between the rock towers of Mullach Fraoch-choire there sometimes forms a fragile cornice that is one of the most beautiful in the Highlands.

A' Chràlaig (1,120 m, 3,674 ft)
   A *Chrah*-lik, The Creel
Mullach Fraoch-choire (1,102 m, 3,615 ft)
   *Mull*ach Frœch Chorra, Summit of the Heather Corrie
Stob Coire na Cràlaig* (1,008 m, 3,307 ft)
   Stop Corra na *Crah*-lik, Peak of the Corrie of the Creel
Coire a' Ghlas-thuill
   Corr a Ghlass *Hoo*-il, Corrie of the Green Hollow
Coire Odhar
   Corr *Oa*-ar, Dun Corrie

Mullach Fraoch-choire faces Ciste Dhubh (route 44) across the defile of An Caorann Mór and is a mountain of similar character, with a tapering summit ridge breaking out into rock towers at some points. When combined with its bulky neighbour A' Chràlaig to the south, the traverse of the connecting ridge makes a sporting route of many contrasts.

Begin where route 44 ends, at the foot of An Caorann Mór, near the west end of Loch Cluanie on the A87. Climb directly up the relentlessly steep grassy hillside to reach the south ridge of A' Chràlaig and continue past the junction with the east ridge to the massive summit cairn. From here, follow the grassy main ridge northwards as it snakes between Coire a'Ghlas-thuill on the left and Coire na Cràlaig on the right to the small pointed top of Stob Coire na Cràlaig. Beyond here, an abrupt swing to the right makes a turning point in the character of the route as the ridge narrows to a bealach and swings back left to the pinnacled crest of Mullach Fraoch-choire's summit ridge. The rock towers provide an exhilarating scramble, but can be bypassed if desired.

The shortest return route from the summit is to retrace your steps to the bealach before Stob Coire na Cràlaig and descend steeply into Coire Odhar to pick up the path through An Caorann Mór back to your starting point.

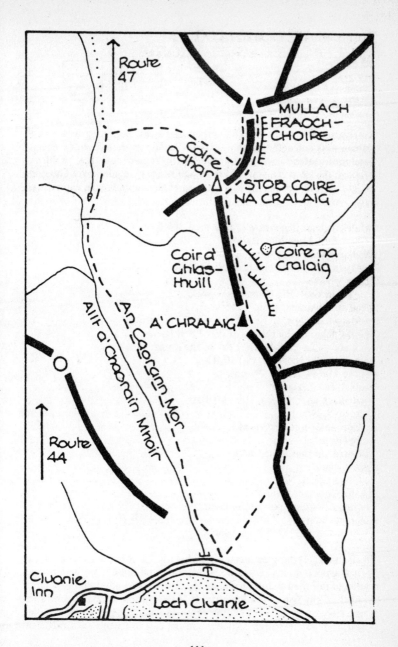

Route 47

MULLACH FRAOCH-CHOIRE

Coire Odhar

STOB COIRE NA CRALAIG

Coire na Cralaig

Coir a' Ghlas-thuill

An Caorann Mor

Allt a' Chaorain Mhoir

A' CHRALAIG

Route 44

Cluanie Inn

Loch Cluanie

111

Route 46: **BEINN FHADA**

OS MAP: 33
GR: 981223
Distance: 8 miles (13 km)
Ascent: 1,140 m (3,750 ft)
Time: 6½ hr

	1	2	3	4	5
Grade				●	
Terrain			●		
Navigation					●
Seriousness			●		

Assessment: a route of two contrasting halves, beginning with a high plateau walk and ending with a scramble amidst impressive rock scenery.
Seasonal notes: under snow the ascent should pose few problems, although the steep exit from Coire an Sgàirne may require care. The ridge to Sgurr a' Choire Ghairbh is a sporting winter route for the experienced only.

Beinn Fhada or Ben Attow (1,032 m, 3,385 ft)
  Ben *Att*a, Long Mountain
Meall a' Bhealaich (c780 m, c2,560 ft)
  Myowl a *Vyal*ich, Hill of the Pass
Plaide Mhór*
  Plah-ja Voar, Big Plain
Meall an Fhuarain Mhóir* (956 m, 3,136 ft)
  Myowl an *Oo*-arin *Voe*-ir, Hill of the Big Springs
Sgurr a' Choire Ghairbh (c870 m, c2,860 ft)
  Skoor a Chorra *Ghirr*av, Peak of the Rough Corrie
Beinn Bhuidhe (c490 m, c1,610 ft)
  Ben *Voo*-ya, Yellow Mountain
Bealach an t-Sealgaire*
  *Byal*ach an *Jal*akera, Hunter's Pass
Coire an Sgàirne*
  Corr an *Scarn*a, Corrie of Rumbling
Coire Gorm*
  Corra *Gorr*am, Blue Corrie
Coire Chaoil*
  Corra Choel, Narrow Corrie
Gleann Chòinneachain
  Glen *Choan*-yachin, Boggy Glen
Abhainn Chonaig
  *Av*in *Chonn*ik, Dog River (poss)

'In Kintail everything culminates. Nothing lacks. It is the epitome of the West Highland scene,' wrote W.H. Murray, and there is no better illustration of this than Beinn Fhada, a long complex mountain that is as large as all the Five Sisters put together. It is a mountain of many contrasts, from steep grassy hillsides on the south to wild crag-girt corries on the north, from vast expanses of plateau in the east to narrow rock ridges in

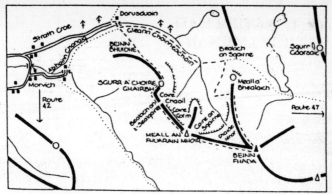

the west. The best circuit of the mountain approaches the summit plateau from the north and returns via the narrow western reaches to show Beinn Fhada in all its moods.

Begin at the Forestry Commission car park at Dorusduain in Strath Coe, at the end of the minor road that leaves the A87 at the head of Loch Duich. Keep right on the Land Rover track to Dorusduain House, and at the gate to the house keep right beside the fence to reach a path down to the bridge over the Abhainn Chonaig. This path joins a good path through the narrow confines of Gleann Chòinneachain (see route 47). Fifteen minutes after crossing the Allt Coire an Sgairne, leave the path at a cairn to follow a good stalkers' path that cuts back right across the hillside into wild Coire an Sgàirne and climbs onto the ridge to the right of Meall a' Bhealaich.

Follow the ridge onto the Plaide Mhór, the vast featureless summit plateau of Beinn Fhada, which provides unbeatable navigational practice in adverse weather, and continue to the summit. Beyond lie further tops stretching away towards Glen Affric, but few venture onwards for there are more exciting tops to hand on the return journey.

Head back across the Plaide Mhór to the southern rim of Coire an Sgàirne and onto Meall an Fhuarain Mhoir, a rounded top beyond which the character of the route changes completely. A rocky ridge narrows around Coire Gorm and descends to the Bealach an t-Sealgaire. Some handwork is called for, but the only section that causes pause for thought is the ascent from the bealach, where the steep sloping rock requires care (awkward when wet).

Continuing onwards around Coire Chaoil to Sgurr a' Choire Ghairbh it is necessary to negotiate the curious nicks in the ridge that are so conspicuous from below, but there is no difficulty. Descend the steep ridge curving round to Beinn Bhuidhe and go straight over the end down steep grass slopes among outcrops to Dorusduain. These last slopes are very steep and require care; if wet they are best avoided by descending westwards from Beinn Bhuidhe towards Morvich.

113

Route 47: **SGURR NAN CEATHREAMHNAN**

OS MAP: 25 or 33
GR: 981223
Distance: 17 miles (27 km)
Ascent: 1,690 m (5,550 ft)
Time: 10½ hr

	1	2	3	4	5
Grade			●		
Terrain		●			
Navigation		●			
Seriousness					●

Assessment: a route through the wilderness to a mountain of great character.

Seasonal notes: in winter, the length of the approach march and the steepness of the east ridge should not be underestimated. A beautiful but dangerous cornice forms on the summit ridge.

Sgurr nan Ceathreamhnan (1,151 m, 3,776 ft)
    Skoor nan *Cerr*anan, Peak of the Quarters
A' Ghlas-bheinn (918 m, 3,011 ft)
    A Ghlass Ven, The Grey Mountain
An Socach* (920 m, 3,018 ft)
    An *Soch*-cach, The Snout
Stob Coire nan Dearcag* (940 m, 3,083 ft)
    Stop Corra nan *Jerr*-cak, Peak of the Corrie of Berries
Sgurr Gaorsaic (c830 m, c2,730 ft)
    Skoor *Gærsik*, obscure
Coire na Cloiche
    Corra na *Cloch*-ya, Stony Corrie
Gleann Gniomhaidh
    Glen *Gree*-ava, Active Glen
Alltbeithe
    Owlt *Bay*-ha, Birch River
Loch a' Bhealaich
    Loch a *Vyali*ch, Loch of the Pass

North of the Glen Shiel hills, and separated from them by the long and beautiful Glen Affric, is a country of wide horizons, where the mountains have a grandeur born of magnificent approaches and long high ridges rising above remote glens. Most of the hills are best approached via Glen Affric (see route 48) but the remote outlier of Sgurr nan Ceathreamhnan is best reached from the west. Like Beinn Fhada to the south, Sgurr nan Ceathreamhnan radiates a number of long ridges that support a cluster of subsidiary tops, but it is more graceful than its neighbour, with a narrow tent-shaped summit ridge, which provides a fine ridge walk.

Of the many possible approach routes to the mountain the shortest and perhaps best is that from Glen Elchaig via the Falls of Glomach, but this is

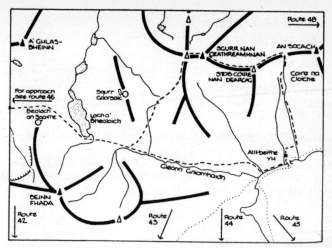

currently impracticable owing to the unenlightened access policy of Glen Elchaig estate (locked gate on access road). Of the remaining approaches that from Strath Croe is much the most interesting.

Begin at the Forestry Commission car park at Dorusduain and take the path up Gleann Chòinneachain (as for route 46) between the steep hillsides of A' Ghlas-bheinn and Beinn Fhada into the wild rocky jaws of the Bealach an Sgàrne. From here the path descends to the mountain sanctuary of Loch a' Bhealaich, as lonely and desolate a spot as you could wish to find, and continues down Gleann Gniomhaidh to Alltbeithe youth hostel. Vehicular access for stalking has reduced the latter stages of this path to mud in some places. Alltbeithe is a haven in the wilderness, more a superior bothy than a modern youth hostel, and on a wild day it may require determination to continue beyond it.

From Alltbeithe, a stalkers' path heads northwards up Coire na Cloiche to the bealach between Sgurr nan Ceathreamhnan and An Socach; this latter Munro (not named on OS map) can be easily bagged if desired. Turning westwards, the ridge climbs over Stob Coire nan Dearcag and narrows across the east top of Sgurr nan Ceathreamhnan to abruptly reach the cairn that crowns the main summit. Beyond lies the narrow summit ridge that leads to the lower west top; although quite exposed in places and requiring some handwork on the crest, it is without difficulty and ends all too soon.

From the west top follow the fence that descends the south ridge and bears right to the saddle below Sgurr Gaorsaic. From here, go down steep grass slopes on the south side of Sgurr Gaorsaic and contour right to rejoin the path along Gleann Gniomhaidh for the long walk back to Dorusduain.

115

Route 48: **MAM SODHAIL and CARN EIGE**

OS MAP: 25
GR: 200234
Distance: 14 miles (22 km)
Ascent: 1,380 m (4,550 ft)
Time: 9 hr

	1	2	3	4	5
Grade		●			
Terrain			●		
Navigation			●		
Seriousness				●	

Assessment: a demanding walk along the twisting and undulating ridges of the spacious Affric hills.

Seasonal notes: a long, but entertaining, winter route, which may have to be curtailed at Carn Eige owing to the difficulty of the continuation to the Garbh-bhealach under snow. Glen Affric is at its most colourful in autumn.

Màm Sodhail (1,181 m, 3,874 ft)
   Mam Soal, Breast (-shaped hill) of the Barns
Carn Eige (1,183 m, 3,881 ft)
   Carn *Aik*a, Cairn of the Notch, or poss should be Eighe (*Ai*-ya, File) or Eite (*Ait*-ya, Extensive)
Sgurr na Lapaich (1,036 m, 3,398 ft)
   Skoor na *Lah*-pich, Peak of the Bog
Mullach Cadha Rainich* (993 m, 3,257 ft)
   Mullach *Ca*ha *Rahn*ich, Summit of the Fern Pass
Stob a' Choire Dhomhain* (1,148 m, 3,766 ft)
   Stop a Chorra *Ghoe*-in, Peak of the Deep Corrie
Sron Garbh*
   Srawn *Garr*av, Rough Nose
Gleann nam Fiadh
   Glen nam *Fee*-a, Glen of the Deer
Garbh-bhealach*
   *Garr*av *Vyal*ach, Rough Pass

Glen Affric is one of the major showpieces for the integration of HEP schemes and forestry plantations into the natural environment, and the road along the glen is one of the most scenic in Scotland. In autumn the view westwards from the road end towards Sgurr na Lapaich is stunningly colourful. Beyond the road end the long glen forms a major east-west through-route past Loch Affric and Alltbeithe youth hostel to Kintail (see route 47). To the north of Loch Affric lies an area of long undulating ridges and high peaks, culminating in the twin summits of Màm Sodhail and Carn Eige, the highest peaks in Britain north of the Great Glen. The traverse of the two mountains around the head of Gleann nam Fiadh makes a strenuous but satisfying high-level tramp.

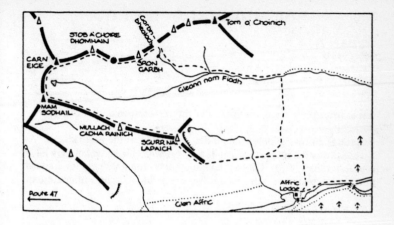

Begin at the car park at the end of the public road and take the Land Rover track to Affric Lodge. Just before the lodge a path goes north up the hillside then west onto the moor beneath Sgurr na Lapaich's craggy east face. Keep to the path until it doubles back away from Sgurr na Lapaich, then head across the moor and climb steep heathery slopes left of the crags to gain the summit. The route onwards is a delightful 2½ mile (4 km) undulating ridge, narrowing across Mullach Cadha Rainich to the final steep slopes of Màm Sodhail. The huge summit cairn on this, the thirteenth highest mountain in Britain, testifies to the mountain's former importance as a survey point during the OS mapping of the Highlands in the nineteenth century.

A sharp descent and reascent around the head of Glean nam Fiadh leads to the even higher dome of Carn Eige, and then the ridge narrows interestingly over a succession of tops towards the Garbh-bhealach. A number of pinnacles on the crest just beyond Stob a' Choire Dhomhain are easily bypassed on the right, and further on a stone staircase eases the rocky descent to the bealach.

Strong walkers may wish to continue to Tom a' Chòinich's mossy top, and masochists may even wish to bag Toll Creagach further east, but this would be something of an anticlimactic finish to the day; most walkers, like the author, will settle for the long walk back to Affric Lodge. From the Garbh-bhealach descend the left bank of the burn to pick up a stalkers' path heading down Gleann nam Fiadh. Leave this path for another that crosses the Abhainn Gleann nam Fiadh, climb the right bank of the burn that comes down from the moor beneath Sgurr na Lapaich's east face and rejoins the ascent route.

Route 49: **THE MULLARDOCH GROUP**

OS MAP: 25
GR: 219316
Distance: 17½ miles (28 km)
Ascent: 1,580 m (5,200 ft)
Time: 10½ hr

	1	2	3	4	5
Grade			●		
Terrain				●	
Navigation					●
Seriousness					●

Assessment: a rough tramp across the remote peaks of Loch Mullardoch.

Seasonal notes: a long winter's day, especially as the east ridges of An Riabhachan and Sgurr na Lapaich may cause problems under snow. The southern ridges of An Riabhachan's south-west top and Sgurr na Lapaich provide escape routes. Glen Cannich is exceptionally beautiful in autumn.

An Socach* (1,069 m, 3,507 ft)
    An *Soch*-ach, The Snout

 Riabhachan (1,129 m, 3,704 ft)
    An *Ree*-avachan, Brindled Hill
Sgurr na Lapaich (1,150 m, 3,772 ft)
    Skoor na *Lah*-pich, Peak of the Bog
Carn nan Gobhar (992 m, 3,254 ft)
    Carn nan *Goe*-ar, Goat's Cairn
Bealach a' Bholla*
    *Byal*ach a *Voll*a, Pass of the Bowl
Toll an Lochain*
    Towl an Lochan, Hollow of the Lochan
Coire Mhàim
    Corra *Va*-im, Corrie of the Breast (-shaped hill)
Coire an t-Sith
    Corr an Jee, Fairy Corrie
Loch Tuill Bhearnach
    Loch *Too*-il *Vyarn*ach, Loch of the Notched Hollow
Allt Taige
    Owlt *Tie*-ka, Stream of Attachment (poss)

North of Glen Affric, the parallel glen of Glen Cannich gives access to the remote mountains lying in the forlorn country between Loch Mullardoch and Loch Monar. The road up the beautifully wooded glen ends at Loch Mullardoch's enormous dam, the largest in Scotland, a desolate and surreal sight on a dreich day. Beyond here the enlarged loch has inundated all tracks and habitations and made journeys into the interior correspondingly more adventurous. The walk along either shore of the 9 mile (14 km) long loch now has a pioneering feel to it, and this has, if anything,

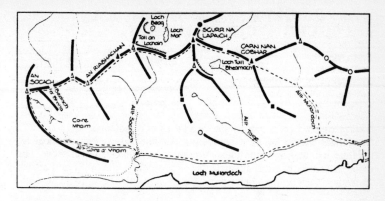

enriched the prizes on the north side of the loch, where four Munros await the intrepid mountain walker.

The route begins at the dam with a 5 mile (8 km) walk along the north shore of the loch. There is a good path as far as the Allt Mullardoch, then sheep tracks can be used to ease the journey to the Allt Taige, beyond which a path continues to the hut at the foot of the Allt Socrach. Cross the burn and take the stalkers' path up the left bank of the Allt Coire a' Mhàim into Coire Mhàim. When the path ends continue straight on to gain the south-east ridge of An Socach and climb easy grass slopes to the summit.

Turning eastwards, the main ridge goes over a short dip, descends more steeply to the Bealach a' Bholla, then narrows up to An Riabhachan's west top. Three more tops follow in quick succession as the surprisingly level summit ridge is followed over the south-west top to the main summit and beyond to the north-east top. Here the character of the route changes as the narrow east ridge drops around the edge of cliffs bordering Toll an Lochain to the Bealach Toll an Lochain. A stiff pull is then required up the south-west shoulder of Sgurr na Lapaich to gain the summit of this most impressive of the Mullardoch mountains. From the summit radiate several interesting ridges, which on the east enclose some fine corries. The route onwards descends the steep rocky east ridge and calls for some handwork; if in doubt about the way off the summit in mist, err south of this ridge towards Loch Tuill Bhearnach.

From the broad grassy saddle at the foot of the east ridge bouldery slopes lead up to the rounded top of Carn nan Gobhar; the first cairn reached is higher than the larger cairn 200 m to the south. Descend directly into Coire an t-Sith, and follow a stalkers' path, on the left bank of the burn, back to the lochside and the dam.

119

Route 50: **SGURR CHOINNICH and SGURR A' CHAORACHAIN**

OS MAP: 25
GR: 066488
Distance: 10½ miles (17 km)
Ascent: 1,160 m (3,800 ft)
Time: 7½ hr

	1	2	3	4	5
Grade			●		
Terrain				●	
Navigation			●		
Seriousness			●		

Assessment: a grand ridge walk with an air of remoteness.
Seasonal notes: Sgurr Choinnich's summit ridge becomes heavily corniced in winter, and both this and the connection to Sgurr a' Chaorachain require care.

Sgurr Choinnich (999 m, 3,277 ft)
 Skoor *Choan*-yich, Bog Peak
Sgurr a' Chaorachain (1,053 m, 3,454 ft)
 Skoor a *Chœra*chin, Peak of the Rowan Berries
Sgurr nan Ceannaichean (915 m, 3,001 ft)
 Skoor nan *Kyanni*chan, Peak of the Merchants
Sgurr na Conbhaire (c880 m, c2,900 ft)
 Skoor na *Conn*avira, Peak of the Dog-men (ie hunters' attendants)
Bidean an Eòin Deirg (1,046 m, 3,431 ft)
 *Beej*an an Yai-*awn Jerr*ak, Red Peak of the Bird
Bealach Bhearnais
 *Byal*ach *Vyarn*ish, Pass of the Gap
Allt a' Chonais
 Owlt a *Chonn*ish, Whin River

The head of Loch Monar is today a remote and lonely place, and climbing in the amphitheatre of surrounding mountains has a wilderness feel to it, yet a thriving community once lived here. Most of the local inhabitants were evicted by the Highland Clearances of the nineteenth century, with the last nail in the coffin being provided by the raising of the water level when Loch Monar was damned for hydro-electric power in 1960. Now only Pait Lodge remains, perhaps the most remote habitation in mainland Britain. The walker who visits the area today, and revels in its wildness, cannot help but feel pangs of guilt for the historical reasons that have made it as it is.

As the track along the western reaches of Loch Monar now lies under water, the best approach to the hills is from Glen Carron to the north. At Craig 2½ miles (4 km) east of Achnashellach a forestry road crosses the railway line and is driveable as far as a parking space near the tree line. Begin here and continue along the track into a broad open glen where the Allt a' Chonais meanders beneath the broken west face of Sgurr nan Ceannaichean—a perfect hidden valley.

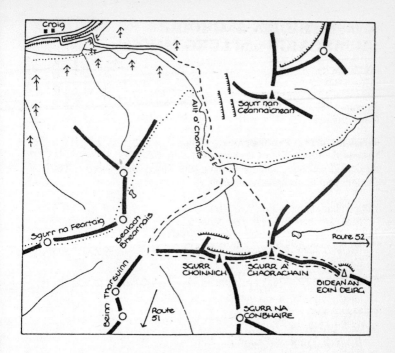

At the end of the plain, beyond a series of cascades, the track veers left round a knoll towards Glenuaig Lodge; at this point fork right on a stalkers' path that crosses the river and meanders up to the Bealach Bhearnais at the foot of Sgurr Choinnich's west ridge. The route to the peaks on the south side of Loch Monar branches off here and is described later (route 51), while the north Loch Monar peaks are described here.

Sgurr Choinnich's west ridge is steep and broken by rock outcrops, which provide scrambling opportunities if taken direct. The final 200 m follows the rim of the fine northern corrie to the castellated summit. From here, a worthwhile detour can be made along the gentle south ridge to Sgurr nan Conbhaire, a rarely visited peak that gives an eagle's view of Loch Monar. The dip between Sgurr Choinnich and Sgurr na Conbhaire is known as The Bowman's Pass, after the bowmen who hunted deer here in the days of James VI of Scotland.

From Sgurr Choinnich, a steep descent and reascent along a rough narrow ridge leads to Sgurr a' Chaorachain, beyond which a broad, stony highway continues to Bidean an Eòin Deirg, the last top of the day perched high above Strath Mhuilich. The best way back is to return to Sgurr a' Chaorachain and descend its grassy north ridge, avoiding some outcrops, to reach the track back along the Allt a' Chonais.

Route 51: **BIDEIN A' CHOIRE SHEASGAICH and LURG MHÓR**

OS MAP: 25
GR: 066488
Distance: 15 miles (24 km)
Ascent: 1,760 m (5,750 ft)
Time: 10½ hr

	1	2	3	4	5
Grade				●	
Terrain				●	
Navigation				●	
Seriousness					●

Assessment: a magnificent expedition with a real mountaineering flavour; remote, long and exciting.
Seasonal notes: a lengthy winter route whose many steep and narrow sections require technical competence.

Beinn Tharsuinn (863 m, 2,831 ft)
  Ben *Har*sin, The Transverse Mountain
Bidein a' Choire Sheasgaich (945 m, 3,100 ft)
  *Beej*an a Chorra *Hays*-kich, Peak of the Corrie of Reeds or Barren Cattle
Lurg Mhór* (986 m, 3,234 ft)
  *Loor*ak Voar, Big Shank
Meall Mór (974 m, 3,195 ft)
  Myowl Moar, Big Hill
Bealach Bhearnais
  *Byal*ach *Vyarn*ish, Pass of the Gap
Bealach an Sgoltaidh
  *Byal*ach an Scoalty, Pass of the Cleft
Allt Bealach Crudhain
  Owlt *Byal*ach *Croo*-in, Stream of the Horseshoe Pass

The circuit of Bidein a' Choire Sheasgaich and Lurg Mhór, the two peaks forming the southern arm of the amphitheatre of peaks that enclose the head of Loch Monar, is one of the finest expeditions in the Western Highlands. They are remote and contrasting mountains, Bidein, a crag-girt pointed cone, and Lurg Mhór, a long, relatively flat ridge, whose traverse turns out to be unexpectedly exciting.

The best approach to the mountains is from Craig via the Bealach Bhearnais (see route 50). From the bealach, the route to Bidein is barred by Beinn Tharsuinn, a grassy lump of a hill that lies across the head of Loch Monar and whose name is doubly apt as it lies on the watershed between the east and west coasts of Scotland. There are no easy ways round Beinn Tharsuinn, and it is necessary to climb over it in order to reach the narrow defile of the Bealach an Sgoltaidh at the foot of Bidein's north ridge. The ascent from here involves some interesting route-finding problems, as a route must be threaded through the tiers of cliffs that rise

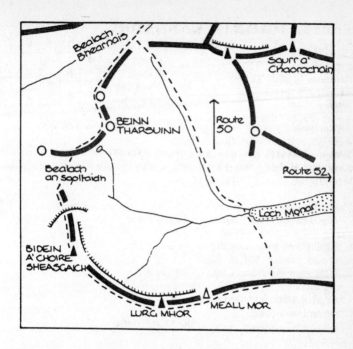

overhead. It is best to keep to the left, following the line of a prominent stone dyke built to channel deer into the bealach for the hunt. The first tier is broken and easy; the next goes by a gully on the left that veers to the right, reaching easier ground at the first of two sparkling lochans. From here, a graceful tapering ridge leads to the summit.

Turning south-eastwards, easy ground descends around the rim of the craggy corrie that separates Bidein from Lurg Mhór. A reascent of 250 m (800 ft) is required to gain the summit of Lurg Mhór, and here the fun begins again. Lurg Mhór is connected to Meall Mór ½ (1 km) to the east by a narrow rocky ridge that at one point has a short hiatus, which involves an awkward move. There is no real difficulty, however, and this exhilarating scramble high above Loch Monar ends all too soon.

To avoid the return over Bidein a' Choire Sheasgaich and Beinn Tharsuinn, continue down the gentle east ridge of Meall Mór for about 1 mile (1½ km), until it is possible to make a steep descent to the head of Loch Monar. Once into the glen, follow a good stalkers' path that climbs the left bank of Allt Bealach Crudhain to the Bealach Bhearnais. Halfway up, the path suddenly ends, but the going remains good for the last weary climb to the bealach, where the stalkers' path leading back down to the Allt a' Chonais is rejoined.

Route 52: **MAOILE LUNNDAIDH**

OS MAP: 25
GR: 203394
Distance: 14 miles (22 km)
Ascent: 970 m (3,200 ft)
Time: 7½ hr

	1	2	3	4	5
Grade	●				
Terrain		●			
Navigation			●		
Seriousness		●			

Assessment: an easy ascent rendered interesting by beautiful surroundings.

Seasonal notes: normally no especial difficulty in winter, when the corries are at their finest. In autumn, no glen is more stunning than Glen Strathfarrar.

Maoile Lunndaidh (1,007 m, 3,303 ft)
    Mæla Loondy, Bare Hill of the Boggy Place
Creag Toll a' Choin* (1,006 m, 3,300 ft)
    Craik Towl a Choan, Crag of the Boggy Hollow
Carn nam Fiaclan (996 m, 3,267 ft)
    Carn nam *Fee*-aclan, Cairn of the Teeth
Creag Breac
    Craik Brechk, Speckled Crag
Creag an Dubh-thuill
    Craik an Doo *Hoo*-il, Crag of the Black Hollow
Fuar-tholl Mór
    Foo-ar Howl Moar, Big Cold Hollow

Maoile Lunndaidh's name and flat plateau summit do not immediately single it out as a prime objective in a region replete with fine hills, but to ignore it would be to do an injustice to the beautiful approach walk and to the deeply cut corries that give the mountain a Cairngorm grandeur and a character unique in this area of the Western Highlands.

The finest approach to the mountain is from the east via Glen Strathfarrar, whose ever-changing vistas form a backdrop to some beautiful river and woodland scenery. Access to the glen is restricted (in the summer months currently from 9am to 6pm, except Sundays 1.30pm to 6pm and Tuesdays no access). A key for the locked gate at the entrance to the glen can be obtained from the cottage beside the gate (phone Struy 260 to check times beforehand).

Begin at the great horseshoe dam of Loch Monar, which dominates the enclosed glen at the end of the public road. A private road continues along the lochside to Monar Lodge, and around the corner is what Iain Thomson described as 'perhaps the most breath-catching shift of scenery in the north'. The view suddenly opens up over the blue waters of Loch Monar, indented by rocky promontories, leading the eye to the corries of Maoile Lunndaidh and its curving plateau summit high in the sky.

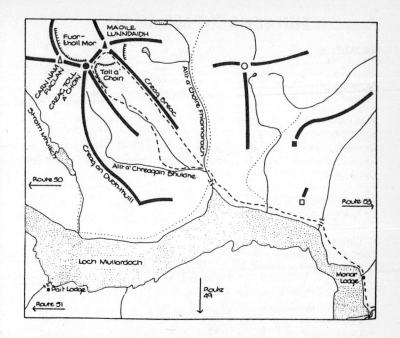

The old path along the north shore of the loch was inundated when the 1960 HEP scheme enlarged the loch, but the new path constructed at that time was well built and remains in excellent condition. It goes past Monar Lodge, through a defile to the right of a knoll and keeps well above the shoreline to reach the bridge over the Allt a' Choire Fhionnaraich. Don't cross the bridge, but keep right on a stalkers' path that crosses the river higher up to climb towards Toll a' Choin. When the path ends, climb easy slopes left of the Toll to reach Creag Toll a' Choin. (Alternatively, devotees of Iain Thomson's book *Isolation Shepherd* may wish to continue along the lochside path to the site of Strathmore Lodge, then reach Creag Toll a' Choin by the path up Strath Mhuilich and Creag an Dubhthuill.)

Creag Toll a' Choin straddles the two corries of Toll a' Choin and Fuar-tholl Mór, a deep trench, containing three lochans, which is Maoile Lunndaidh's finest feature. The undistinguished summit of Maoile Lunndaidh lies less than $^1/_2$ mile (1 km) north-east. To complete the circuit of Toll a' Choin, descend Maoile Lunndaidh's south-east ridge over Creag Breac to regain the stalkers' path and the ascent route below the corrie.

Route 53: **THE STRATHFARRAR SIX**

OS MAP: 25
GR: 283386
Distance: 15 miles (24 km)
Ascent: 1,550 m (5,100 ft)
Time: 8½ hr

	1	2	3	4	5
Grade		●			
Terrain			●		
Navigation			●		
Seriousness	●				

Assessment: a fine tramp around the compact Strathfarrar Six.
Seasonal notes: a lengthy, but normally straightforward, winter route.
If time is short the southern ridges of Sgurr a' Choire Ghlais and Creag
Ghorm a' Bhealaich provide routes back down to the glen. In autumn the
glen and hillsides are beautifully golden.

Sgurr na Ruaidhe (993 m, 3,257 ft)
   Skoor na *Roo*-iya, Red Peak
Carn nan Gobhar (992 m, 3,254 ft)
   Carn nan *Goe*-ar, Goat's Cairn
Sgurr a' Choire Ghlais (1,083 m, 3,553 ft)
   Skoor a Chorra Ghlash, Peak of the Green Corrie
Creag Ghorm a' Bhealaich (1,030 m, 3,379 ft)
   Craik *Ghorr*am a *Vyal*ich, Blue Crag of the Pass
Sgurr Fhuar-thuill (1,049 m, 3,441 ft)
   Skoor *Oo*-ar *Hoo*-il, Peak of the Cold Hollow
Sgurr na Fearstaig (1,015 m, 3,330 ft)
   Skoor na *Fyar*stak, Peak of the Thrift (poss)
Sgurr na Muice (891 m, 2,923 ft)
   Skoor na *Much*ka, Pig Peak
Garbh-charn (854 m, 2,801 ft)
   *Garr*av Charn, Rough Cairn

The traverse of the six 914 m (3,000 ft) peaks, which bound the north
side of upper Glen Strathfarrar, makes an interesting ridge walk but one
that must be accomplished against the clock, owing to access restrictions
at Struy Bridge (see route 52). Begin in Glen Strathfarrar a few hundred
metres east of the bridge over the Allt Coire Mhuillidh and take the Land
Rover track, that becomes a path, up into Coire Mhuillidh. Once across
the burn coming down from the bealach between Sgurr na Ruaidhe and
Garbh-charn, climb easy grass slopes directly to the rounded summit of
Sgurr na Ruaidhe.

The peaks can now be picked off one by one. A pleasant, grassy
descent to the Bealach nam Brogan is followed by an ascent of stony Carn
nan Gobhar, beyond which the ridge twists westwards to Sgurr a' Choire
Ghlais, Creag Ghorm a' Bhealaich, Sgurr Fhuar-thuill and Sgurr na
Fearstaig. The final three peaks are closely grouped and provide the most

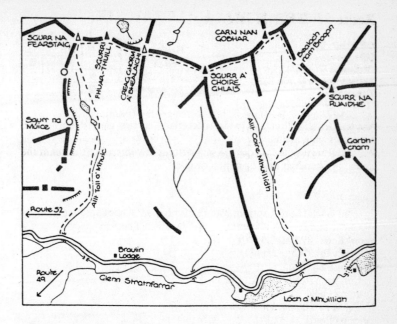

interesting walking, with broken crags on the north side and a fine view over the remote western reaches of Loch Monar.

From the last top, descend directly towards Loch Toll a' Mhuic and pick up a stalkers' path that passes left of the loch then crosses to the right bank of the Allt Toll a' Mhuic beneath the craggy east face of Sgur na Muice. The path becomes a Land Rover track to reach the roadside 3¹/₂ miles (6 km) west of your starting point.

Route 54: **BEINN BHAN**

OS MAP: 24
GR: 834423
Distance: 8 miles (13 km)
Ascent: 940 m (3,100 ft)
Time: 6 hr

	1	2	3	4	5
Grade			●		
Terrain					●
Navigation		●			
Seriousness		●			

Assessment: a circuit of wide spectacular corries gouged out of the Applecross mountains.
Seasonal notes: the corries are magnificent in winter, but the exit from Coire am Fhamhair may be impracticable.

Applecross
    from Gaelic Apor Crossan, Mouth of the River Crossan, in modern
    Gaelic known as A' Chomraich, A *Chom*rich, The Sanctuary
Beinn Bhan (896 m, 2,939 ft)
    Ben Vahn, White Mountain
Coir' an Eich
    Corr an Yaich, Horse Corrie
Coire na Feola
    Corra na *Fay*ola, Flesh Corrie
Coire na Poite
    Corra na *Poa*-tya, Cauldron Corrie
Coire an Fhamhair*
    Corr an *A*vir, Giant's Corrie

On the coast of Wester Ross lies the remote and romantic-sounding peninsula of Applecross, where, since the founding of a monastery by St Maelrubha in 673, all kinds of fugitives have found sanctuary over the centuries. Applecross owes its remoteness to the rough barrier of old red sandstone mountains that straddle the peninsula to the east, their eastern faces gouged out by glacial action into huge terraced corries. The highest, and most spectacular, of the mountains is Beinn Bhan, whose four impressive corries make a fascinating and unusual mountain route.

Begin at the bridge over the Kishorn River on the minor road that leaves the A896 at Tornapress. A path heads north low down on the moor beneath the corries of Beinn Bhan. Follow it until the first corrie (Coir' an Eich) comes into view, then strike directly across the moor into this shallowest of the four corries. Traverse beneath the spur into Coire na Feola, then beneath the more pronounced shoulder into Coire na Poite, passing Lochan Coire na Poite. Climb up over the rock lip into the inner corrie to view two hidden lochans cradled beneath the dramatic 350 m (1,200 ft) walls.

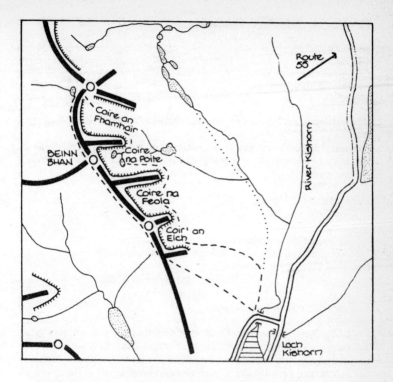

Continue round into the fourth corrie, Coire an Fhamhair, whose left-hand wall is one of the steepest in Scotland, and from here gain the summit plateau of Beinn Bhan via the head of the corrie. Return around the rim of the corries to descend directly to your starting point.

Route 55: **BEINN DAMH**

OS MAP: 24/25
GR: 887541
Distance: 8 miles (13 km)
Ascent: 1,110 m (3,650 ft)
Time: 6¹/₂ hr

	1	2	3	4	5
Grade			●		
Terrain				●	
Navigation			●		
Seriousness			●		

Assessment: a steep buttress ascent in a fine situation well off the beaten track.

Seasonal notes: under snow, the steepness of the eastern buttress should not be underestimated; it is probably best to ascend by the Coire Roill descent route.

Beinn Damh (902 m, 2,959 ft)
    Ben Daff, Stag Mountain
Sgurr na Bana Mhoraire (687 m, 2,253 ft)
    Skoor na *Banna Vorr*ar, The Peak of the Lady (placed on top by a
    cruel Lord and fed with shellfish whose shells can still be seen!)
Drochaid Coire Roill
    *Droch*itch Corra *Roe*-il, Bridge of the Dripping Saliva
Creag na h-Iolaire
    Craik na *Hill*era, Eagle's Crag

From the west, Beinn Damh's 2 mile (3 km) long western wall is an arresting sight, especially the curious Stirrup Mark immediately beneath the summit. Yet the mountain presents an even more dramatic aspect to the east, where a good stalkers' path gives access to a part of the mountain rarely visited.

Begin at the bridge over the Allt Coire Roill 5 miles (9 km) east of Shieldaig on the A896. Fifty metres west of the bridge, a path goes through a gate and climbs pleasantly through woods, among rhododendron bushes and past a high waterfall into Coire Roill. Above the trees the path forks; take the left branch, which crosses the river 200 m further on and climbs to the Drochaid Coire Roill. Leave the path at the Drochaid and cut right beneath a rocky knoll to the foot of the steep east buttress. The next buttress along looks more interesting but is deceptive; its steep heather slopes are best left to mountain goats. Climb the east buttress directly; it rises steeply in a fine situation and ends with a short scramble up the summit rock tower.

From the summit, follow the main ridge northwards across two lower tops to the saddle below Sgurr na Bana Mhoraire. This last summit appears distant, but the uninterrupted view it affords over Loch Torridon is ample recompense for its ascent. Returning to the saddle, descend into Coire Roill on a path that rejoins the route of the ascent.

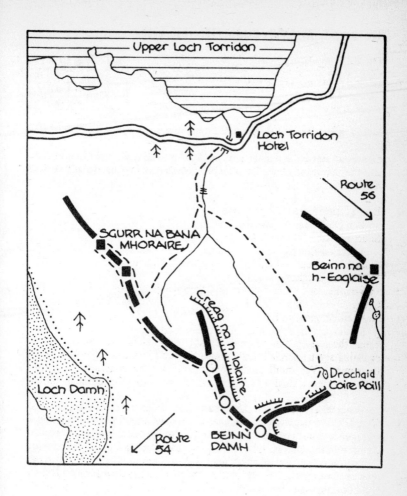

Route 56: **MAOL CHEAN-DEARG**

OS MAP: 25
GR: 958451
Distance: 10 miles (16 km)
Ascent: 910 m (3,000 ft)
Time: 7 hr

	1	2	3	4	5
Grade			●		
Terrain					●
Navigation				●	
Seriousness				●	

Assessment: a tough walk around some secret corners of the Coulin deer forest.

Seasonal notes: in winter conditions, the eastern side of Maol Chean-dearg is best avoided, but an ascent via the south-east ridge should remain practicable.

Maol Chean-dearg (933 m, 3,060 ft)
    Mœl Chan-*jerr*ak, Bare Redheaded Hill
An Ruadh-stac (892 m, 2,926 ft)
    An *Roo*-a Stachk, The Red Stack
Bealach na Lice
    *Byal*ach na *Leek*a, Slabby Pass
Fionn-abhainn
    Fyoon *Av*in, White (ie Clear) River
Clach nan Con-fionn
    Clach nan Coan-fyoon, Stone of the White Dogs
Coire Fionnaraich*
    Corra *Fee*-on-*arr*ich, Cool Corrie
Loch an Eion (should be Eoin)
    Loch an Yai-*awn*, Bird Loch

East of Beinn Damh (route 55) lies the Coulin deer forest, a complex area of bold, cliff-girt peaks, wild lochans and hidden corners, crisscrossed by a maze of scenic paths that are ideal for backpacking and provide easy access to the interior. Most prominent and intimidating of the Coulin mountains is the isolated, bare pate of Maol Chean-dearg, whose ascent from the east penetrates the heart of the area and provides a good test of route-finding capabilities on rocky terrain.

Begin at the bridge over the Fionn-abhainn 5 miles (8 km) north-east of Lochcarron village on the A890, taking the bulldozed road on the left bank of the river to join the old path up the glen. After 1½ miles (2 km) the path crosses the river and passes a well appointed bothy to reach the Clach nan Con-fionn, the curious finger of rock to which the legendary Fingal tethered his hounds while hunting. Five hundred metres further on, keep right at a fork to pass the shores of Loch Coire Fionnaraich, then keep left at another fork to reach the Bealach na Lice beneath the east face of Maol Chean-dearg, with the islands of lovely Loch an Eion spread out below.

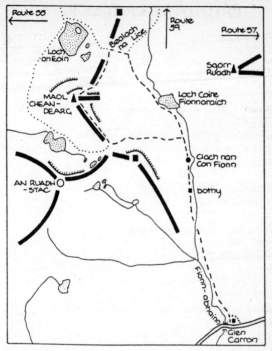

Leave the path at the bealach, and climb left along the edge of the escarpment overlooking Loch an Eion to reach the foot of Maol Chean-dearg's craggy north-east face. According to choice, either (1) ascend the obvious grassy rake (becoming a stone shoot), which goes diagonally right to reach the skyline at the notch just right of the summit dome, or (2) pick a route among outcrops up an open gully to reach the ridge to the right of the east buttress that forms the left-hand skyline, or (3) follow a complex cairned route that goes right and weaves among the crags of the north face. In mist, any ascent from this side is best avoided.

The summit dome is isolated from its steep supporting slopes and is a good viewpoint. Descend via the tough south-east ridge, on awkward boulders at first and then over a section of shattered quartzite, tilted sharply upwards by folding. On the bealach between Maol Chean-dearg and An Ruadh-stac nestles one of the most beautiful lochans in the Highlands, its bleached white quartzite walls giving it the appearance of a swimming pool. Only the most dedicated will continue beyond it and make the steep stony ascent of An Ruadh-stac. Most, like the author, will settle for the stalkers' path that descends from the bealach to rejoin the route of ascent along the Fionn-abhainn.

Route 57: **THE COIRE LÀIR SKYLINE**

OS MAP: 25
GR: 005484
Distance: 9¹/₂ miles (15 km)
Ascent: 1,640 m (5,400 ft)
Time: 9 hr

	1	2	3	4	5
Grade			●		
Terrain					●
Navigation					●
Seriousness				●	

Assessment: a long tough round of an extensive corrie with some memorable situations.

Seasonal notes: a fine winter ridge walk of exceptional length which may give considerable problems in many sections. The route can be curtailed halfway round at the Bealach Coire Làir.

Coire Làir*
  Corra Lahr, Low Corrie
Beinn Liath Mhór (925 m, 3,034 ft)
  Ben *Lee*-a Voar, Big Grey Mountain
Sgorr Ruadh (960 m, 3,149 ft)
  Skorr *Roo*-a, Red Peak
Fuar Tholl (907 m, 2,975 ft)
  Foo-ar Howl, Cold Hollow
Bealach Mhóir*
  *Byal*ach *Voe*-ir, Big Pass
Mainreachan Buttress*
  obscure

The majority of the high peaks of the Coulin deer forest rim the extensive basin of Coire Làir, and the round of the corrie skyline makes the finest and toughest expedition in the area. Begin at the road to Achnashellach Station on the A890. Walk up to the station and cross the railway line onto a forestry road. At a crossroads after a short distance turn left, and when the road approaches the River Lair cut left onto a path along the left bank. This path continues up into Coire Làir, through woods and rhododendron bushes, above gorges studded with waterfalls and gnarled pines.

Once into Coire Làir, keep right at a first fork then right again at a second to reach the bealach south-east of Beinn Liath Mhór, then climb steep slopes of heather and boulders to gain the south-east top. The main summit lies 1¹/₂ miles (2 km) distant along a ridge of alternating quartzite and sandstone, which is quite narrow in parts, especially at one point along the edge of a buttress overlooking Coire Làir. The quartzite at the summit is purgatorially sharp, but the views of Liathach and Beinn Eighe are without compare.

Continuing around the corrie skyline, the descent to the Bealach Coire Làir is complicated by lines of cliffs and a craggy knoll that guards the jaws of the bealach. The best line keeps to the crest of the ridge to reach

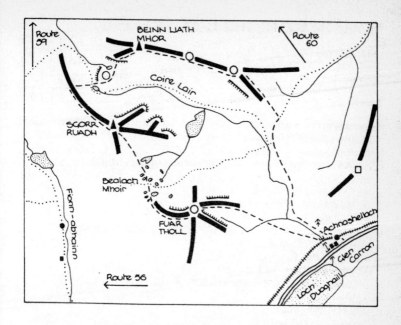

the knoll then descends left around it to reach the bealach. Gain the north ridge of Sgorr Ruadh by a grassy depression, which trends right beneath outcrops, and scramble up to the tapering summit. A rough descent leads down to the Bealach Mhóir, a long complex bealach studded with sparkling lochans. On a hot day it is entirely possible that you may not wish to continue beyond here, especially as a path descends from here to rejoin the Coire Làir path.

The next mountain on the round, however, is Fuar Tholl, which with its peculiarly scalloped hillsides and awesome Mainreachan Buttress, is the finest mountain in the area. Climb its northern slopes directly, easily breaching a band of cliffs halfway up, and cross the top of the Mainreachan Buttress to reach the summit. Continuing over towards Achnashellach, you are immediately confronted with the cliff edge of the deep-cut south-east corrie. Descend the interesting left-hand rim, which is quite sharp and exposed near the top, though of no technical difficulty. When the ridge levels off, cut down right to the lochan in the corrie, then aim directly for the junction of the River Lair and the railway line. The long descent through boulder-strewn heather is as tough as they come. If river conditions permit, it is better to cross to the path on the left bank.

135

Route 58: **BEINN ALLIGIN**

OS MAP: 24
GR: 869577
Distance: 6 miles (10 km)
Ascent: 1,190 m (3,900 ft)
Time: 6½ hr

	1	2	3	4	5
Grade					●
Terrain				●	
Navigation			●		
Seriousness					●

Assessment: a good introduction to Torridonian 'hillwalking' on a mountain full of fascinating features, with all hard scrambling avoidable if necessary.
Seasonal notes: a major winter mountaineering expedition.

Beinn Alligin (985 m, 3,231 ft)
 Ben *Ahl*igin, Jewelled Mountain
Na Rathanan★
 Na *Rahn*an, The Horns (literally pulleys, ie deep notches)
Sgurr Mhór (985 m, 3,231 ft)
 Skoor Voar, Big Peak
Tom na Gruagaich (922 m, 3,024 ft)
 Towm na *Groo*-agich, The Maiden's Knoll
Eag Dhuibh★
 Aik Ghoo-y, Black Notch
Coire an Laoigh★
 Corr an *Lœ*-y, Calf Corrie
Abhainn Coire Mhic Nobuil
 *Av*in Corra Veechk *Noe*bil, River of MacNoble's Corrie
Bealach a' Chomhla
 *Bya*lach a *Chaw*la, Pass of the Gate
Allt a' Bhealaich
 Owlt a *Vyal*ich, River of the Pass
Toll a' Mhadaidh★
 Towl a' *Vah*ty, The Fox's Hollow

Glen Torridon is one of the scenic gems of the Northern Highlands. It may not be as picturesque as Loch Maree nor as wild as The Great Wilderness, but its austere beauty and majestic, sculptured, sandstone peaks impose themselves upon the imagination as nowhere else. The Torridonian mountains are often regarded as the oldest mountains in the world (the sandstone from which they were formed is over 1,000 million years old), and there is certainly something primeval about their bulky shapes crouching on the moor like prehistoric monsters.

 The three major peaks on the north side of Glen Torridon (routes 58–61) exhibit all that is characteristic of walking in the area: rough approaches, narrow ridges, exhilarating scrambling, and superb situations. Beinn Alligin is the most westerly and least complex of the

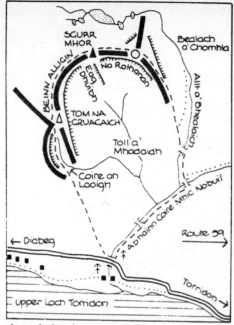

three, and makes a good introduction to the delights of Torridonian hill-walking. Viewed across Upper Loch Torridon it is seen to consist of three tops, two of which look extremely interesting, the centre top being split by the enormous gash of the Eag Dhuibh and the right-hand top consisting of three rocky prongs—the famous Rathanan or Horns of Alligin, where a good head for heights is required.

Begin on the minor road from Torridon to Diabeg, at the car park at the bridge over the Abhainn Coire Mhic Nobuil. Take the path through the pines on the left bank of the gorge, ignoring a boggy path that branches left over a bridge after 15 mins. Beyond the confluence with the Allt a' Bhealaich, the path crosses the river (bridge) and forks. Keep left along the left bank of the Allt a' Bhealaich, following the path that crosses to the right bank (bridge) and continues to the Bealach a' Chomhla right of Beinn Alligin. Leave the path, and climb the ridge rising up to The Horns, which provide exciting scrambling on exposed sandstone terraces but which can be bypassed on steep grass slopes to the left. Beyond the Horns, a steep, narrow ridge leads to the summit of Sgurr Mhór, Beinn Alligin's highest top.

Continuing round Toll a'Mhadaidh, the ridge broadens past the edge of the Eag Dhuibh. This remarkable cleft plunges 550 m (1,800 ft) into the corrie, where its boulder debris makes for interesting exploration but purgatorial going. Beyond a dip, the ridge narrows again to the summit of Tom na Gruagaich, perched high above the precipices of Toll a' Mhadaidh and the best viewpoint on the mountain. From the dip to the west of the summit, descend into Coire an Laoigh, following the burn down out of the corrie and then aiming back across the moor (cairned) to your starting point.

Route 59: **LIATHACH**

OS MAP: 25
GR: 936567
Distance: 6 miles (10 km)
Ascent: 1,340 m (4,400 ft)
Time: 7¹/₂ hr

	1	2	3	4	5
Grade					●
Terrain				●	
Navigation			●		
Seriousness					●

Assessment: a spectacular and thrilling scramble, with some fine situations and lots of atmosphere.
Seasonal notes: a major winter mountaineering expedition.

Liathach
  Lee-aghach, The Grey Place
Spidean a' Choire Léith (1,054 m, 3,457 ft)
  *Speej*an a Chorra Lay, Peak of the Grey Corrie
Mullach an Rathain (1,023 m, 3,356 ft)
  *Mull*ach an Rahn, Summit of the Pulley (ie two rocks near the summit as seen from Loch Torridon)
Bidean Toll a' Mhuic* (975 m, 3,198 ft)
  *Beej*an Towl a Vuchk, Peak of the Pig's Hollow
Am Fasarinen* (927 m, 3,041 ft)
  Am *Fahs*rinnen, The Teeth
Stuc a' Choire Dhuibh Bhig (913 m, 2,995 ft)
  Stoochk a Chorra Ghoo-y Veek, Peak of the Little Black Corrie
Meall Dearg (960 m, 3,149 ft)
  Myowl *Jerr*ak, Red Hill
Toll Bhan*
  Towl Vahn, White Hole
Allt an Doire Ghairbh*
  Owlt an Durra *Ghirr*av, River of the Rough Thicket

There are few more imposing sights in Scotland than the primeval bulk of Liathach rising fortresslike above Glen Torridon. Its steep terraced slopes appear impregnable from below, but it can be breached at either end to give access to a sensational ridge whose traverse constitutes one of the most spectacular scrambles on the mainland.

Begin just east of Glen Cottage in Glen Torridon at the bridge over the Allt an Doire Ghairbh, taking the path on the left bank of the burn which climbs steeply up the craggy hillside. Leave the path to thread your way up through broken rock bands to reach the further of two obvious gullies on the right. This debouches into the main ridge just west of Stuc a' Choire Dhuibh Bhig, which should be climbed for the view of Beinn Eighe (route 60) before turning westwards along the ridge.

As far as Spidean a' Choire Léith (Liathach's highest summit), the narrowest section of ridge remains hidden, but the immediate prospect

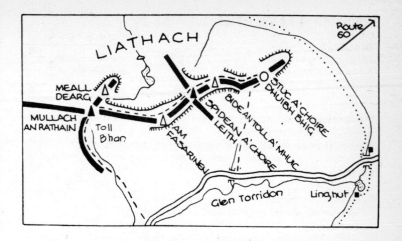

ahead is impressive enough, with the narrow quartzite ridge curving round above the great sandstone buttresses of Coire Léith. The stony ridge begins with a stroll around the corrie to the foot of Bidean Toll a' Mhuic, then ascends more steeply over the twin tops of that peak to the summit of Spidean a' Choire Leith.

A 150 m (500 ft) descent down Spidean's stony, south-west slopes (confusing in mist) leads to a short, level, grassy section that heralds the onset of the most exciting scramble of the day—the traverse of the pinnacled crest of Am Fasarinen. A good head for heights is required, one section having to be taken *à cheval*, but most of the 'difficulties' can be avoided by a track lower down on the south side if necessary. The situation and the exposure are spectacular.

Beyond the pinnacles, a pleasant stroll leads onto Mullach an Rathain, the last top of the day and a fine perch from which to contemplate the beautiful western seascape. To the north, the pinnacles of the north ridge beckon towards Meall Dearg, but they are best left to those with rock climbing experience.

From the Mullach, the most interesting descent to the glen is via the south-west ridge, which provides an entertaining scramble near the top and a breathtaking aerial view of Torridon village if a direct line is taken. When the ridge veers south-east, cut left into the Toll Bhan and follow the stream down; to avoid all scrambling on the descent descend into the Toll directly from the top of the south-west ridge. The day ends with a short walk back along the glen to your starting point.

Route 60: **BEINN EIGHE (WEST)**

OS MAP: 19/25
GR: 977578
Distance: 12 miles (19 km)
Ascent: 1,280 m (4,200 ft)
Time: 9 hr

	1	2	3	4	5
Grade					●
Terrain				●	
Navigation				●	
Seriousness					●

Assessment: a memorable ridge walk and scramble amidst awesome scenery.

Seasonal notes: in winter the ridges and steep hillsides of Beinn Eighe require technical competence; the descent of the Ceum Grannda is for experts only.

Beinn Eighe
    Ben *Ai*-ya (usually pronounced Ai), File Mountain
Spidean Coire nan Clach★ (972 m, 3,188 ft)
    *Speej*an Corra nan Clach, Peak of the Stony Corrie
Sgurr Ban (971 m, 3,185ft)
    Skoor Bahn, White Peak
A' Choinneach Mhór★ (975 m, 3,198 ft)
    A *Choan*-yach Voar, The Big Moss
Ruadh Stac Mór (1,010 m, 3,313 ft)
    Roo-a Stachk Moar, Big Red Stack
Sail Mhór (981 m, 3,218 ft)
    Sahl Voar, Big Heel
Coire an Laoigh
    Corr an Lœ-y, Calf Corrie
Coire Mhic Fhearchair★
    Corra Veechk *Err*achar, MacFarquhar's Corrie

The sprawling scree-girt mass of Beinn Eighe is a complex mountain range in miniature, which contains seven peaks over 914 m (3,000 ft). Its most interesting features lie at each end of a narrow quartzite ridge that extends for 3 miles (5 km) along the north side of Glen Torridon. Two routes are recommended, one (route 61) covering the eastern end of the ridge and one (described here) covering the western end, where exciting scrambling leads to perhaps the most magnificent corrie in the Northern Highlands.

Begin 5 miles (8 km) towards Glen Torridon from Kinlochewe, where a path passes to the right of a small plantation of trees and climbs into Coire an Laoigh. Once into the corrie bear left onto its bounding rocky east ridge and scramble around the corrie skyline and up shifting quartzite slopes to reach the main ridge 200 m west of Spidean Coire nan Clach. From here the route goes west along the main ridge, but first scramble to the summit and, if time and energy permit, continue eastwards across a

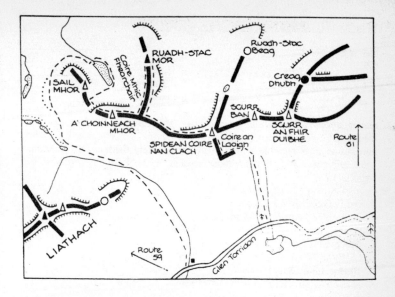

dip and a pleasant level bouldery section to Sgurr Ban, to view the Black Carls at the eastern end of the ridge (route 61).

Heading westwards from Spidean Coire nan Clach, the main ridge reaches the grassy summit plateau of A' Choinneach Mhór at the head of Coire Mhic Fhearchair. This corrie is one of the scenic wonders of Scotland, its 300 m (1,000 ft) Triple Buttresses providing an awesome backdrop to a sparkling lochan. Before continuing to the summit of A' Choinneach Mhór at the west end of the plateau, cross the saddle to the north around the rim of the corrie and ascend Ruadh Stac Mór, Beinn Eighe's highest peak.

From the saddle, a stone shoot can be descended into the corrie, but a much better route for the fit and capable is to return to A' Choinneach Mhór's summit plateau and climb the short distance to the summit at the edge of the Triple Buttresses. Continuing over the top towards Sail Mhór, the Ceum Grannda (Ugly Step) is encountered. No place less deserves its name, for its lovely clean slabs of rock provide engrossing scrambling, giving one a flavour of the exposed climbing on the Triple Buttresses. The last few metres are probably best descended facing inwards.

Continue over a rocky knob to the foot of Sail Mhór's south-east ridge and descend grass slopes into Coire Mhic Fhearchair. A path leads round the lochan, from where the view of the Triple Buttresses is unforgettable. The path continues down between Beinn Eighe and Liathach to reach the roadside 1½ miles (2 km) from your starting point.

141

Route 61: **BEINN EIGHE (EAST)**

OS MAP: 19/25
GR: 025611
Distance: 6 miles (10 km)
Ascent: 950 m (3,100 ft)
Time: 5½ hr

	1	2	3	4	5
Grade					●
Terrain				●	
Navigation		●			
Seriousness		●			

Assessment: a spectacular scramble over the fearsome Black Carls.
Seasonal notes: in winter, the traverse of the Black Carls is a major mountaineering expedition and, if the path around them is obliterated by snow, this section of the ridge is best avoided by walkers.

Creag Dhubh (929 m, 3,047 ft)
   Craik Ghoo, Black Crag
Sgurr an Fhir Duibhe* (963 m, 3,159 ft)
   Skoor an Eer *Doo*-ya, Peak of the Black Men
Black Carls*
   Black Men
Coire Domhain
   Corra *Doe*-in, Deep Corrie
Allt a' Chuirn
   Owlt a Choorn, Stream of Cairns

'I was presently aware of an obstacle that, looming through the cloud, wore an exceedingly forbidding appearance. It was a pinnacle on the top of my ridge—one of the three, known as the Black Regiment, which you can see from the valley. I learned afterwards that those pinnacles are not as bad as they look; they certainly could not be as formidable as that half-seen menace suggested.'

      W. KERSLEY HOLMES (*Tramping Scottish Hills*, 1946)

From Kinlochewe, the high quartzite ridges of Beinn Eighe's eastern reaches bring to mind Principal Shairp's evocative description of the mountain in his poem on Glen Torridon: 'magnificent alp blanched bare and bald and white'. Above a skirt of grass and scree the Black Carls, which etch the skyline of Coire Domhain, hold out an irresistible challenge.

   Begin at Cromasaig ½ mile (1 km) towards Glen Torridon from Kinlochewe, taking the path that leaves the road 50 m north of the Allt a' Chuirn and follows the wooded left bank of the river up into Coire Domhain. From here climb Creag Dhubh's stony east ridge to gain the skyline, then follow the main ridge south-west over another top to reach the Black Carls. Do not be put off by the fearsome appearance and reputation of these pinnacles, for they provide a sporting scramble on

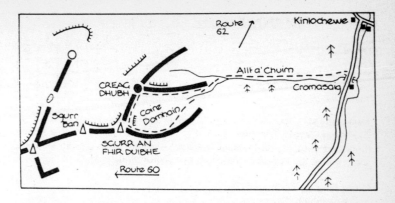

good holds. A path weaves among them, and indeed some of them are best bypassed, but many can be taken direct. The only real problem is the final 10 m (30 ft) wall up to the summit slopes of Sgurr an Fhir Duibhe, and this too provides excellent holds for a direct ascent. Alternatively, climb a gully on the left, or avoid all difficulties by a path that circumvents the crag further left.

Complete the round of Coire Domhain by descending Sgurr an Fhir Duibhe's east ridge, dropping down into the corrie when the ridge levels off and picking up the path back to Cromasaig.

Route 62: **SLIOCH**

OS MAP: 19
GR 033624
Distance: 12 miles (19 km)
Ascent: 1,130 m (3,700 ft)
Time: 7½ hr

	1	2	3	4	5
Grade		●			
Terrain			●		
Navigation			●		
Seriousness			●		

Assessment: a beautiful approach and an impressive mountain walk on The Spear.

Seasonal notes: under snow, the ridge between the east top and the north top makes a good introduction to narrow winter ridge walking.

Slioch (980 m, 3,215 ft)
   Slee-och, The Spear
Sgurr an Tuill Bhain (933 m, 3,060 ft)
   Skoor an *Too*-il *Va*-in, Peak of the White Hollow
Beinn a' Mhuinidh (692 m, 2,270 ft)
   Ben a Voony, Mountain of Urinating (after the waterfall; a more vulgar interpretation of the name would be more precise)
Gleann Bianasdail
   Glean Bee-*ann*asdil, Valley of the Hides (poss)
Abhainn an Fhasaigh
   Avin an *Ah*-ssy, River of the Dwelling (poss)

Slioch is a bold chunk of a mountain that dominates beautiful Loch Maree, its base a plinth of ice-scoured gneiss, its summit a great pyramid of Torridonian sandstone guarded by cliffs on three sides and allowing easy access only from the south.

Take the Incheril turn-off ½ mile (1 km) east of Kinlochewe on the A832, then turn left at the crossroads. From the road end a delightful path goes along the beautifully wooded right bank of the Kinlochewe River beneath the cliffs of Beinn a' Mhuinidh, from which tumbles a 100 m (300 ft) waterfall—a tremendous sight when in spate. After 3 miles (5 km) cross the Abhainn an Fhasaigh (bridge) and turn right on the path up deep-cut Gleann Bianasdail, which separates Beinn a' Mhuinidh from Slioch and provides a route to Lochan Fada (see route 64) as well as onto Slioch itself. After ½ mile (1 km) branch left on a path that climbs northwards towards Slioch's great south-east corrie and continue up to the south-east ridge and summit of Sgurr an Tuill Bhain.

From here, follow the 1 mile (1½ km) long narrow ridge leading to the north top, perched above the cliffs of the impressive north-west face, then go south across a shallow dip to reach the main summit. Continue around the south-east corrie, descend past a hanging lochan and over the end of Slioch's south-east ridge to regain the Gleann Bianasdail path.

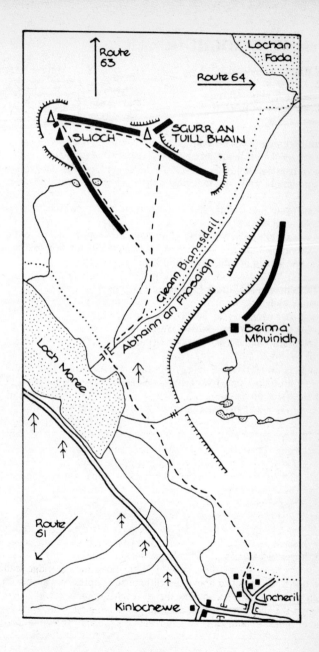

Route
63

Route 64 →

Lochan
Fada

SLIOCH

SGURR AN
TUILL BHAIN

Gleann Bianasdail

Abhainn an Fhasaigh

Loch Maree

Beinn a'
Mhuinidh

Route
61

Kinlochewe

Incheril

145

Route 63: **A' MHAIGHDEAN**

OS MAP: 19
GR: 872790
Distance: 25 miles (41 km)
Ascent: 1,280 m (4,200 ft)
Time: 12½ hr

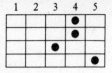

	1	2	3	4	5
Grade				●	
Terrain				●	
Navigation			●		
Seriousness					●

Carnmore approach (each way):
9 miles (15 km), out 260 m (850 ft) back 80 m (250 ft), 3½ hr
Ascent from Carnmore:
7 miles (11 km), 940 m (3,100 ft), 5½ hr

Assessment: a testing and unforgettable route on the most remote mountain in Britain.
Seasonal notes: A' Mhaighdean's remoteness makes its ascent a unique winter expedition. The north-west ridge is a difficult proposition under snow and it may be best to ascend via the descent route.

A' Mhaighdean (967 m, 3,172 ft)
A *Va*-ijan, The Virgin
Ruadh Stac Mór (918 m, 3,011 ft)
Roo-a Stachk Moar, Big Red Stack
Sgurr na Laocainn (c660 m, c2,165 ft)
Skoor na *Læk*in, Peak of the Hero
Fuar Loch Mór (Beag)
Foo-ar Loch Moar (Bake), Big (Little) Cold Loch
Allt Bruthach an Easain
Owlt *Broo*-ach an *Ess*an, River of the Slope of the Waterfall

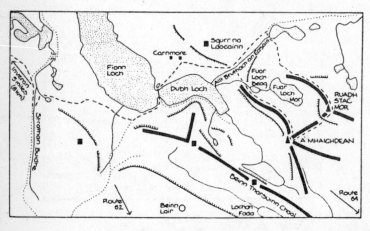

East of Slioch (route 62) lies The Great Wilderness, an area of unsurpassed remoteness and solitude that forms the greatest stretch of wild land remaining in Britain. Uncrossed by road and virtually untouched by the hand of man, the area consists of well over 100 square miles of water, peat bog and mountain. The mountains are remote and serious undertakings on tough terrain, the most remote of all being the shapely peak of A' Mhaighdean, which lies about 9 miles (15 km) equidistant from Poolewe, Kinlochewe and Dundonnell; to climb it in a single day requires fitness and determination. All the approaches to the mountains of The Great Wilderness are of considerable interest: the Kinlochewe approach is explored by route 64 and the Dundonnell approach by route 67, while the Poolewe approach is the shortest route to A' Mhaighdean and is described here.

From Poolewe, a private road leaves the A832 and runs along the east side of the River Ewe to Inveran and Kernsary (ring Poolewe 346 to obtain permission to use the road as far as a locked gate near Inveran and to obtain a key for the gate at Poolewe if locked). From the gate, continue past Kernsary, taking the track up into the wood and keeping right on the path that holds to the left bank of the Allt na Creige onto the shoulder of Beinn Airigh Charr. The path makes a short detour to cross the Strathan Buidhe and then heads down to the causeway between the Fionn (White) Loch and the Dubh (Black) Loch to reach Carnmore Lodge and bothy. This is a fine spot, with A' Mhaighdean rising majestically over the Dubh Loch.

Take the path which climbs east beneath the cliffs of Sgurr na Laocainn into the glen of the Allt Bruthach an Easain. Cross the burn into the corrie of Fuar Loch Beag and continue up A' Mhaighdean by its stepped north-west ridge, which breaks out into pinnacles at one point (easily bypassed; care when wet). The summit dome of A' Mhaighdean provides just reward for your endeavours, for the view and the situation are tremendous.

Close at hand is Ruadh Stac Mór and, after coming all this way, it is worth threading a way up through its fringe of broken sandstone crags to add its summit to the round. Descend from the bealach between A' Mhaigdean and Ruadh Stac Mór on a stalkers' path which descends above Fuar Loch Mór across Ruadh Stac Mór's north-west shoulder to rejoin the path along the Allt Bruthach an Easain. In front of you lies the long walk out to Carnmore and Inveran to complete an unforgettable day.

Route 64: **MULLACH COIRE MHIC FHEARCHAIR**

OS MAP: 19
GR: 039624
Distance: 20 miles (32 km)
Ascent: 1,400 m (4,600 ft)
Time: 11½ hr

	1	2	3	4	5
Grade				●	
Terrain					●
Navigation				●	
Seriousness					●

Lochan Fada approach (each way):
  7 miles (11 km), out 300 m (1,000 ft) back 80 m (250 ft), 3 hr
Ascent from Lochan Fada:
  6 miles (10 km), 1,020 m (3,350 ft), 5½ hr

Assessment: a tough remote route around the rocky ridges of The Great Wilderness.
Seasonal notes: the pinnacled section of Sgurr Dubh is a serious proposition under snow; the south ridge of Meall Garbh provides an easier descent route.

Mullach Coire Mhic Fhearchair (1,019 m, 3,343 ft)
  Mullach Corra Veechk *Err*achar, Summit of MacFarquhar's Corrie
Beinn Tarsuinn (936 m, 3,070 ft)
  Ben *Tar*sin, Transverse Mountain
Meall Garbh* (c830 m, c2,750 ft)
  Myowl *Garrav*, Rough Hill
Sgurr Dubh (918 m, 3,011 ft).
  Skoor Doo, Black Peak
Sgurr Ban (989 m, 3,244 ft)
  Skoor Bahn, White Peak
Lochan Fada
  Lochan *Fatt*a, Long Lochan
Loch an Sgeireach
  Loch an *Skair*-ach, Loch of Skerries
Gleann na Muice
  Glen na *Much*ka, Pig Glen

The route begins at Incheril, as for Slioch (see route 62); at the crossroads in Incheril keep straight on to a locked gate at the road end. A Land Rover track continues to the Heights of Kinlochewe, where it forks. Take the left branch that climbs Gleann na Muice and becomes a path leading past Loch Gleann na Muice and Loch an Sgeireach to the shores of Lochan Fada, a remote and beautiful spot.

From the end of the path, head northwards into the labyrinth of peat sloughs that encompass Lochan Fada and form some of the toughest terrain in the Highlands. Gain the south-east ridge of Beinn Tarsuinn to the right of the line of crags facing Lochan Fada and climb without

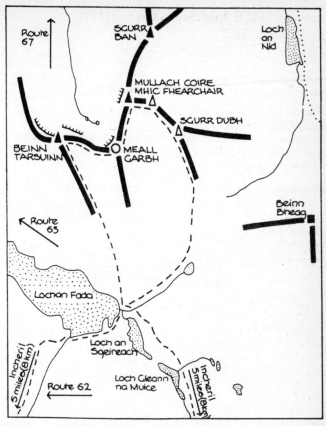

incident to the summit, which was elevated to Munro status in 1974. If
time permits, a detour should be made westwards around the rim of the
northern corrie for an interesting scramble.

Eastwards from Beinn Tarsuinn the lump of Meall Garbh stands
astride the ridge to Mullach Core Mhic Fhearchair; this can be traversed
or bypassed according to inclination before attacking the shattered
quartzite slopes of the highest peak in the group. Beyond Mullach Core
Mhic Fhearchair purgatorial going leads to Sgurr Ban, but this is best left
to terminal Munro baggers in favour of the much finer south-east ridge.
This leads across the east top to terminate in some easy pinnacles at Sgurr
Dubh, from where a descent of the south ridge leads back across the moor
to Lochan Fada. To complete a memorable circuit, return to Incheril via
Gleann Bianasdail, picking up a good path at the south-west corner of
Lochan Fada (see route 62).

Route 65: **THE FANNICHS**

OS MAP: 20
GR: 221660
Distance: 10½ miles (17 km)
Ascent: 1,340 m (4,400 ft)
Time: 7½ hr

	1	2	3	4	5
Grade	●				
Terrain		●			
Navigation					●
Seriousness				●	

Assessment: a spacious walk around a clutch of Munros in high rolling country.

Seasonal notes: a magnificent winter tramp, which can be curtailed or extended according to time and inclination. The road to Fannich Lodge is often blocked by snow.

The Fannichs
    The Gentle Slopes (poss) or named after windswept Loch Fannich
    (poss meaning Surging)
An Coileachan (923 m, 3,028 ft)
    An *Cull*-yachan, The Cockerel
Meall Gorm (949 m, 3,113 ft)
    Myowl *Gorr*am, Blue Hill
Meall nan Peithirean* (974 m, 3,195 ft)
    Myowl nan *Peh*-iran, Foresters' Hill
Sgurr Mór (1,110 m, 3,641 ft)
    Skoor Moar, Big Peak
Carn na Criche (961 m, 3,152 ft)
    Carn na *Creecha*, Cairn of the Boundary
Sgurr nan Clach Geala (1,093 m, 3,585 ft)
    Skoor nan Clach *Gyall*a, Peak of the White Stones
Sgurr nan Each (923 m, 3,028 ft)
    Skoor nan Yech, Horse Peak
Beinn Liath Mhór Fannaich (954 m, 3,129 ft)
    Ben *Lee*-a Voar Fannich, Big Grey Mountain of the Fannichs
Meall a' Chrasgaidh (934 m, 3,064 ft)
    Myowl a Chrashky, Hill of the Crossing
Am Biachdaich
    Am *Bee*-achdich, The Feeding Place
Garbh Choire Mór
    *Garr*av Chorra Moar, Big Rough Corrie

A rough private road to Fannich Lodge leaves the A835 Garve-Achnasheen road just east of Grudie Bridge (GR 312626); ring Fannich Lodge (Garve 227) or Fannich Estate (Almondbank 236) to obtain permission to use the road and a key for the locked gate. Begin at a fork just before the lodge, taking the rough track on the right that climbs around the lodge grounds and across a stream (bridge 200 m downstream,

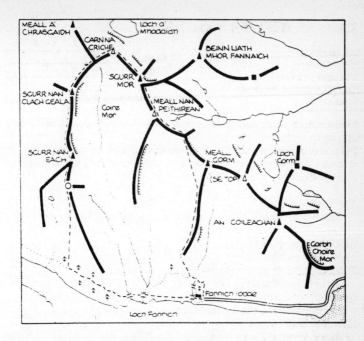

if in spate). Two hundred metres beyond the stream take the excellent stalkers' path on the right that climbs steadily up the south ridge of Meall Gorm. At 700 m (2,300 ft) the path forks; take the left branch that contours round Meall Gorm's broad summit to the flat ridge beyond.

From Meall Gorm, the ridge sweeps across Meall nan Peithirean to Sgurr Mór, the crowning peak of The Fannichs; the going is delightfully easy on moss and flat rocks, steepening towards the summit of Sgurr Mór. To the west, the outlying Munro of Beinn Liath Mhór Fannaich can be added to the route by intrepid walkers. The main ridge descends steeply towards flat-topped Carn na Criche then swings sharply south-west across the rich pastures of Am Biachdaich to climb along the edge of the impressive buttresses of Sgurr nan Clach Geala. Another appreciable detour to the north-west would enable Meall a' Chrasgaidh to be included in the round.

Continuing southwards from Sgurr nan Clach Geala on grassy slopes the route clings to the craggy west side of deep-cut Coire Mór to reach the final Munro of Sgurr nan Each. A direct descent from here to Fannich Lodge is beset by boggy ground, and it is better to descend southwards to pick up the rough road along the lochside (not marked on OS map) back through the lodge grounds to your starting point.

Route 66: **BEN WYVIS**

OS MAP: 20
GR: 412673
Distance: 8 miles (13 km)
Ascent: 940 m (3,100 ft)
Time: 5 hr

	1	2	3	4	5
Grade	●				
Terrain	●				
Navigation			●		
Seriousness	●				

Assessment: an unusual stroll across an ecologically unique mountain summit.

Seasonal notes: in autumn, the summit moss colours are beautiful; in normal winter conditions the mountain provides a good introduction to winter walking.

Ben Wyvis
    Ben *Wiv*is, from Gaelic Fhuathas (*Oo*-ash, Spectre) or Uais (*Oo*-ash, Noble) or Uamhas (*Oo*-ash, Terror)
An Cabar (950 m, 3,116 ft)
    An *Cabb*ar, The Antler
Glas Leathad Mór (1,046 m, 3,431 ft)
    Glass *Lye*-at Moar, Big Green Slope
Tom a' Choinnich (955 m, 3,133 ft)
    Towm a *Choan*-yich, Knoll of the Bog
Allt a' Bhealaich Mhóir
    Owlt a *Vyal*ich *Voe*-ir, River of the Big Pass

Although Ben Wyvis is not a mountain to immediately catch the eye of the connoisseur, its vast isolated bulk and unique summit plateau repay closer investigation. It is a walker's mountain par excellence, with seven tops over 914 m (3,000 ft) and an easy route to the summit, normally without undue difficulty even under the snow that lies late into the year (there are proposals for a downhill ski development here, which includes a railway from Strathpeffer to the summit ridge).

The ascent is relatively straightforward, despite extensive forestry plantations. Begin on the A835 Dingwall-Ullapool road 500 m south of Garbat at the bridge over the Allt a' Bhealaich Mhóir. Follow a path up the clearing on the right bank of the river, then bear left above the forest to climb An Cabar, the southernmost top of the Wyvis group. Here begins the ecologically unique Glas Leathad Mór, a soft carpet of moss, which extends for 1 mile (2 km) along the roof of the mountain to the summit, perhaps the most unusual mountain terrain in Scotland. Under the right atmospheric conditions, with mist clinging to the glen or shafts of light piercing brooding clouds over the hills to the west, many a more shapely peak is easily forgotten.

It is possible to make a circuit back to Garbat across the boggy moorland and through the labyrinthine forest, but this is likely to lead to

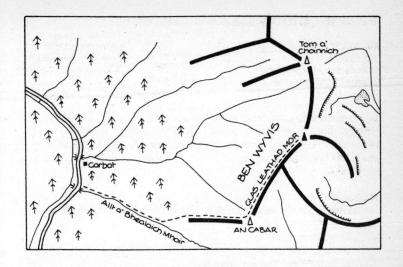

aggravation rather than to the roadside, and for once it is probably best to descend via the ascent route.

Historical note: Ben Wyvis's late-lying snow made it possible for the MacKenzie Earls of Cromarty to rent their land from the Crown on condition that they could produce a snowball at any time of year. Today, the mountain's unique ecological character is recognised by its designation as a National Nature Reserve and a Site of Special Scientific Interest.

153

Route 67: **BEINN DEARG MHÓR**

OS MAP: 19
GR: 114850
Distance: 16 miles (25 km)
Ascent: 1,530 m (5,050 ft)
Time: 10½ hr

	1	2	3	4	5
Grade			●		
Terrain					●
Navigation					●
Seriousness					●

Approach to Shenavall (each way):
4½ miles (7 km), out 360 m (1,200 ft) back 300 m (1,000 ft), 2½ hr
Ascent from Shenavall:
7 miles (11 km), 870 m (2,850 ft), 5½ hr

Assessment: a long, arduous circuit on a magnificent hidden mountain.
Seasonal notes: in winter, the steep slopes of Beinn Dearg Mhór are for experts only.

Beinn Dearg Mhór (Mor on OS map) (908 m, 2,978 ft)
  Ben *Jerr*ak Voar, Big Red Mountain
Beinn Dearg Bheag (818 m, 2,683 ft)
  Ben *Jerr*ak Vake, Little Red Mountain
Gleann Chaorachain
  Glen *Chœr*achin, Glen of Rowan Berries
Coire nan Clach*
  Corra nan Clach, Stony Corrie
Strath na Sealga
  Stra na *Shal*aka, Strath of Hunting
Abhainn Gleann na Muice
  *Av*in Glen na *Much*ka, River of the Pig Glen
Loch Toll an Lochain
  Loch Towl an Lochan, Loch of the Hollow of the Lochan

On the northern edge of The Great Wilderness lie the two awesome peaks of An Teallach (route 68) and Beinn Dearg Mhór. Beinn Dearg Mhór is a compelling mountain with a unique purity of line, consisting almost entirely of a crescent-shaped ridge which encloses the deeply sculptured and exquisitely proportioned Coire nan Clach. The approach to the mountain, in a magnificent setting above the hidden mountain fastness of Strath na Sealga, is long and arduous, but the rewards are commensurate.

Begin at the layby 100 m south of the bridge over the Allt Gleann Chaorachain on the A832 2½ miles (4 km) south of Dundonnell. A cart track heads south up the glen and crosses the river to a high point on the moor beneath the pinnacled ridges of An Teallach. One hundred metres beyond the high point, branch right on a path that contours round An Teallach's south-east shoulder to descend to lonely Shenavall bothy,

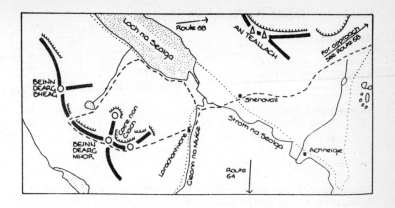

magnificently sited on the flats of Strath na Sealga near the head of Loch na Sealga.

Across the strath, Beinn Dearg Mhór is an irresistible attraction, but reaching its foot is not easy. First ford the Abhainn Strath na Sealga below Shenavall (aim for two trees on the river bank), then follow the grassy river flats round beside extremely marshy ground to the Abhainn Gleann na Muice and ford this second river close to Larachantivore cottage. Both rivers are wide and, in spate, impassable. Climb the steep, earthy rake left of the north-east ridge of Beinn Dearg Mhór to reach the east top. The ridge itself is a mostly simple scramble, well worth exploring during the ascent, but in places it is exposed and vegetated.

From the east top, follow the rim of Coire nan Clach round behind an impressive overhanging prow to the main summit, an eyrie between The Great Wilderness and the sea, which has a unique aura of solitude. The rocky ridge, which forms the western arm of the corrie, narrows to a castellated north top well worth investigation, but there is no way off the end. The route onwards from the main summit goes westwards for a short distance, then descends north-westwards down steep, earthy slopes to the bealach below Beinn Dearg Bheag. Climb Beinn Dearg Bheag if you have time, for its summit ridge is exhilaratingly narrow, with a succession of rocky tops leading north-westwards towards Gruinard Bay.

From the bealach descend grassy rakes between cliffs (great care required in mist) to reach the sandy shores of Loch Toll an Lochain, beyond which lies merely a tough descent to Loch na Sealga, more river crossings and the long walk out from Shenavall.

Route 68: **AN TEALLACH**

OS MAP: 19
GR: 111858
Distance: 8½ miles (14 km)
Ascent: 1,450 m (4,750 ft)
Time: 8 hr

	1	2	3	4	5
Grade					●
Terrain				●	
Navigation			●		
Seriousness					●

Assessment: a thrilling scramble on one of the most spectacular of all Scottish mountains.

Seasonal notes: a major winter mountaineering expedition.

An Teallach
   An *Tyell*ach, The Forge
Glas Mheall Mór (981 m, 3,218 ft)
   Glass Vyowl Moar, Big Green Hill
Bidein a Ghlas Thuill (1,062 m, 3,484 ft)
   *Beej*an a Ghlass *Hoo*-il, Peak of the Green Hollow
Sgurr Fiona (1,059 m, 3,474 ft)
   Skoor Fyoona, Fair Peak or Wine Peak
Lord Berkeley's Seat (1,047 m, 3,434 ft)
Corrag Bhuidhe (1,036 m, 3,398 ft); Buttress* (929 m, 3,047 ft)
   *Corr*ak *Voo*-ya, Yellow Finger
Stob Cadha Gobhlach* (959 m, 3,146 ft)
   Stop *Ca*ha *Goal*ach, Peak of the Forked Pass
Sail Liath (954 m, 3,129 ft)
   Sahl *Lee*-a, Grey Heel
Toll an Lochain*
   Towl an Lochan, Hollow of the Lochan
Garbh Allt*
   *Garr*av Owlt, Rough River
Coir' a' Ghuibhsachain
   Corr a *Gews*achin, Corrie of Pines

An Teallach is regarded by many as the finest peak in Scotland, and certainly, when viewed from the A832 Dundonnell road, it is an awe-inspiring sight, a sturdy wedge of old red sandstone whose sharp tops tower over the moorland. When struck red by the rays of the setting sun, or when mists curl like smoke around its pinnacles, it admirably suits its evocative Gaelic name. The traverse of the whole mountain has much in common with Torridonian routes and, if taken direct, the scramble around Toll an Lochain is harder than any of them, involving some sensational situations on a succession of rock towers—though there is also a path round most of the more awkward sections.

    The finest features of An Teallach's complex topography are the two eastern corries (Coire a' Ghlas Thuill and Toll an Lochain) and the ridges

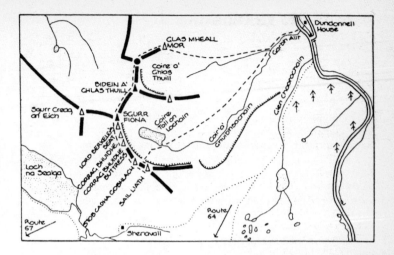

that enclose them; the best route on the mountain makes a circuit of their skylines. Begin at the foot of the Garbh Allt near Dundonnell House on the A832, taking the path that begins 10 m north of the bridge and tunnels through the rhododendrons on the left bank of the burn. At the confluence with the burn coming down from Coire a' Ghlas Thuill keep right to follow that burn up into the corrie, then leave it and climb the steep slopes of Glas Mheall Mór directly to the summit. The hard work over, there follows a pleasant stroll round the corrie rim to Bidein a' Ghlas Thuill, and then a steep descent and reascent of 150 m (500 ft) to Sgurr Fiona, An Teallach's highest top.

The view ahead from Sgurr Fiona may well bring to mind Pennant's 1772 description of An Teallach: 'horrible and awful with summits broken, sharp and serrated and springing into all terrific forms'. The first rock tower is Lord Berkeley's Seat, a simple scramble over sandstone terraces; it can be bypassed on the right, but should be ascended for the vertiginous view over the edge to Loch Toll an Lochain. Next come the Corrag Bhuidhe pinnacles, hard, airy scrambles that can again be avoided on the right, and Corrag Bhuidhe Buttress. To avoid the descent at the end of Corrag Bhuidhe Buttress, on which walkers have fallen to their deaths, follow the path out right to a short, exposed scramble where care is required.

The remainder of the ridge develops into a pleasant walk over Stob Cadha Gobhlach to Sail Liath. Descend by returning to the first of the two gullies of Cadha Gobhlach and going down into Toll an Lochain, from where easy going over a quartzite escarpment leads back down Coir' a' Ghuibhsachain to your starting point.

Route 69: **BEINN DEARG and CONA' MHEALL**

OS MAP: 20
GR: 267750
Distance: 11 miles (17 km)
Ascent: 1,180 m (3,850 ft)
Time: 7½ hr

	1	2	3	4	5
Grade				●	
Terrain				●	
Navigation					●
Seriousness					●

Assessment: a majestic skyline circuit in rough lonely country, with plenty of route-finding problems.

Seasonal notes: in winter, the ascent to and traverse of Cona' Mheall's south-east ridge are not for beginners, and the summit dome of Beinn Dearg requires extra care in adverse weather; in normal conditions an easier ascent/descent route is via the head of Coire Ghrannda.

Beinn Dearg (1,084 m, 3,556 ft)
    Ben *Jerr*ak, Red Mountain
Cona' Mheall (980 m, 3,215 ft)
    Conna Vyowl (usually pronounced Connaval), Adjoining Hill or Hill of Meeting
Coire Ghrannda*
    Corra *Ghrann*da, Ugly Corrie
Allt a' Gharbhrain
    Owlt a *Ghar*ravrin, Rough River
Loch an Eilean
    Loch an *Ail*an, Loch of Islands
Dirrie More
    Great Ascent

When driving north across the Dirrie More on the A835 to Ullapool, the craggy summits of Beinn Dearg and Cona' Mheall can be seen rising over the wild moorland north of Loch Glascarnoch. They are an irresistible attraction, especially as between the two lies misnamed Coire Ghrannda, yet another of those remote and magnificent hidden corries for which the Northern Highlands are famous. A circuit of the corrie skyline, which takes in the two summits, provides a problematical and engrossing route in lonely country.

Even the start of the route may be difficult to find. Four hundred metres north-west, along the road from the layby at the south-east end of Loch Droma, a path (no longer marked on OS map) cuts north-east up the hillside (look for the small causeway of stones that carries the path over the roadside ditch). After 50 m the path turns right along an old drove road, then turns left uphill again after a similar distance, improving with height. It contours round the hillside to end at the ruins of an old shieling near Loch a' Gharbhrain.

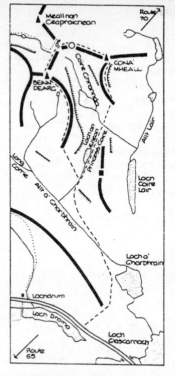

Follow the Allt a' Gharbhrain up into the boggy Long Corrie, crossing the river wherever practicable (this is notoriously difficult to do dryshod and may be impossible in spate). Once across, aim diagonally up the hillside into the rough heathery trough of the Princess Corrie. Here the serrated skyline of Cona' Mheall is seen for the first time, mirrored in Loch nan Eilean. Continue through the corrie, descending slightly across the entrance to Coire Ghrannda, and pick a steep route up among rock outcrops to Cona' Mheall's south-east ridge, from where Coire Ghrannda's lochan and encircling 450 m (1,500 ft) cliffs look spectacular.

The ridge is narrow and slabby, but of little difficulty, unless the rock is wet and grassy, when care is required. Short scrambles are required to descend to a level section of the ridge and to reascend to the high point of the ridge; beyond here a short dip leads to gentle boulder slopes curving right to the summit. The route to Beinn Bearg goes west around the head of Coire Ghrannda, contouring to lochans on the Bealach Coire Ghrannda at the foot of Beinn Bearg's rough north-east slopes. From here climb directly to Beinn Deag's summit dome, following the line of a dry stone wall most of the way.

The most interesting descent route follows the ridge that forms the western rim of Coire Ghrannda (difficult to locate in mist). Hold to the ridge when it rises across a saddle, then bear right above the crags bordering the Princess Corrie to descend to the corrie entrance and rejoin the route of ascent.

Route 70: **SEANA BHRAIGH**

OS MAP: 20
GR: 324951
Distance: 12½ miles (20 km)
Ascent: 880 m (2,900 ft)
Time: 7 hr

	1	2	3	4	5
Grade				●	
Terrain		●			
Navigation		●			
Seriousness			●		

Assessment: an exhilarating scramble on a peak well off the beaten track whose dramatic inner recesses are well worth seeking out.
Seasonal notes: the traverse of An Sgurr is a major expedition in winter, and it is best to descend Seana Bhraigh via the ascent route.

Seana Bhraigh (927 m, 3,041 ft)
  Shenna Vri, Old Upland
An Sgurr* (c890 m, c2,920 ft)
  An *Skoor*, The Peak
Luchd Coire*
  Luchk Corra, Corrie of the People (poss) or Load (poss)
Feich Coire*
  poss should be Feidh (pron Fay, Deer) or Feith (pron Fay, Bog)
Corriemulzie
  Corra Mooly, Mill Corrie
Loch a'Choire Mhóir
  Loch a Chorra *Voe*-ir, Loch of the Big Corrie

From the Beinn Dearg group (route 69) Seana Bhraigh appears as a wearisome featureless plateau hardly worthy of consideration and well deserving its Gaelic name. From the north, however, it shows its true colours as a mountain of dramatic features, notably the pointed spur of An Sgurr, which forms the eastern boundary of the great Luchd Coire, whose cliffs rise 400 m (1,300 ft) from the lochan cupped in its depths. From Strathmulzie, a circuit of Luchd Coire combines an easy ascent with an exciting scramble over An Sgurr.

From Oykel Bridge on the A867, take the minor road up Glen Einig to Duag Bridge and beyond to Corriemulzie Lodge. Begin here, continuing up Strath Mulzie along a Land Rover track that becomes a path leading to Loch a' Choire Mhóir. When the path crosses the Corriemulzie River, leave it, and climb west up easy grass slopes to the summit of Seana Bhraigh, perched at the edge of Luchd Coire. Across the corrie, An Sgurr looks particularly impressive, while to the north the isolated mountains of Sutherland fringe the horizon like a string of beads.

Follow the edge of the plateau around the rim of the corrie to the narrow arete between Luchd Coire and Feich Coire that develops into an exciting scramble onto the summit tower of An Sgurr. To regain the path

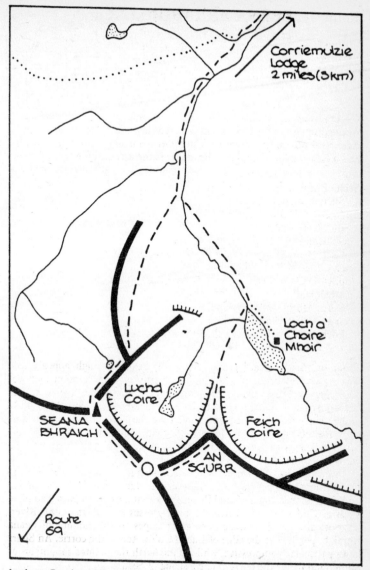

Corriemulzie Lodge 2 miles (3km)

Loch a' Choire Mhóir

Luchd Coire

Feich Coire

SEANA BHRAIGH

AN SGURR

Route 69

back to Corriemulzie Lodge, make a direct descent of An Sgurr's north-west ridge (all difficulties avoidable) and cross the Corriemulzie River below Loch a' Choire Mhóir.

Route 71: **SGURR AN FHIDHLEIR and BEN MÓR COIGACH**

OS MAP: 15
GR: 139066
Distance: 9½ miles (15 km)
Ascent: 1,020 m (3,350 ft)
Time: 6½ hr

	1	2	3	4	5
Grade			●		
Terrain				●	
Navigation					●
Seriousness				●	

Assessment: a rough walk amidst stunning rock scenery and coastal views.

Seasonal notes: in winter, the gully beside the prow of The Fiddler becomes a steep snow climb, and the Garbh Choireachan ridge may also require care.

Ben Mór Coigach (743 m, 2,437 ft)
   Ben Moar *Coe*-igach, Big Mountain of the Fifths (division of land into fifths was an ancient Gaelic practice)
Sgurr an Fhidhleir (703 m, 2,306 ft)
   Skoor an *Ee*lir, The Fiddler's Peak
Garbh Choireachan (c720 m, c2,360 ft)
   *Garr*av *Chorr*achan, Rough Corries
Speicin Coinnich (c700 m, c2,300 ft)
   Spaich-kin *Coan*-yich, Boggy Peak
Beinn Tarsuinn (c530 m, c1,740 ft)
   Ben *Tars*in, Transverse Mountain
Lochan Tuath
   Lochan Too-a, North Lochan
Allt Claonaidh
   Owlt Clœny, Bent Stream

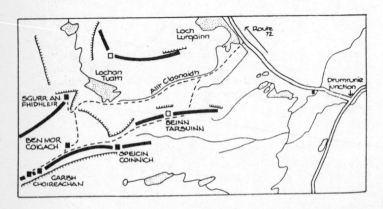

In the north-west corner of Ross and Cromarty, jutting out into The Minch, lies the district of Coigach. It is an area of shattered sandstone peaks rearing in dramatic isolation above desolate moor of bog and lochan. Although the hills are not high by Scottish standards, they provide spectacular walking, and none more so than the breathtaking summits of Sgurr an Fhidhleir and Ben Mór Coigach.

Begin 2 miles (3 km) along the minor road that leaves the A835 at Drumrunie junction 9 miles (15 km) north of Ullapool. Cross the river below the road, just east of where it enters Loch Lurgainn (stepping stones), and make for the right bank of the Allt Claonaidh. An attempt at a path climbs beside the river, which forms some fine pools and cascades, but the going is very boggy. Follow the course of the river to Lochan Tuath at the foot of the impressive prow of The Fiddler. When viewed across the sandy bays of the loch, this awesome wedge of rock, unique in Scotland, has an air of impregnability and unreality; not until 1962 was it climbed direct.

The walkers' route to the summit goes up the obvious steep heather gully to the left of the prow; the going is better on the left bank of the burn, if anything, making the most of sheep tracks. The gully debouches onto the plateau between The Fiddler and Ben Mór Coigach, and easy boulder slopes on the right lead up to The Fiddler's summit. With care, a spectacular view of Lochan Tuath 430 m (1,400 ft) beneath your feet can be obtained.

To reach Ben Mór Coigach, retrace your steps to the plateau and climb easy grass slopes to the summit; in adverse weather good navigation is required here. From the summit, a 1 mile (1½ km) narrow ridge beckons seawards to the twin tops of the Garbh Choireachan, with tremendous views southwards over Loch Broom and westwards over the Summer Isles. It is a wonderful walk, with opportunities for scrambling, to be savoured at leisure.

From the Garbh Choireachan retrace your steps along the ridge, bypassing the summit of Ben Mór Coigach and continuing as far as the bealach beneath Speicin Coinnich (which can be climbed by a short scramble). Descend open slopes below the bealach towards Beinn Tarsuinn and climb to its summit for a classic view of The Fiddler. Continue over the summit and descend a few hundred metres to a level section of ridge; at the end of this head directly down steep heather slopes, circumventing one or two outcrops, to reach the Allt Claonaidh and the route of ascent.

Route 72: **STAC POLLAIDH**

OS MAP: 15
GR: 107095
Distance: 2 miles (3 km)
Ascent: 560 m (1,850 ft)
Time: 4 hr

	1	2	3	4	5
Grade					●
Terrain		●			
Navigation	●				
Seriousness			●		

Assessment: a scrambler's paradise on pinnacled ridges high above the wilds of Assynt.

Seasonal notes: in winter, the ascent route becomes a steep snow slope and the summit ridge requires great care when iced.

Stac Pollaidh (613 m, 2,011 ft)
    Stachk Powly (usually anglicised to Stack Polly), Muddy Stack
Coire Gorm
    Corra *Gorra*m, Blue Corrie
Loch Lurgainn
    Loch *Loor*akin, Shank Loch (Fingal, grabbing his mother by the hair
    and throwing her over his shoulder while escaping from some giants,
    discovered he had *only* her hair and threw it into the loch!)

'Then the sun came out and the traverse of the ridge from end to end was sheer delight. There is nothing like it in all Britain, for it consists of a sucession of little needles and pinnacles with lateral ridges sticking out on either side, and whose grotesque appearance baffles description.'

BEN HUMBLE (*On Scottish Hills*, 1946)

Stac Pollaidh is the smallest mountain in this book, but what it lacks in stature it more than makes up for in character. The traverse of its prickly summit ridge calls for some tricky manoeuvres amidst spectacular rock architecture.

Begin at the car park at the bridge over the burn coming down from Coire Gorm, 5 miles (8 km) along the minor road from Drumrunie junction on the A835. Climb the very steep, earthy path which, making no concessions to contouring, takes a *directissima* route up the grassy hillside to the low point on the summit ridge, gaining height fast. Visit the east top first, scrambling across a notch, which many will prefer to bypass on a path lower down. The ridge to the west and higher top bristles with weird pinnacles and towers, like the splintered ruins of an ancient fortress. A maze of paths provides endless choices of route, easy or spectacular depending on inclination. Note especially the second gully from the end (Pinnacle Basin), which contains the peculiar Lobster's Claw among other fantastic formations.

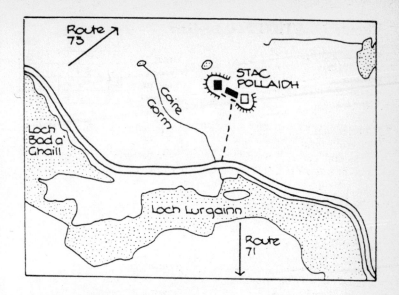

Guarding the summit stands the one unavoidable barrier—a rock tower that must be climbed direct. It is easier than it looks, with good ledges for feet and a good jug handle halfway up, but remember that you will have to reverse it. To descend, return to the low point on the ridge for a knee-breaking jog down to the roadside.

Route 73: **SUILVEN**

OS MAP: 15
GR: 107220
Distance: 13 miles (21 km)
Ascent: 880 m (2,900 ft)
Time: 8 hr

	1	2	3	4	5
Grade					●
Terrain			●		
Navigation	●				
Seriousness					●

Assessment: an attractive approach and a spectacular ascent make for an enthralling route on Scotland's Pillar Mountain.
Seasonal notes: a major winter mountaineering expedition, when even the stone shoot may become a steep snow climb.

Suilven
   Sool-ven, Pillar Mountain
Caisteal Liath (731 m, 2,398 ft)
   *Cash*tyal *Lee*-a, Grey Castle
Meall Mheadhonach★
   Myowl *Vee*anach, Middle Hill
Meall Bheag★
   Myowl Vake, Little Hill
Bealach Mór
   *Byal*ach Moar, Big Pass
Allt na Clach Airigh
   Owlt na Clach Arry, River of the Stone Shieling

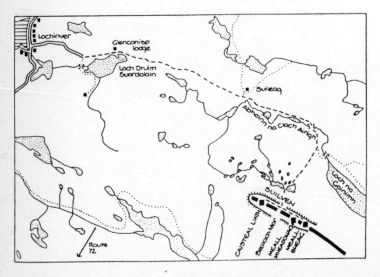

The striking sandstone peak of Suilven rises boldly above the lochan-studded Sutherland moors like an impregnable monolith, its formidable western buttress as seen from Lochinver prompting the Vikings to name it Pillar Mountain. To the Gaels it became known as the Grey Castle, and to a more recent invasion of tourists it has become the Sugar Loaf. Despite its seeming unscalability, the 1 mile (1½ km) long summit ridge is, in fact, easily reached using stone shoots on either side, but the traverse of the three sharp tops is an altogether more exciting affair, calling for careful and exposed scrambling in superb situations.

The best approach is from the road to Glencanisp Lodge that leaves the A837 at the south end of Lochinver. Begin 1 mile (2 km) along the road at a junction, where there is a parking space. Continue along the road, through the grounds of the lodge, and take the track around the end of Loch Druim Suardalain. Leave some ruined buildings by the lochside on your right and take the excellent well drained stalkers' path, which strikes eastwards towards Suilven, undulating beside a chain of lochans among rock outcrops typical of gneiss terrain.

Keep right at a cairned fork near Suileag to draw slowly alongside the north face of Suilven, which from here has the appearance of a beached galleon. The access stone shoot can be seen leading up to the lowest point on the ridge (the Bealach Mór). About 600 m after the path crosses the Abhainn na Clach Airigh, branch right on a side path that crosses the moorland to a shelf of attractive lochans and climbs steeply up the stone shoot. At the Bealach Mór, turn right for an easy but exposed scramble (care if the path is muddy) to the table-top summit of Caisteal Liath, for a magnificent view of the western seascape.

The two eastern tops are trickier than Caisteal Liath, but are well worth exploring if you feel capable. Return to the Bealach Mór and scramble up Meall Mhead-honach, avoiding some awkward towers by a path on the right if necessary. The top is surprisingly level and grassy, but soon drops steeply to a narrow bealach from where the climb up Meall Bheag is the most sensational on the ridge, requiring exposed scrambling on loose rocky terraces. Keep left to find the easiest line, and remember that you will have to reverse it.

The return route is as for the approach. On a hot summer's day the shelf of lochans at the foot of the stone shoot is a seductive place to recuperate after the heat of battle and before the long walk out.

Route 74: **CONIVAL and BEN MORE ASSYNT**

OS MAP: 15
GR: 251218
Distance: 11½ miles (18 km)
Ascent: 1,130 m (3,700 ft)
Time: 7½ hr

	1	2	3	4	5
Grade					●
Terrain					●
Navigation				●	
Seriousness				●	

Assessment: an unusual route across startling changes of terrain on Assynt's highest mountains.

Seasonal notes: in winter, the south-east ridge of Ben More Assynt should be left well alone by walkers.

Conival (987 m, 3,238 ft) (an anglicisation of Cona' Mheall)
usually pronounced Connaval (Gaelic Conna Vyowl), Adjoining Hill or Hill of Meeting
Ben More Assynt (998 m, 3,274 ft)
Ben Moar Assynt, Big Mountain of Assynt
Beinn an Fhurain* (860 m, 2,821 ft)
Ben an *Oo*rin, Mountain of the Spring
Breabag Tarsuinn
Brepak *Tar*sin, Transverse Mountain of the Little Kick (ie cleft)
Garbh Choire
*Garr*av Chorra, Rough Corrie
Gleann Dubh
Glen Doo, Black Glen
Traligill
Giant's Ravine
Cnoc nan Uamh*
Crochk nan *Oo*-a, Knoll of the Cave
Dubh Loch Mor
Doo Loch Moar, Big Black Loch
Allt a' Bhealaich
Owlt a *Vyal*ich, River of the Pass

Conival and Ben More Assynt are the crowning hills of the Sutherland district of Assynt, an area of great geological and historical interest. The name Assynt is probably derived from a Norse word meaning rocky and, if so, these two mountains are worthy representatives of the area, for their connecting ridge sports an enormous collection of quartzite stones, more like a beach than a mountain top. The circuit of the two mountains passes through an absorbing variety of rock scenery, from limestone caves to shattered quartzite summits and a narrow gneiss ridge, which calls for some sporting scrambling in parts.

168

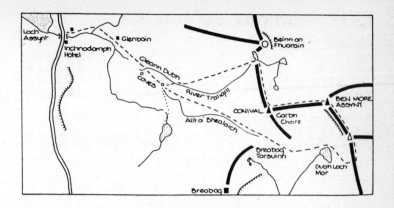

Begin near Inchnadamph Hotel on the A837, taking the private road along the right bank of the River Traligill to Glenbain Cottage. A path continues beyond the cottage, crossing the river and passing the Cnoc nan Uamh cave system, whose underground river can easily be reached beneath an arched cave entrance (both torch and care required). The whole area is rich in caves and is still yielding new finds; some of the caves show the earliest traces of human habitation in Scotland (c6,000 BC).

Leave the path to follow the course of the Traligill up Gleann Dubh, taking time to explore the limestone river bed of this Giant's Ravine as you go, then aim diagonally up the grassy south-west slopes of Beinn an Fhurain to reach the bealach between it and Conival. A further stiff 250 m (800 ft) climb over shattered quartzite leads to the summit of Conival.

The summit of Ben More Assynt lies 1 mile (1½ km) east across a broad ridge of similar shattered quartzite. The terrain is featureless, almost surreal, and in mist it can be difficult to distinguish the summit from any other heap of stones. At the summit the route turns south-eastwards, leaving the quartzite behind and unexpectedly encountering a ridge of mo.e reliable gneiss, the oldest rock in the world, here reaching a greater height than anywhere else in Scotland. Above Dubh Loch Mor the ridge narrows to a sharp arete, which has been flatteringly compared to Aonach Eagach (route 20), with several unexpectedly awkward moves across exposed slabs requiring care (especially when wet).

The ridge leads to the south top of Ben More Assynt, from where there is a good view of the fine Garbh Choire of Conival cupped high beneath the summit. About 500 m beyond the south top, a way can be made down towards Dubh Loch Mor, steeply at first but becoming easier lower down. To return to your starting point, make for the narrow defile between Conival and Breabag Tarsuinn, which leads to a descent by the Allt a' Bhealaich into Gleann Dubh.

169

Route 75: **QUINAG**

OS MAP: 15
GR: 232274
Distance: 8 miles (13 km)
Ascent: 1,040 m (3,400 ft)
Time: 6 hr

	1	2	3	4	5
Grade			●		
Terrain			●		
Navigation			●		
Seriousness			●		

Assessment: an undulating ridge walk, narrow in parts, across the many tops of the Milking Pail.

Seasonal notes: under snow, many sections of the ridge require extreme care and are not for the inexperienced.

Quinag
    Kwin-yak, Milking Pail (from Gaelic Cuinneag, pron *Coon*-yak
Spidean Coinich (764 m, 2,506 ft)
    *Speej*an *Coan*-yich, Boggy Peak
Sail Gorm (776 m, 2,545 ft)
    Sahl *Gorr*am, Blue Heel
Sail Gharbh (808 m, 2,650 ft)
    Sahl *Gharr*av, Rough Heel
Bealach a' Chornaidh
    *Byal*ach a Chorny, Pass of the Folding Cloth

Quinag is the most northerly of the chain of great sandstone peaks that rise in the north-west of Scotland. It is a peculiar Y-shaped mountain that looks different from every bend in the roads that almost encircle it. From Kylesku to the north, the buttresses of the two northern 'heels' of the Y are particularly impressive. The entire mountain consists of six tops linked by ridges, which are narrow in parts but nowhere difficult. The drops between the tops are of sufficient depth to test resolve in bagging them all, but the complete traverse makes an exhilarating tramp amidst typically spacious Assynt scenery.

Begin on the A894 4 miles (7 km) north of Inchnadamph; there is a large parking space on the east side of the road and a stalkers' path heads up towards Lochan Bealach Cornaidh on the west side. Aim directly across the moor to the foot of the south-east ridge of Spidean Coinich. A cairned path ascends the edge of the escarpment, which becomes increasingly steep and boulder-strewn as height is gained. From the summit, there is a fine view over Loch Assynt to Conival (route 74), and to the north Foinaven (route 76) is prominent.

The most interesting section of the route now begins, with a short, sharp descent to a narrow level ridge, followed by another steep descent to an enticing lochan. From here grass slopes lead up to a sharp top, and then a path goes without fuss straight down the narrow crest of the twisting north-west ridge to the Bealach a' Chornaidh.

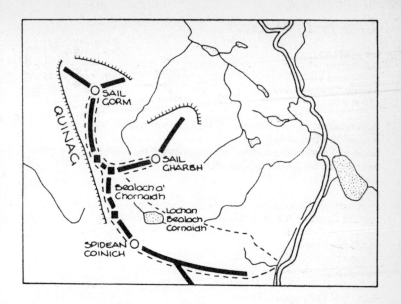

Another steep ascent on grass leads to the centre top of Quinag at the junction of the two heels of the Y; a rock band, halfway up, is easily avoided on the right. The two heels can now be visited in turn. Begin with the ascent of Sail Gorm to the north, which first involves the negotiation of a bold rocky hump that bars the way; steep but straightforward. Then follows a long climb along a gentle ridge, at one point passing along the edge of a spectacular buttress, to reach the eyrie of Sail Gorm, from where the view of the western seaboard is mesmerising.

It is tempting to linger, but there is still much to do. Make the return trip to the centre top, re-negotiating the rocky hump, and cross a short dip to Quinag's other heel and highest top, Sail Gharbh. To descend, return to the dip and go down steep grass slopes to pick up a cairned path leading across the flat moor left of Lochan Bealach Cornaidh. This becomes an excellent stalkers' path that leads back to your starting point.

Route 76: **FOINAVEN**

OS MAP: 9
GR: 306564
Distance: 14 miles (22 km)
Ascent: 1,280 m (4,200 ft)
Time: 9 hr

	1	2	3	4	5
Grade			●		
Terrain					●
Navigation			●		
Seriousness					●

Assessment: an engrossing walk along the shattered ridges of a crumbling mountain.
Seasonal notes: in the right winter conditions, beautiful snow aretes form along the ridge, but their traverse should not be attempted by the inexperienced.

Foinaven
    Fun-ya-ven, Wart Mountain (from Gaelic Foinne Bheinn)
Ceann Garbh (901 m, 2,956 ft)
    Kyown *Garr*av, Rough End
Gannu Mór (908 m, 2,978 ft)
    Big Wedge (poss from Gaelic geinn, pron gain)
A' Cheir Ghorm
    A Cheer *Ghorr*am, The Blue Comb
Cadha na Beucaich*
    *Ca*ha na *Bai*-achkich, Pass of the Bellowing
Coire na Lice*
    Corra na Leeka, Corrie of Slabs
Coire Duail
    Corra *Doo*il, Corrie of the Fold
Strath Dionard
    Stra *Jee*-onard, Strath of the High Shelter
Loch Tarbhaidh
    Loch *Tarr*avy, Bull Loch

In the desolate wastes of north-west Sutherland the shattered quartzite peak of Foinaven dominates a wild and savagely indifferent landscape pitted with water. The traverse of the long summit ridge is an exceptionally interesting expedition, although the remote and disintegrating nature of the terrain can be an unsettling experience.

Begin at Gualin House on the A838 4½ miles (7 km) north of Rhiconich. Cross the moor left of Loch Tarbhaidh, patiently threading your way through the maze of bog and lochan that obstructs the approach to Foinaven's north-west shoulder. With relief negotiate craggy slopes onto the shoulder and climb uniform boulder slopes to the summit of Ceann Garbh, Foinaven's most northerly top.

A path leads off along the summit ridge, initially narrow and stony, but soon broadening to provide a delightful grassy stroll, with superlative

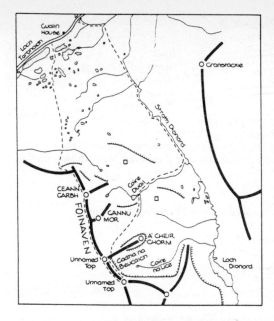

views on either side. Leaving the greenery behind for good, the ridge curves upwards in a perfect arc to Gannu Mór, Foinaven's highest summit. Note in mist that the high point lies beyond the first cairn reached, at the end of a short ridge jutting eastwards. From the first cairn, descend onto a level section of ridge that narrows over a short rise and down to a bealach, then climbs more steep-ly to an unnamed top above A' Cheir Ghorm.

The return route descends towards A' Cheir Ghorm, but first follow the main ridge round Coire na Lice amidst the most spectacular scenery of the day. The route narrows across the prominent buttress known as Lord Reay's Seat to reach the Cadha na Beucaich, where a pinnacle astride the ridge is easily bypassed, then the route climbs to another unnamed top above some of the remotest cliffs in Britain, whose full climbing potential was not realised until the 1960s.

Returning to the top above A' Cheir Ghorm, descend the steep east ridge to the bealach between these two tops. It is worth wandering out along the shattered ridge to the end point of A' Cheir Ghorm (with some exposed scrambling in places if the crest is adhered to) for the perspective on the main ridge and the eerie sound of falling quartzite as the mountain disintegrates around you.

From the bealach, descend mobile slopes on the north side (please leave some mountain behind for the next person) and follow the river down between cliffs into Coire Duail. Continue down beside the river into remote and forlorn Strath Dionard to meet a welcome path that leads back to the roadside ½ mile (1 km) north of Gualin House. Note that the path hugs the left bank of the River Dionard and should not be confused with the muddy sloughs caused by motorised stalking parties.

Route 77: **BEN HOPE**

OS MAP: 9
GR: 462477
Distance: 6 miles (10 km)
Ascent: 910 m (3,000 ft)
Time: 5 hr

	1	2	3	4	5
Grade			●		
Terrain		●			
Navigation				●	
Seriousness		●			

Assessment: an uncommon route of surprises and panoramic views on Scotland's most northerly Munro. (The direct ascent of the rock step is Grade 5.)
Seasonal notes: the north ridge is a major winter mountaineering expedition and it is best to ascend via the descent route.

Ben Hope (927 m, 3,041 ft)
    Mountain of the Bay (ie Loch Eriboll, from Norse hop)
Dubh-loch na Beinne
    Doo Loch na *Ben*-ya, Black Loch of the Mountain
Loch na Seilg
    Loch na *Shell*ik, Loch of the Hunt

Historical note: Strathmore is a desolate and lonely area, perhaps reflecting its troubled history. The greatest time of suffering was during the brutal Sutherland Clearances when, in October 1819, 100 young men of Strathmore and their families were shipped off to Ontario; all were lost at sea in winter storms. Their houses were demolished 'because they showed the devastation where people had lived' and the stones used to lay the foundations of the Road of Desolation.

The craggy wedge of Ben Hope makes a fitting most northerly Munro, rising in splendid isolation beside the Road of Desolation in wild Strathmore south-east of Loch Eriboll. The best route of ascent attacks the interesting north ridge and its sensational rock step.

    Begin in Strathmore near a cowshed 2 miles (3 km) north of Dun Dornaigil broch. A path (signpost: 'Ben Hope way up') ascends the left bank of a stream, but leave it when it heads up to a breach in the cliffs (the normal route) and continue northwards beside the main stream past Dubh-loch na Beinne until the north ridge can be gained (in mist continue to Loch na Seilg before attempting to gain the ridge).

    The ridge rises to a cairn, beyond which a short dip leads to a spectacular 10 m (30 ft) section of exposed scrambling on the edge of the west face. Try it if you have the nerve, otherwise take the not surprisingly well-worn path up the gully 30 m to the left, regaining the ridge above all difficulties. The ridge continues narrowly to the summit dome, which has an air of spaciousness unequalled on the mainland. Descend via the normal route (path) down the relentless south-west slopes, bearing right at

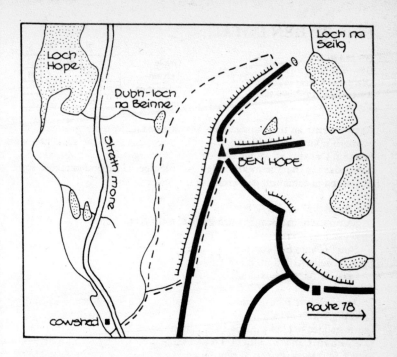

a height of 400 m (1,300 ft) through a breach in the cliffs and down beside a stream to regain the route of ascent (care in mist; if in doubt continue southwards to the Allt na Caillich and descend a path to Alltnacaillich in Strathmore).

Route 78: **BEN LOYAL**

OS MAP: 10
GR: 583539
Distance: 9½ miles (15 km)
Ascent: 880 m (2,900 ft)
Time: 6½ hr

	1	2	3	4	5
Grade			●		
Terrain					●
Navigation			●		
Seriousness		●			

Assessment: an undulating route across a scrambler's playground high above the Pentland Firth.

Seasonal notes: in winter, the descent from Sgor a' Chleiridh may be impracticable, otherwise the route is of no especial difficulty except for iced rocks on summit tors.

Ben Loyal
    Law Mountain (from Norse laga-fjall)
Sgor Chaonsaid (708 m, 2,322 ft)
    Skorr *Chæn*sitch, obscure
Sgor a' Bhatain (700 m, 2,296 ft)
    Skoor a *Vahti*n, Boat Peak
An Caisteal (764 m, 2,506 ft)
    An *Cash*-tyal, The Castle
Heddle's Top* (741 m, 2,431 ft)
Cairn an Tionail (714 m, 2,342 ft)
    Cairn an *Tyinn*al, Cairn of the Collecting
Sgor a' Chleiridh (642 m, 2,106 ft)
    Skorr a Chlairy, Peak of the Cleric
Loch Fhionnaich
    Loch Ee-*oon*ich, Cool Loch (poss)

Ben Loyal is a distinctive feature of the north coast of Scotland. Its granite tops, reminiscent of Cairngorm tors, set some enjoyable bouldering problems and form an attractive frieze, which has given rise to the mountain's flattering epithet 'Queen of the Scottish Peaks'.

The best circuit of the major tops begins on the old road around the Kyle of Tongue. 1½ miles (2 km) south of Tongue village, take the minor road that ends at farm buildings just beyond Ribigill Farm. Begin walking here, following the farm track towards Cunside Cottage. A path passes the cottage on the right and climbs the left bank of the burn coming down from the craggy north face of Sgor Chaonsaid. Climb steep grass and heather left of the face to reach the summit tors.

From here, Ben Loyal's tops can be visited one by one. Firstly the tors of Sgor a' Bhatain, then crag-girt An Caisteal (the highest top), then Heddle's Top and finally Cairn an Tionail, beyond which lower bumps lead down to the moor. From Cairn an Tionail, contour back to the broad west ridge of Heddle's Top and walk out to Sgor a' Chleiridh, the sharpest

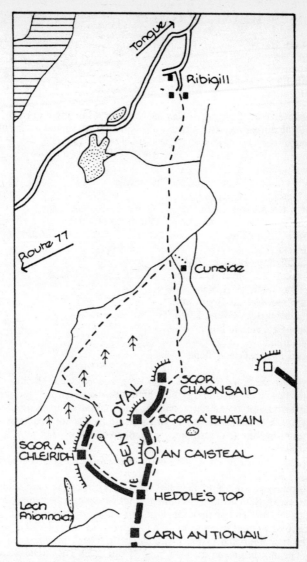

Route 77

of all Ben Loyal's tops with an impressive south-west face. With care pick a route down the south-east ridge among outcrops, then follow sheep tracks down the right bank of the burn through fine birch woods to reach the moor. From here make a beeline back to the Cunside path.

Route 79: **BEINN A' GHLO**

OS MAP: 43
GR: 901718
Distance: 14½ miles (23 km)
Ascent: 1,420 m (4,650 ft)
Time: 9 hr

	1	2	3	4	5
Grade		●			
Terrain			●		
Navigation				●	
Seriousness			●		

Assessment: a wild tramp across the windswept Mountain of Mist.
Seasonal notes: a classic winter walk whose length should not be under-estimated.

Beinn a' Ghlo
    Ben a Ghloe, Mountain of the Veil or Mist
Carn Liath (975 m, 3,198 ft)
    Carn *Lee*-a, Grey Cairn
Braigh Coire Chruinn-bhalgain (c1,070 m, c3,500 ft)
    Bra-i Corra *Chroo*-in *Val*akin, Upland of the Corrie of Round Little
    Blisters
Airgiod Bheinn (1,061 m, 3,480 ft)
    *Err*akat Ven, Silver Mountain
Carn nan Gabhar (1,129 m, 3,704 ft)
    Carn nan *Goe*-ar, Goat Cairn
Meall a'Mhuirich (898 m, 2,946 ft)
    Myowl a *Voor*ich, obscure
Glas Leathad
    Glass *Lye*-at, Green Slope

'As we left the wood we came upon such a lovely view—Beinn a'Ghlo straight before us—and under these high hills the River Tilt gushing and winding over stones and slates, and the hills and mountains skirted at the bottom with beautiful trees; the whole lit up by the sun; and the air so pure and fine; but no description can at all do it justice'.

QUEEN VICTORIA describing a drive up Glen Tilt in 1844.

The complex mountain of Beinn a' Ghlo rises out of the bare landscape north-east of Blair Atholl. According to an old sporting legend, its three Munros support no less than nineteen corries, in any one of which a rifle can be fired without being heard in any other.

The best approach to the mountain is the rough private road along Glen Tilt that begins on the west bank of the River Tilt at Old Bridge of Tilt near Blair Atholl. Ring Atholl Estate (Blair Atholl 355) to obtain permission to drive the 4 miles (7 km) to the start of the route at the bridge just past Marble Lodge. From here, climb diagonally up the hillside to the low ridge on the south side of the glen, then cross windswept moors

178

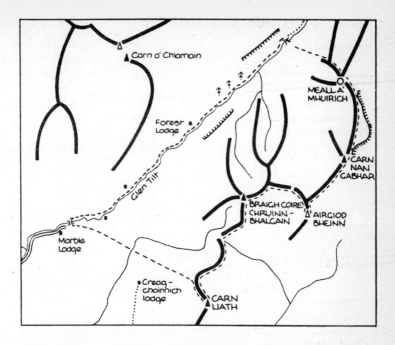

and negotiate steep heathery slopes to reach the summit of Carn Liath.

The route onwards is a bracing high-level walk along the broad grassy main ridge as it sweeps round to Braigh Coire Chruinn-bhalgain, twists right and left to a small rise, then turns immediately right again (care in mist) across a bealach to reach the final summit ridge. Bear right for Airgiod Bheinn, then return along the ridge to Carn nan Gabhar, Beinn a' Ghlo's highest top.

Descend over Meall a' Mhuirich to regain Glen Tilt. Cross the River Tilt by the bridge at the foot of Glas Leathad and end the day with a pleasant walk back down the confines of the glen.

Route 80: **DRIESH and MAYAR**

OS MAP: 44
GR: 283761
Distance: 9 miles (15 km)
Ascent: 980 m (3,200 ft)
Time: 6 hr

	1	2	3	4	5
Grade	●				
Terrain	●				
Navigation			●		
Seriousness		●			

Assessment: a pleasant route along delightful paths through fine corries and glens.
Seasonal notes: a generally easy winter route, although the exit from Corrie Fee may pose problems.

Driesh (947 m, 3,106 ft)
   Dreesh, Place of Brambles
Mayar (928 m, 3,044 ft)
   Mayar, Place of Delight (poss) or Place of the Plain (poss)
Corrie Fee*
   Boggy Corrie (poss, from Gaelic feith, pron fay)
Glen Doll
   Glen Dole, Meadow Glen

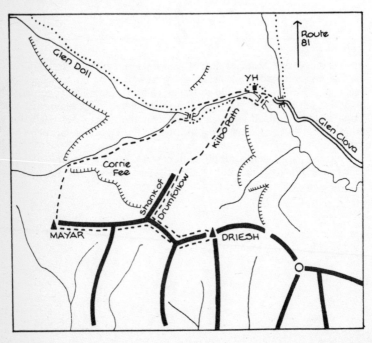

The mountain summits of the great rolling tableland of the White Mounth, south of Deeside, are no more than minor excrescences on the moor, but Driesh and Mayar on the southern perimeter are flanked by interesting glens and corries, which make their ascent well worth investigation. They are reached by the B955 road along Glen Clova, one of the finest examples of glacial scenery in Scotland.

Begin at the car park at the road end and take the track (Jock's Road), past the youth hostel, along the densely wooded Glen Doll. Ignore a left turn to the Kilbo path and continue to a fork, leaving Jock's Road for a forestry track that crosses the White Water and follows the right bank of the tumbling Fee Burn up into Corrie Fee. This beautiful corrie is full of interesting moraines and is ringed by crags that are a favourite haunt of Dundonian climbers. Follow the path across the corrie flats and up zigzags beside a fine waterfall, then trend left onto the open plateau to reach the summit of Mayar. The continuation to Driesh is a pleasant stroll across the plateau waymarked by a broken fence.

To descend, retrace your steps to the Shank of Drumfollow and descend it to the forest fence at its foot, with fine views left into Corrie Fee. Pick up the Kilbo path, which descends the Shank below its crest and provides a delightful and effortless descent back to Jock's Road.

Route 81: **LOCHNAGAR**

OS MAP: 43/44
GR: 186911
Distance: 12 miles (19 km)
Ascent: 910 m (3,000 ft)
Time: 7½ hr

	1	2	3	4	5
Grade				●	
Terrain					●
Navigation			●		
Seriousness			●		

Assessment: a beautiful woodland walk and rock scramble lead to one of the great corries of the Scottish Highlands.

Seasonal notes: the north-east corrie is magnificent under snow, but the prow of the Stuic is no place for walkers and is best avoided by ascending the western rim of Coire nan Eun.

Lochnagar
    Loch-na-*gahr*, Loch of the Noise (ie wind among rocks)
Cac Carn Beag (1,155 m, 3,789 ft), (Mór, 1,150 m, 3,772 ft)
    Cachk Carn Bake (Moar), Little (Big) Shit Cairn (vulgar)
The Stuic (1,093 m, 3,585 ft)
    The Stoochk, The Pinnacle
Carn a' Coire Boidheach* (1,118 m, 3,667 ft)
    Carn a Corra *Baw*-yach, Cairn of the Beautiful Corrie
Coire nan Eun*
    Corra nan *Yai*-an, Bird Corrie
Garbh Allt
    *Garr*av Owlt, Rough Stream

The vast tableland of the White Mountain ends abruptly in the north where the great granite peak of Lochnagar towers over the rivers and forests of Deeside. Artists and poets as well as climbers have long been attracted here to the dramatic scenery of the north-east corrie, a spectacular crescent of cliffs enclosing the dark lochan that gives the mountain its name. There are many routes to the summit, but by far the most interesting is by Ballochbuie Forest and the prow of The Stuic. This was the approach favoured by Byron, whose atmospheric poem did much to further the fame of the mountain, with its stirring references to 'the steep frowning glories of dark Lochnagar'.

Begin at Invercauld Bridge where the A93 crosses the Dee 3 miles (5 km) east of Braemar. Forest roads leave each side of the bridge to join on the south side of the old bridge and enter magnificent Ballochbuie Forest, purchased by Queen Victoria in 1878 to preserve it from felling and now the finest stand of pines in the Highlands. (*NB:* the road is private and permission to use it should be sought at the house by the old bridge.) At a fork after 500 m take the right branch, keep straight on at the next crossroads and join another track up the left bank of the Garbh

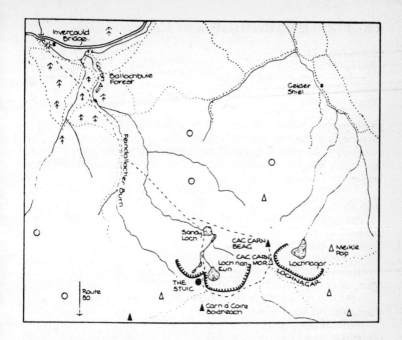

Allt. Unlike modern forestry roads, these Victorian ones blend beautifully with the trees and make enchanting walking.

At a hairpin bend, keep left on a path past the wild and mysterious Falls of Garbh Allt to rejoin the forest road higher up. Follow the road up the left bank of the Feindallacher Burn until the trees begin to thin out, then cut left over a low ridge to the Allt Lochan nan Eun and cross the rough heathery moor to Sandy Loch. The Stuic begins to look decidedly interesting from here, its steep prow bisecting Coire nan Eun into two halves, each cradling lochans. Bear right into the corrie and climb the prow direct, a fine easy scramble on secure blocks of granite.

At the top follow the path round the corrie rim (bagging the dreary Munro of Carn a' Coire Boidheach en route if you so desire) to Cac Carn Mór and Cac Carn Beag, the unfortunately named twin tops of Lochnagar. Both tops lie on the rim of the north-east corrie, and as you stroll between them you should keep close to the edge to contemplate the vertiginous cliffs and the dark lochan far below. To descend, boulder hop down the north-west ridge to reach Sandy Loch and return via the approach route.

Route 82: **BRAERIACH and CAIRN TOUL**

OS MAP: 36
GR: 915087
Distance: 22 miles (35 km)
Ascent: 1,580 m (5,200 ft)
Time: 12¹/₂ hr

	1	2	3	4	5
Grade		●			
Terrain			●		
Navigation					●
Seriousness					●

Assessment: probably the best high-level plateau walk in Scotland.
Seasonal notes: the plateau and its corniced rims are spectacular in winter, but the route is a formidable undertaking best attempted only in excellent conditions. Note that the exit from Coire Dhondail is very steep and may be corniced.

Braeriach (1,296 m, 4,251 ft)
    Bri-*ree*-ach, Brindled Upland
Cairn Toul (1,291 m, 4,235 ft)
    Cairn Towl, Cairn of the Barn
Sgor an Lochain Uaine (1,258 m, 4,127 ft)
    Skorr an Lochan Oo-*an*-ya, Peak of the Green Lochan
Carn na Criche* (1,265 m, 4,150 ft)
    Carn na *Creech*a, Cairn of the Boundary
Einich Cairn (1,237 m, 4,058 ft)
    Ennich Cairn, Marsh Cairn (named after Glen Einich)
Sròn na Lairige (1,814 m, 3,884 ft)
    Srawn na *Lahr*ika, Nose of the Pass
Coire Dhondail
    Corra *Ghown*til, obscure
An Garbh Choire
    An *Garr*av Chorra, The Rough Corrie
Coire Bhrochain
    Corra *Vroch*in, Porridge Corrie
Lairig Ghru
    Lahr ik Ghroo, poss Oozing Pass (from Gaelic drudhadh, after the River Druie) or poss Gloomy Pass (from Gaelic grumach)

Begin at Whitewell car park, at the end of the minor road that leaves the B970 south-east of Inverdruie. A signposted path goes down to join the Land Rover track along Gleann Einich, which is followed all the way to wild Loch Einich in the heart of the mountains.

Just before reaching the loch, take the path on the left that rises across the hillside into the grassy hollow of Coire Dhondail and zigzags up the head of the corrie to end on the plateau. From here make a rising traverse eastwards to the bealach below Sgor an Lochain Uaine, where massive An Garbh Choire comes into view.

Follow the cliff edge over Sgor an Lochain Uaine and around Coire an

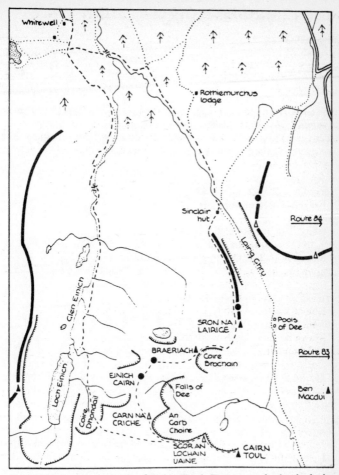

Lochan Uaine to the summit of Cairn Toul. Return to the bealach, leave the corrie rim and follow the plateau skyline round to Braeriach, across a gravel desert that is a navigational test piece in foul weather.

Reach the summit of Braeriach at the lip of the 230 m (750 ft) cliffs of Coire Bhrochain, then continue round the narrowing cliff edge, following an indistinct path to a dip, then go left over the two tops of Sròn na Lairige and down the rough north ridge. At the foot of the ridge a good path leads to the welcoming Sinclair Memorial Hut and the Lairig Ghru path, which provides a delightful descent through Rothiemurchus pine woods back to the Glen Einich track.

Route 83: **BEN MACDUI**

OS MAP: 36/43
GR: 068898
Distance: 19 miles (30 km)
Ascent: 1,020 m (3,350 ft)
Time: 10 hr

	1	2	3	4	5
Grade	●				
Terrain	●				
Navigation				●	
Seriousness					●

Assessment: a long easy walk amidst constantly changing scenery that shows the many moods of the Cairngorm landscape.

Seasonal notes: a fine but lengthy winter's day; the exposed summit plateau of Ben Macdui is best avoided in adverse weather.

Ben Macdui (1,309 m, 4,294 ft)
  Ben Mac*doo*-y, MacDuff's Mountain
Sròn Riach (1,110 m, 3,641 ft)
  Srawn *Ree*-ach, Brindled Nose
Creagan a'Choire Etchachan (1,108 m, 3,635 ft)
  *Craik*an a Chorr *Ait*-yachan, Crag of the Juniper Corrie
Coire Sputan Dearg
  Corra *Spoot*an *Jerr*ak, Corrie of the Red Spouts (ie Scree)
Lochan Uaine
  Lochan Oo-*an*ya, Green Lochan
Lairig an Laoigh
  *Lahr*ik an Loe-y, Calf Pass

Ben Macdui is the second highest mountain in Scotland. Until well into the last century it was thought to be the highest, and this may account for the historical popularity of a mountain that lies well hidden in the centre of the Cairngorms. Famous ascents include those by Gladstone, Queen Victoria (on a pony in 1859) and Professor Collie, the celebrated mountaineer, one of many who have fled from the mountain before its legendary spectre, the Big Grey Man. It is certainly an eerie, desolate place and testaments to the Big Grey Man abound, but the undeterred walker will find its ascent a route of constant interest that shows the variegated Cairngorm landscape in all its many forms.

Begin at the foot of Glen Lui near the Linn of Dee west of Braemar. Take the rough road that crosses the broad flats beside the Lui Water (where large numbers of deer are often to be seen) to Derry Lodge in a fine situation at the junction of Glen Derry and Glen Luibeg. Cross the Derry Burn (footbridge) and take the Lairig an Laoigh path (signposted) through an enchanted forest of native pines to rejoin a Land Rover track from Derry Lodge further up Glen Derry.

The track becomes a path leading through the desolate upper glen below Coire an Lochan Uaine, a favourite haunt of the eighteenth-century Gaelic poet-cum-poacher, William Smith. At the head of the glen, the

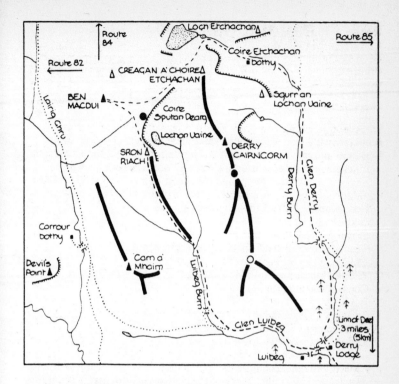

Route 82

path forks, the right branch continuing to Aviemore; take the left branch that curves round into Coire Etchachan, a deep basin backed by crags and sporting a hut (the Hutchison Memorial Hut), which gives the place an Alpine flavour. Beyond the hut, the path climbs beside the burn to the corrie rim and debouches into an unexpected higher corrie filled by Loch Etchachan, the largest loch above the 3,000 ft (914 m) contour in the Highlands and frozen for much of the year. The scenery is more Arctic than Alpine.

The path climbs left to the rim of Coire Sputan Dearg, yet another (and probably the finest) of Macdui's corries, and then veers right across the plateau to the summit boulderfield, strewn with stone howffs (care in mist). Return to the rim of Coire Sputan Dearg and follow it down to the small top of Sròn Riach, beneath whose crags sparkles lovely Lochan Uaine, a prime example of why Macdui's collection of high lochans is said to be the finest in the Cairngorms. Continue down the south-east ridge of Sròn Riach, picking up a path leading down to Glen Luibeg and the Lairig Ghru path, whose wide sandy swathes provide a beautiful route through the pines back to Derry Lodge.

187

Route 84: **BYNACK MORE and CAIRN GORM**

OS MAP: 36
GR: 983086
Distance: 17 miles (27 km)
Ascent: 1,520 m (5,000 ft)
Time: 10¹/₂ hr

	1	2	3	4	5
Grade		●			
Terrain		●			
Navigation				●	
Seriousness					●

Assessment: a wild walk around some secret corners of Cairn Gorm.
Seasonal notes: a long and spectacular winter route, but the ascent from The Saddle and the descent into Coire an Lochan are very steep and not for the inexperienced. The summit plateau of Cairn Gorm is best avoided in adverse weather; the easiest descent from the summit goes northwards to the Ptarmigan Restaurant and down into Coire Cas.

Cairn Gorm (1,245 m, 4,084 ft)
    Cairn *Gorr*am (usually anglicised to *Cairn*gorm), Blue Cairn
Bynack More (1,090 m, 3,576 ft)
    *By*nack Moar, Big Little Mountain (poss, from Gaelic Beinneag)
A' Chòinneach (1,017 m, 3,336 ft)
    A *Choan*-yach, The Boggy Place
Stob Coire an t-Sneachda* (1,176 m, 3,858 ft)
    Stop Corra an *Drech*ka, Peak of the Snow Corrie
Cairn Lochan (1,215 m, 3,986 ft)
    Cairn of the Lochan
Fiacaill an Leth-choinn* (1,083 m, 3,553 ft)
    Fee-acil an *Lye*-chonn, Tooth of the Half-dog or Lurcher
Coire Cas
    Corra Cas, Steep Corrie
An Lochan Uaine
    An Lochan Oo-*an*-ya, The Green Lochan
Allt Mór*
    Owlt Moar, Big River
Strath Nethy, poss from Gaelic neithich (pure stream)
Ryvoan, from Gaelic ruighe a' bhothain (shieling of the cottage)

Begin on the Cairn Gorm ski road just before it crosses the Allt Mór for the second time; a road on the right is marked 'Danger High Voltage'. Take the forestry track on the left which crosses the Allt Mór and continues straight on (ignore all branches) to join the track from Glen More into the Pass of Ryvoan, a wonderfully Alpine pass with pines and crags overlooking the deep green eye of An Lochan Uaine.

    Keep right at a fork to reach the corrugated iron bothy of Bynack Stable at the foot of Strath Nethy. From here a finely graduated path crosses the shoulder of Bynack More into Glen Avon, providing an effort-

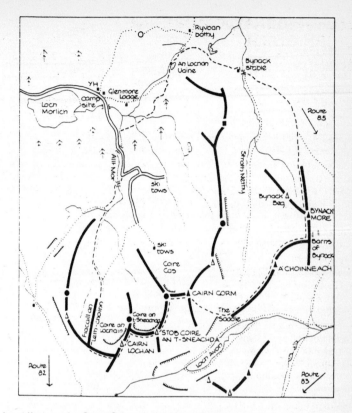

less climb to the foot of the north ridge. Once onto the shoulder leave the path and climb the ridge to the tumble of granite boulders that form the summit. Continue over A' Chòinneach to The Saddle, pausing on the way to explore the rocky tors of the Little Barns of Bynack.

From The Saddle, pick a route up the steep slopes rising 400 m (1,300 ft) to the broad, stony summit of Cairn Gorm, where the most spectacular section of the route begins, hugging the edge of the boulder-strewn plateau around the rims of Coire an t-Sneachda and Coire an Lochain. Note especially the huge walls of Coire an Lochain, the remote haunt of climbers far from the skiing areas (and may it ever remain so).

Descend into the corrie on the path from the dip before Fiacaill an Leth-choin. If there is snow on the ground a direct descent here can be misleadingly steep, and you may prefer to continue over the Fiacaill and descend further along. The path crosses the wild open moors below Coire an Lochain and eventually reaches a bridge over the Allt Mór to join the ski road not far above your starting point.

Route 85: **BEN AVON**

OS MAP: 36
GR: 162165
Distance: 24 miles (39 km)
Ascent: 990 m (3,250 ft)
Time: 12½ hr

	1	2	3	4	5
Grade	●				
Terrain		●			
Navigation					●
Seriousness					●

Approach to Inchrory (each way):
   6 miles (10 km), out 80 m (250 ft) back 30 m (100 ft), 2½ hr
Ascent from Inchrory:
   12 miles (19 km), 880 m (2,900 ft), 7½ hr

Assessment: a long walk of great interest on one of Scotland's most remote and unusual mountains. (The summit tor is Grade 3.)
Seasonal notes: in winter the length, remoteness and navigational difficulty of the route make it a serious proposition best undertaken only in excellent conditions.

Ben Avon
   Ben Ahn, Fair Mountain (poss, after the River Avon)
Leabaidh an Daimh Bhuidhe (1,171 m, 3,841 ft)
   Lyeppy an Deff *Voo*-ya, Bed of the Yellow Stag
Beinn a' Bhuird (1,196 m, 3,923 ft)
   Ben a Voort, Table Mountain
Meall Gaineimh (911 m, 2,988 ft)
   Myowl Gahny, Sandy Hill
Stob Bac an Fhurain (1,076 m, 3,530 ft)
   Stop Bachk an Oorin, Peak of the Bank of the Spring
Clach Bhàn
   Clach Vahn, Stone of the Women
Clach Bun Rudhtair
   Clach Boon *Root*ir, Stone at the Foot of the Mounds (poss)
Builg Burn
   *Bool*ik Burn, Bubbling Burn

Prepare yourself for a lengthy and testing tramp across the desolate tableland of the eastern Cairngorms. This largest of all Cairngorm plateaux consists of two mountain groups, Ben Avon and Beinn a' Bhuird, separated by the high saddle known as the Sneck. Ben Avon is the most interesting of the two, its slopes bristling with fascinating rock tors rearing up to 30 m (80 ft) in height, and it is best approached from the north in order to explore the best of these.

   Just reaching the foot of the mountain is an exercise in logistics for it lies distant from any public road; the best approach is that from Tomintoul, which has more to recommend it than most during the 6 mile

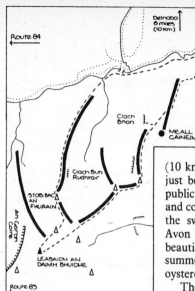

Route 84

Route 83

(10 km) haul into the interior. Begin just beyond Delnabo at the end of the public road south-west of Tomintoul and continue along a private road beside the swift-flowing waters of the River Avon to Inchrory Lodge. The glen is beautifully wooded at first and in summer the riverbanks are alive with oystercatchers.

The road continues past the lodge into upper Glen Avon; follow it until 200 m beyond the Builg Burn, then take a left branch up the hillside. At last bulldozed roads are left behind (although many can be seen scarring the hillsides) and a path climbs the north ridge of Meall Gaineimh to the shallow bealach between its summit and Clach Bhàn, the largest of Ben Avon's tors. Make a short detour to explore Clach Bhàn's rocks and hollows, particularly the chair formations, visited by pregnant women until the latter part of the nineteenth century in the belief that this would ensure an easy birth.

It is still a long haul to the summit of Ben Avon over several subsidiary tops, especially if diversions are made to explore the numerous interesting tors. The summit itself (Leabaidh an Daimh Bhuidhe) is the second highest tor on the mountain, set in the midst of a stony plateau which is no place to be in mist. The tor's high point is an easy scramble from the north side. Beyond, the vast plateau continues to the flat summit of Beinn a' Bhuird, visible behind the Sneck and the huge basin of An Garbh Choire, but only the most dedicated will contemplate going further.

To return to Glen Avon descend north-east then north over Stob Bac an Fhurain and continue down the north ridge past the weird fingers of Clach Bun Rudhtair, Ben Avon's highest tor. From the foot of the ridge a Land Rover track is soon reached which leads back past the foaming Linn of Avon to Inchrory Lodge and the long walk out.

191

Route 86: THE WEST GLEN ROSA PEAKS (ARRAN)

OS MAP: 69
GR: 999378
Distance: 8½ miles (14 km)
Ascent: 1,020 m (3,350 ft)
Time: 6½ hr

	1	2	3	4	5
Grade			●		
Terrain				●	
Navigation				●	
Seriousness				●	

Assessment: a pleasant introduction to Arran ridge walking with the option of exploring the island's most thrilling scramble (the A' Chir ridge: Grade 5).

Seasonal notes: A' Chir under snow is no place for walkers, and rather than descend from Beinn Tarsuinn to the Bealach an Fhir-bhogha it is easier to follow the south-east ridge out towards Beinn a' Chliabhain.

Caisteal an Fhinn (792 m, 2,598 ft)
    Cash-tyal an Een, Hero's Castle (poss)
Beinn Nuis (792 m, 2,598 ft)
    Ben Noosh, (should be Gnuis, pron Groosh, Face Mountain)
Beinn Tarsuinn (825 m, 2,706 ft)
    Ben *Tars*in, Transverse Mountain
A' Chir (712 m, 2,335 ft)
    A Cheer, The Comb
Beinn a' Chliabhain (653 m, 2,142 ft)
    Ben a *Chlee*-avin, Creel Mountain
Bealach an Fhir-bhogha
    *Byal*ach an Eer *Voe*-a, Bowman's Pass
Coire a'Bhradain
    Corr a *Vrah*tin, Salmon Corrie
Garbh Allt*
    *Garr*av Owlt, Rough Stream

The rough granite mountains of Arran provide spectacular walking. The shapely peaks, the narrow pinnacled ridges and an island setting all combine to produce exciting and addictive mountain country that is easily accessible from central Scotland. All the major peaks could be climbed in a single long day, many of them between ferries, but it is better to savour the experience with the three routes recommended in this book (routes 86–8).

The main mountain group lies north of Brodick in a rough H shape, with Glen Sannox bisecting the upper half and Glen Rosa the lower. The ridge on the west side of Glen Rosa divides into two to enclose Coire a' Bhradain, and the round of the corrie makes a good introduction to the delights of Arran ridge walking.

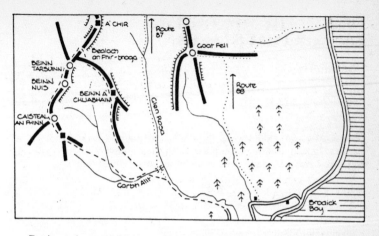

Begin at the end of the road up Glen Rosa that leaves the B880 200 m west of its junction with the A841. Continue along the cart track through the farmlands of the lower glen until a pipeline crosses the river just before the Garbh Allt. Branch left here on a path that climbs diagonally across the hillside to a small dam on the Garbh Allt, then cross the stream and make your way across boggy ground and up the south-west ridge of Caisteal an Fhinn. On reaching the stony south top, turn right to gain the main summit. As on all Arran's ridges a good path makes the going easy.

Continuing along the ridge, an extremely pleasant stroll on moss and grass leads along the edge of the cliffs of Beinn Nuis, whose central chimney became notorious after an early party was forced during its ascent to attempt a human pyramid of three. Beyond Beinn Nuis the ridge continues easily to Beinn Tarsuinn, from where a contrasting steep, rocky descent to the Bealach an Fhir-bhogha requires some handwork. Ahead lies the south ridge of A' Chir, the most difficult of Arran's peaks. This ridge is not included in the itinerary because it is exposed and hard, but it is the finest scramble on Arran and should on no account be missed by capable scramblers, who may even wish to explore beyond the summit to the infamous bad step, which all but the bravest will leave for another day.

From the Bealach an Fhir-bhogha take the path that contours beneath the cliffs of Beinn Tarsuinn's east face to join the broad ridge leading round to Beinn a' Chliabhain, with spectacular views of A' Chir and Cir Mhór. The path goes over the summit of Beinn a' Chliabhain and down the south ridge towards the Garbh Allt, where the route of ascent is rejoined.

Route 87: **THE WEST GLEN SANNOX PEAKS (ARRAN)**

OS MAP: 69
GR: 016454
Distance: 8 miles (13 km)
Ascent: 1,070 m (3,500 ft)
Time: 7½ hr

	1	2	3	4	5
Grade				●	
Terrain					●
Navigation					●
Seriousness				●	

Assessment: an exhilarating ridge walk, with ample scrambling opportunities, superb situations and magnificent rock scenery.
Seasonal notes: a major winter mountaineering expedition.

Suidhe Fhearghas (634 m, 2,080 ft)
   Su-ya *Erra*ghas, Fergus's Seat
Ceum na Caillich
   Kame na *Kyle*-yich, Old Woman's Step
Caisteal Abhail (859 m, 2,818 ft)
   Cash-tyal *Avi*l, Ptarmigan Castle
Cir Mhór (798 m, 2,618 ft)
   Keer Voar, Big Comb

Commercial barytes mining in Glen Sannox became uneconomical at the end of World War II, yet a good deal of the mineral still remains (look for its white veins). Sannox miners are said to have collected £50 worth of gold dust from the River Sannox. There are also stories of gold grains

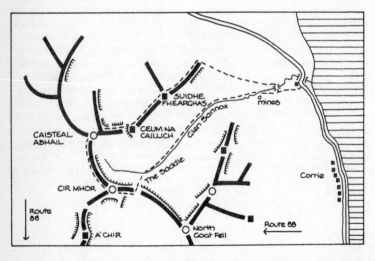

combed out of sheep fleeces in Glen Rosa, and tales of even greater secret finds, but beware iron pyrites (fool's gold).

For wildness and ruggedness, few mountain prospects equal the view up Glen Sannox. The round of the sharp skyline is a magnificent but considerable undertaking, however, and it is best to leave the eastern peaks for another day (route 88) in order to allow more time for the exploration of the exciting western arm of the glen.

Begin at Glen Cottage 200 m south of the bridge over the River Sannox on the A841 and take the car track beside the cottage up Glen Sannox. Leave the track after 10 min, cross the river (bridge) and head across the moor to climb the rough north-east shoulder of Suidhe Fhearghas, keeping well to the right to outflank all outcrops. At the summit the rock towers, which stand astride the ridge leading onwards to Caisteal Abhail, burst into view, producing a shiver of anticipation.

As far as the summit platform of the first rock tower, the ridge is easy and pleasant, but take note of paths descending to the right as you will most likely need to use them to contour into the 50 m (150 ft) gap of the Ceum na Caillich that lies beyond. The direct descent into the gap is an unforgettable experience, but is recommended for experienced scramblers only; it begins in a groove to the right of the summit boulder and lower down requires an awkward thrutch down an exposed 30° slab.

From the gap, easier scrambling leads up and over a succession of rock tors to the crag-girt summit of Caisteal Abhail. The route onwards from here is barred by a line of crags that must be circumvented on the right after retracing your steps a short distance. Gentler slopes then sweep down around the head of Glen Sannox to the foot of Cir Mhór, Arran's most spectacular mountain. The ascent to its narrow summit platform is without difficulty, but the ensuing descent to The Saddle is long and steep, requiring some handwork near the top and care on loose granite granules.

Beyond The Saddle rises Goat Fell and its satellites (route 88), but most people will have had enough excitement for one day and opt for the descent into Glen Sannox. This itself is not without interest as the steep stony path uses an eroded basalt dyke to breach a band of cliffs and gain the level confines of the glen. The path crosses the river and is boggy until the lower glen is reached, but the views of the encircling peaks compensate. Recross the river at stepping stones just before old mine workings (see opposite) or at the bridge just beyond to rejoin the cart track back to Glen Cottage.

Route 88: **GOAT FELL (ARRAN)**

OS MAP: 69
GR: 006369
Distance: 13 miles (21 km)
Ascent: 1,220 m (4,000 ft)
Time: 8½ hr

	1	2	3	4	5
Grade				●	
Terrain				●	
Navigation			●		
Seriousness				●	

Assessment: an easy ascent of Arran's highest mountain followed by an entertaining scramble.

Seasonal notes: in winter, the ridge between Goat Fell and Cioch na h'Oighe may be impracticable for walkers.

Goat Fell (874 m, 2,867 ft)
　　Mountain of Wind (from Gaelic goath) or Goat Mountain (from
　　Norse geita)
Mullach Buidhe (819 m, 2,686 ft)
　　*Mull*ach *Boo*-ya, Yellow Summit
Cioch na h-Oighe (661 m, 2,168 ft)
　　Kee-och na *Hu*ya, The Virgin's Breast
Cnocan Burn
　　Crochkan Burn, Burn of the Knoll

Goat Fell is the highest mountain on Arran; its ascent is straightforward but enlivened by tremendous seaward views and the prospect of the sporting north ridge that lies in wait.

Begin at the exit road from Brodick Castle, just north of the junction of the A841 and the B880. Walk up the road past the Cnocan Burn and take the track on the left behind the kennels. Keeping straight on, follow the signposted Goat Fell path up beside the Cnocan Burn and across the moorland to the boulder-strewn east ridge. Reach the summit without difficulty and continue to North Goat Fell along the north ridge, which is punctuated with rock tors whose negotiation provides some entertaining scrambling; paths bypass all the interest. Beyond North Goat Fell easy going leads to the flat summit of Mullach Buidhe and then probably the most interesting scrambling of the day is encountered as the ridge narrows out to Cioch na h-Oighe above the crags of the Punch Bowl.

From Cioch na h-Oighe return to North Goat Fell and descend the steep north-west ridge to The Saddle; hands and care are required near the top. The day ends with a long walk out down Glen Rosa beside the sparkling waters of the Glenrosa Water, reaching the B880 a short distance from your starting point.

NB: the approach can be shortened by beginning at the car park in Glen Rosa and fording the Glenrosa Water to reach the castle grounds.

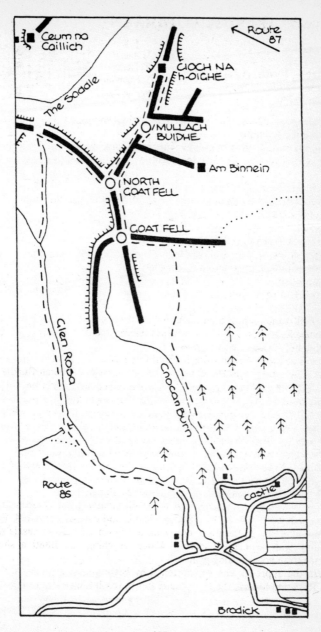

Ceum na Caillich

The Saddle

CIOCH NA h-OIGHE

MULLACH BUIDHE

Am Binnein

NORTH GOAT FELL

GOAT FELL

Glen Rosa

Cnocan Burn

Route 85

castle

Brodick

Route 87

Route 89: THE PAPS (JURA)

OS MAP: 61
GR: 544721
Distance: 10 miles (16 km)
Ascent: 1,630 m (5,350 ft)
Time: 8½ hr

	1	2	3	4	5
Grade		●			
Terrain					●
Navigation					●
Seriousness					●

Assessment: a tough but memorable walk across the inimitable mountains of Jura.

Seasonal notes: the quartzite hillside may be easier to tackle under certain snow conditions, but their uniform steepness requires great care.

Beinn Mhearsamail (c490 m, c1,600 ft)
    Ben *Vair*samil, obscure
Beinn a' Chaolais (734 m, 2,408 ft)
    Ben a *Chœl*ish, Mountain of the Narrows
Beinn an Oir (784 m, 2,572 ft)
    Ben an *Oa*-ir, Mountain of Gold (from Gaelic Or) or Mountain of the
    Shore or Boundary (from Gaelic Oir)
Beinn Shiantaidh (755 m, 2,477 ft)
    Ben *Hee*-anty, Sacred Mountain
Corra Bheinn (569 m, 1,866 ft)
    Corra Ven, Pointed Mountain
Loch an t-Siob
    Loch an *Jee*-op, Drift Loch

Jura is one of the wildest and loneliest of all the major Scottish islands. Its cave-riddled west coast is untracked and uninhabited, but it is the three distinctive Paps in the south of the island that are the main attraction for walkers. Their scree-girt quartzite domes are separated by deep bealachs, defended by miles of boggy moorland and require a determined assault, yet just as artists have been attracted here over the centuries so no mountain lover could fail to be lured to their commanding summits.

Begin at the bridge over the Corran River just north of Lergybreck on the island's one and only road. Contour above the boggy right bank of the river, around the eastern slopes of Beinn Mhearsamail and above Loch an t-Siob to reach the bealach between Beinn Mhearsamail and Beinn a'Chaolais. The going is tough and adders may provide an additional hazard, but the obvious route directly up Beinn Mhearsamail's eastern shoulder is worse.

From the bealach, climb steeply to gain the summit of Beinn a'Chaolais, the first Pap, then lose height again immediately with a long descent to the bealach beneath Beinn an Oir. Large quartzite boulders on the bealach make awkward going, and the long scree-strewn haul up to the summit of Beinn an Oir, the second and highest Pap, hardly provides

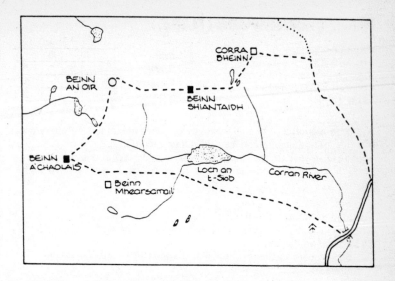

relief. Scientists as well as walkers have been attracted by Beinn an Oir; in 1812 experiments were conducted here on the effect of altitude on the boiling point of water.

From the summit, descend a short distance along the north ridge to reach the causeway of stones built to aid OS surveyors in the nineteenth century. The route onwards to Beinn Shiantaidh, the third Pap, veers eastwards from here to the low bealach between the two mountains and climbs Beinn Shiantaidh's west ridge. It is another long descent and reascent and, despite the superb island views, it is tempting to descend from Beinn Shiantaidh to Loch an t-Siob and so to the road. The complete traverse of the Paps, however, should ideally include the lower Corra Bheinn, the 'fourth Pap', so fortify yourself with the knowledge that the record for the Paps of Jura fell race (including Corra Bheinn) stands at just over three hours and continue the round.

There follows another long steep descent to a broad lochan-studded bealach, from where the ascent to the last top of the day is fittingly less severe. Pause at the summit to congratulate yourself on an exhausting but memorable achievement, then descend eastwards to pick up a path that crosses the island. On easy going, at last, reach the roadside not far from your starting point.

Route 90: **BEN MORE (MULL)**

OS MAP: 48
GR: 507368
Distance: 6½ miles (11 km)
Ascent: 1,050 m (3,450 ft)
Time: 5½ hr

	1	2	3	4	5
Grade				●	
Terrain			●		
Navigation	●				
Seriousness	●				

Assessment: after some initial hard ascent work the route develops into a fine ridge scramble of Hebridean splendour and interest.
Seasonal notes: the east ridge is a major undertaking under snow but rarely in condition, and the route is really one to be savoured in high summer.

Ben More (966 m, 3,170 ft)
    Ben Moar, Big Mountain
An Gearna
    An *Gerr*ana, obscure (poss same derivation as An Gearanach—see route 22)
A' Chioch
    A *Chee*-och, The Breast
Gleann na Beinne Fada
    Glen na *Ben*-ya *Fatt*a, Glen of the Long Mountain
Loch na Keal
    Loch na *Kee*-al, Loch of the (Monastic) Cells
Abhainn na h-Uamha
    *Avi*n na Hoo-*ah*-a, River of the Cave

Mull is a fascinating island that has much to offer the pedestrian explorer, notably the ascent of Ben More, prominent from all over the island and the only Munro in the Hebrides outside Skye. Begin on the north shore of Loch na Keal at the bridge over the Abhainn na h-Uamha, 6½ miles (11 km) south of Salen on the B8035 Bunessan road. Climb directly up the steep grass slopes of An Gearna and onto the summit of the Ben itself. The ascent is somewhat tedious, but console yourself with the knowledge that the French geologist Saint Fond failed to reach the summit in 1784, declaring that 'in my journeys among the High Alps I have never found so much difficulty as here'. In any case the view, which only a Hebridean island could provide, is worth any effort.

If the ascent lacks interest, the remainder of the route more than compensates, for the east ridge connecting Ben More to A' Chioch narrows to a sharp rocky crest that provides an extremely pleasant scramble. There is no difficulty, but the occasionally loose basalt rocks (Ben More is all that remains of one of the most recently active volcanoes

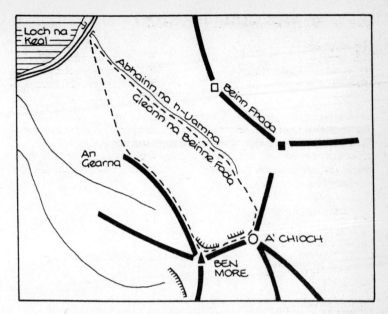

in Western Europe) require care. Continue over the rocky hump of A' Chioch and descend the open grass slopes of Gleann na Beinne Fada to your starting point. During the descent keep close to the burn, whose idyllic pools and waterfalls tempt one to linger on a hot summer's day.

Route 91: **THE CUILLIN (RUM)**

OS MAP: 39
GR: 402995
Distance: 12½ miles (20 km)
Ascent: 1,900 m (6,250 ft)
Time: 11 hr

	1	2	3	4	5
Grade					●
Terrain				●	
Navigation					●
Seriousness					●

Assessment: a superb long scramble across the unforgettable peaks of the forbidden island.
Seasonal notes: a major winter mountaineering expedition.

Barkeval (591 m, 1,938 ft)
    Boat Mountain (poss)
Hallival (723 m, 2,372 ft)
    Mountain of Slabs
Askival (812 m, 2,664 ft)
    Ash (tree) Mountain
Trallval (702 m, 2,303 ft)
    Giant's Mountain
Ainshval (781 m, 2,562 ft)
    obscure
Sgurr nan Gillean (764 m, 2,506 ft)
    Skoor nan *Geel*-yan, Peak of the Gullies
Bealach an Oir
    *Byal*ach an *Oa*-ir, Pass of Gold (from Gaelic Or) or Pass of the Shore
    or Boundary (from Gaelic Oir)
Bealach an Fhuarain
    *Byal*ach an *Oo*-arin, Pass of the Spring
Coire Dubh
    Corra Doo, Black Corrie
Allt Slugan a' Choilich
    Owlt *Slook*an a *Chull*ich, Stream of the Cockerel's Gullet

Climbing on the wild and mysterious island of Rum is an exercise in logistics and commitment, yet this book would be incomplete without at least one route across its rugged peaks. Before it became a National Nature Reserve, in 1957, access to the 'forbidden island' was discouraged by the owners, and even today authorisation to climb must be obtained from the Nature Conservancy (12 Hope Terrace, Edinburgh; 031–447–4784). An overnight stay will be required (hotel accommodation or camping) and all provisions must be carried in.

There is much to see on the island, notably the great sea cliffs and stacks and the mountains themselves, the Cuillin of Rum, which form the shape of a question mark in the southern half of the island. They are certainly 'one heap of rude mountains', as MacCulloch described them in

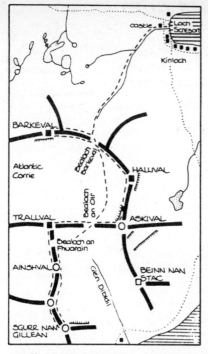

1824. Their traverse is the best route in the islands outside Skye, with unforgettable views and situations and many sections of exciting scrambling on mostly excellent rock closely related to Sky gabbro.

Begin at Kinloch and take the path up the left bank of the Allt Slugan a Choilich into Coire Dubh, from where the Bealach Barkeval is easily reached. Climb Barkeval for the view of northern Rum and the main ridge, then return to the bealach and climb Hallival. Beyond Hallival the ridge narrows to a sharp rocky arete leading to Askival, Rum's highest peak. Askival's north ridge is the sharpest of the day and provides the most spectacular scrambling, although the only real difficulty is the steep step of the so-called Askival Pinnacle, which can be bypassed on the left.

From Askival, the main ridge turns west for a long descent to the Bealach an Oir and reascent to the twin tops of Trallval, the scramble over the airy summit ridge connecting them requiring care. Another long descent to the Bealach an Fhuarain separates you from the last major ascent of the day, the intimidating north ridge of Ainshval. The rock here is quartzite, loose and greasy when wet, and care is required, but on closer acquaintance all difficulties are avoidable. The final section of ridge over a subsidiary top to Sgurr nan Gillean is relatively straightforward, and this last summit of the day makes a fitting finish to the traverse, for before you the ground drops away steeply and ahead lies only the sea.

The easiest return route is to redescend to the Bealach an Fhuarain and contour the slopes of Trallval to the Bealach an Oir. From here descend slightly and traverse beneath Askival and Hallival around the head of the Atlantic Corrie to reach the Bealach Barkeval and the route of ascent.

Route 92: **BRUACH NA FRITHE (SKYE)**

OS MAP: 32
GR: 480298
Distance: 8½ miles (14 km)
Ascent: 990 m (3,250 ft)
Time: 7 hr

	1	2	3	4	5
Grade			●		
Terrain				●	
Navigation					●
Seriousness					●

Assessment: one of the easiest ascents on the main Cuillin ridge, but of no less character for all that and passing through some stunning rock scenery.
Seasonal notes: a major winter mountaineering expedition.

Bruach na Frithe (958 m, 3,143 ft)
  Broo-ach na *Free*-ha, Slope of the Forest
Bealach a' Mhaim (346 m, 1,134 ft)
  *Byal*ach a *Va*-im, Pass of the Moor
Bealach nan Lice (c885 m, c2,900 ft)
  *Byal*ach nan *Leek*a, Pass of the Slabs
Sgurr a' Fionn Choire* (935 m, 3,067 ft)
  Skoor a Fyoon Chorra, Peak of the Fair Corrie
Sgurr a' Bhasteir (900 m, 2,952 ft)
  Skoor a *Vash*-tyir, Peak of the Executioner
Am Basteir (936 m, 3,070 ft)
  Am *Bash*-tyir, The Executioner

Few mountain ranges attract as much devotion as the Cuillin of Skye. There is something about the nature of the rough gabbro peaks, the ambience of their setting above the blue expanse of the Sea of the Hebrides and the quality of the light suffusing them that attracts the visitor again and again. They are scramblers' mountains supreme. For 7 miles (11 km) between Glen Sligachan and Glen Brittle the main Cuillin ridge presents a twisting arete of naked rock, sharp and pinnacled, hollowed out by idyllic corries, never dipping below 2,500 ft (760 m) and containing 14 peaks over 3,000 ft (914 m). Many sections of the ridge are the preserve of the rock climber, and in adverse weather the compass-deflecting properties of the rock and the complexity of the rock architecture should deter the uninitiated from venturing high. But on a fine summer's day there is nothing to match the magic of the Cuillin, and the five routes recommended in this book (routes 92–6, in order of increasing difficulty) will provide memories for a lifetime.

The easiest route (some would say the only easy route) in the Cuillin is the ascent of Bruach na Frithe from Sligachan. It requires no real scrambling but passes through some spectacular rock scenery and is probably the best viewpoint on the ridge. Begin 700 m from Sligachan Hotel on the A863 Dunvegan road and take the path past Alltdearg House

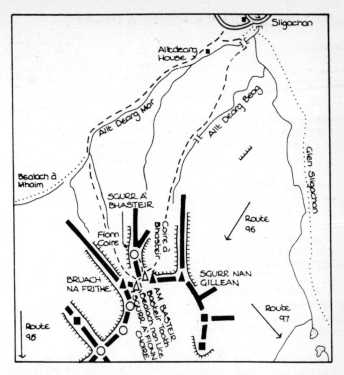

up the left bank of the Allt Dearg Mór. The path crosses the Bealach a'
Mhaim to Glen Brittle, and from the bealach a path climbs Bruach na
Frithe's north-west ridge. More interestingly, leave the path before
reaching the bealach at the confluence of the Allt Dearg Mór and the burn
coming down from Fionn Coire, and climb easy ground into this untypical
Cuillin corrie, carpeted with grass.

The route out of the corrie is cairned and debouches onto the ridge at
the Bealach nan Lice, from where it is a short stroll over Sgurr a' Fionn
Choire to Bruach na Frithe. Return to the Bealach nan Lice and wander
out along the south ridge of Sgurr a' Bhasteir to study the Pinnacle Ridge
of Sgurr nan Gillean and the spectacular wedge of rock known as the
Basteir Tooth below Am Basteir. For a descent in complete contrast to the
approach route, return to the junction with the main ridge and descend
scree slopes into secluded Coire a' Bhasteir. Pick up a cairned route to the
left of and well above the rocky gorge of the Allt Dearg Beag; this leads
out of the corrie and passes some idyllic pools on its way back across the
moor to Sligachan.

205

Route 93: **SGURR DEARG (SKYE)**

OS MAP: 32
GR: 414205
Distance: 5 miles (8 km)
Ascent: 990 m (3,250 ft)
Time: 6 hr

	1	2	3	4	5
Grade				●	
Terrain					●
Navigation					●
Seriousness					●

Assessment: an essentially straightforward (though loose) scramble rendered exciting by sensational surroundings.

Seasonal notes: a major winter mountaineering expedition.

Sgurr Dearg (978 m, 3,208 ft)
    Skoor *Jerr*ak, Red Peak
Inaccessible Pinnacle* (986 m, 3,234 ft)
An Stac (953 m, 3,126 ft)
    An Stachk, The Stack
Sgurr Mhic Choinnich (948 m, 3,110 ft)
    Skoor Veechk *Choan*-yich, Mackenzie's Peak (after John Mackenzie,
    the famous Skye guide)
Sròn na Ciche* (859 m, 2,818 ft)
    Srawn na *Keech*a, Promontory of the Breast
Coire Lagan
    Corra *Lahk*an, Corrie of the Hollow
Loch an Fhir-bhallaich
    Loch an Eer *Vall*ich, Loch of the Spotted Man

'Inaccessible as it looks, this pinnacle may be surmounted by experienced climbers who love to do what no one else has done and to boast thereof for ever after.'

J.A. MACCULLOCH on the Inaccessible Pinnacle (*The Misty Isle of Skye*, 1905)

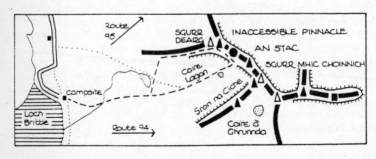

The round of Coire Lagan is a long-standing scrambler's test piece. It develops into what is technically a rock climb, but the ascent of Sgurr Dearg, which begins the round, has no great difficulty, providing a route through probably the most spectacular situations in a mountain range full of spectacular situations.

From Glen Brittle campsite take the well worn Coire Lagan path that climbs the hillside behind the toilet block (beware of keeping too far to the right on the coastal path). The path contours right to a shallow ravine, then climbs unmistakably across the gently rising moorland towards Coire Lagan. Once beyond Loch an Fhir-bhallaich, leave the path and cut left up the broad stony lower slopes of Sgurr Dearg's west ridge. Higher up, the ridge narrows and provides an easy scramble to the sharp summit.

There can be few more dramatic mountain tops than that of Sgurr Dearg, for even higher looms the preposterous blade of rock known as the Inaccessible Pinnacle, the only Munro that requires a rock climb for its ascent. Its very presence is enough to give some people vertigo. The route onwards descends rough ground to the neck of rock between Sgurr Dearg and the 'In Pin', with vertiginous drops left to Coruisk, and contours round the base of the pinnacle on the right to the foot of its east ridge. Many backsides of breeches have been worn out here. From the foot of the east ridge a short detour should be made out to the summit of An Stac for the best view of the In Pin, then return and continue along the broad undercut shelf that traverses beneath the crest of An Stac. Take care to continue left round a corner (cairn), rather than right down some tempting scree, to reach the Bealach Coire Lagan.

The route onwards up Sgurr Mhic Choinnich along probably the sharpest crest in the Cuillin can be explored by those not of a nervous disposition, but the continuation to the Bealach Mhic Choinnich along the airy Collie's Ledge (a Moderate rock climb) is judged outside the scope of this book. From the Bealach Coire Lagan descend fast scree slopes (An Stac screes) to the heart of Coire Lagan and pause beside the lochan to admire the scale of your surroundings. The path down to Glen Brittle descends from the right-hand corner of the lochan beside boiler plate slabs, which lounge at the water's edge like enormous hippopotami. It is a pleasant descent across the moor, with the climber's Mecca of Sròn na Ciche cliffs to your left and in front of you the endless sea.

Route 94: **THE SOUTH CUILLIN RIDGE (SKYE)**

OS MAP: 32
GR: 414205
Distance: 9½ miles (15 km)
Ascent: 1,560 m (5,100 ft)
Time: 10 hr

	1	2	3	4	5
Grade				●	
Terrain					●
Navigation					●
Seriousness					●

Assessment: a long and magnificent scramble of ceaseless interest amidst unearthly rock scenery and hypnotic seaward views. (The scrambles up to the Cioch and up Sgurr Alasdair are Grade 5).
Seasonal notes: a major winter mountaineering expedition.

An Caisteal* (829 m, 2,719 ft)
   An *Cash*-tyal, The Castle
Sgurr nan Eag (924 m, 3,031 ft
   Skoor nan Aik, Notched Peak
Sgurr a' Choire Bhig* (875 m, 2,870 ft)
   Skoor a Chorra Veek, Peak of the Little Corrie
Gars-bheinn (895 m, 2,936 ft)
   Garsh-ven, Echoing Mountain
Sgurr Dubh na Da Bheinn* (938 m, 3,077 ft)
   Skoor *Doo* na *Dah Ven*, Black Peak of the Two Mountains
Sgurr Dubh Mór (944 m, 3,097 ft)
   Skoor Doo Moar, Big Black Peak
Sgurr Sgumain (947 m, 3,106 ft)
   Skoor, *Skoo*man, Mound Peak
Sgurr Alasdair (993 m, 3,257 ft)
   Skoor Alastir, Alexander's Peak (after Alexander Nicolson, who first climbed it in 1873)
Sgurr Thearlaich* (984 m, 3,228 ft)
   Skoor *Hyar*lach, Charles' Peak (after Charles Pilkington, who was the first to climb the Inaccessible Pinnacle, with his brother Lawrence, in 1880)
The Cioch*
   The *Kee*-och, The Breast
Coir a' Ghrunnda
   Corr a *Ghrunn*da, The Floored Corrie

There are few routes in Scotland that offer the mountain walker as much constant interest, satisfaction and exhilaration as the South Cuillin Ridge, which never becomes tedious no matter how often repeated over the years. Begin at Glen Brittle campsite on the Coire Lagan path. At the ravine after ½ mile (1 km) cross the burn, turn immediately left along the far

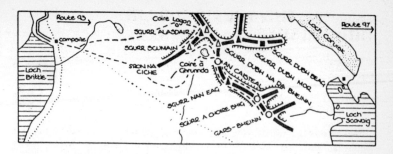

bank and follow a path that climbs diagonally around the south-west slopes of Sròn na Ciche into Coir a' Ghrunnda. The path keeps high above the Allt Coir a' Ghrunnda, but you may wish to explore the fantastic boiler plate slabs in the centre of the corrie and scramble up from there. The skyline in front of you is the lip of the upper corrie, behind which lies one of those idyllic Cuillin lochans whose beckoning waters on a hot day end many a stirring plan.

Gain the main ridge by scrambling up the staircase of huge boulders to the left of the rock bastion of An Caisteal at the back of the corrie. The rock here is so sharp and pitted that the climbing potential of gabbro will soon become painfully obvious. The ridge is reached through a rock window, beyond which a path leads round the far side of An Caisteal to the summit of Sgurr nan Eag. A sharp descent leads on across the shattered quartzite top of Sgurr a' Choire Bhig to Garsbheinn at the end of the main ridge, providing wonderfully airy ridge walking.

Returning from Gars-bheinn, continue around Coir a' Ghrunnda, behind An Caisteal once more, contouring beneath the crags of Sgurr Alasdair to Bealach Coire a' Ghrunnda. En route you may wish to climb Sgurr Dubh na Da Bheinn and Sgurr Dubh Mór. From the bealach two worthwhile possibilities present themselves. The shortest and easiest is the descent to the Coire Lagan path beneath the awesome cliffs of Sròn na Ciche, pausing at a jumble of huge boulders to view the famous Cioch (an improbable knob of rock, which can be reached by a hard scramble left up a sloping terrace).

Probably more rewarding, however, is the ascent of Sgurr Sgumain and Sgurr Alasdair, from where the renowned stone shoot (descending from the Alasdair-Thearlaich bealach) provides an easy descent into Coire Lagan and the path back to Glen Brittle. This alternative involves much harder scrambling and routefinding, especially at the Bad Step just above the foot of the ridge to Sgurr Alasdair (which can be bypassed on the right, using a small chimney), but what better way to end a magnificent day than atop the Cuillin's highest peak?

Route 95: **THE COIRE A' GHREADAIDH SKYLINE (SKYE)**

OS MAP: 32
GR: 410225
Distance: 6 miles (10 km)
Ascent: 1,340 m (4,400 ft)
Time: 8½ hr

	1	2	3	4	5
Grade					●
Terrain					●
Navigation					●
Seriousness					●

Assessment: a long sporting scramble with some memorable situations.
Seasonal notes: a major winter mountaineering expedition.

Sgurr Thuilm (879 m, 2,883 ft)
  Skoor *Hool*am, Peak of the Knoll or Holm
Sgurr a' Mhadaidh (918 m, 3,011 ft)
  Skoor a Vahty, Peak of the Foxes
An Dorus (847 m, 2,778 ft)
  An *Dorr*us, The Door
Sgurr a' Ghreadaidh (973 m, 3,192 ft)
  Skoor a Gretta, Peak of the Clear Waters
Sgurr Thormaid* (927 m, 3,041 ft)
  Skoor *Hurr*amitch, Norman's Peak (after Norman Collie, the great
  Cuillin pioneer and discoverer of the Cioch)
Sgurr na Banachdich (965 m, 3,165 ft)
  Skoor na *Ban*achdich, Milkmaid's Peak or Smallpox Peak
Sgurr nan Gobhar (631 m, 2,070 ft)
  Skoor nan *Goe*-ar, Goat Peak

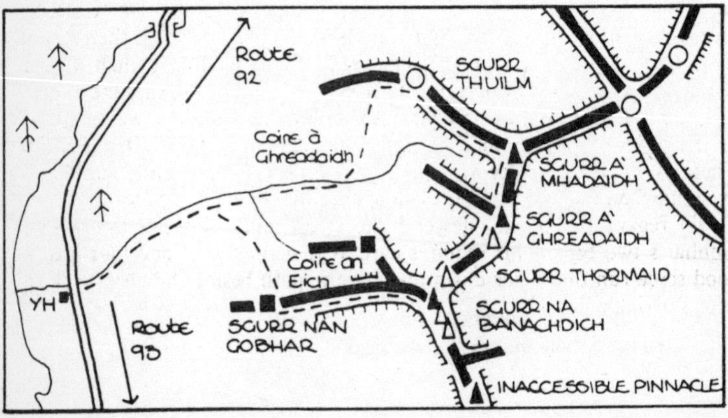

The meaning of the name Cuillin is obscure; possibilities include High Rocks (from Norse Kjölen), Holly (from Gaelic Cuilion) and Worthless (from Celtic). Despite what tourist guides say, it is unlikely that the range is named after Prince Cuchullin of Antrim.

Coire a' Ghreadaidh is less immediately dramatic than most Cuillin corries as it is more open and has less clean climbing rock than elsewhere, but for the walker its attractions are many. The two enclosing ridges, which project westwards to Sgurr Thuilm and Sgurr nan Gobhar, are the longest on this side of the Cuillin and provide a high-level scramble around the corrie that is both long and exciting.

Begin at the youth hostel in Glen Brittle and take the path up the left bank of the burn past innumerable waterfalls, pools and gorges. At the burn coming down from Coir an Eich the path veers right to Sgurr na Banachdich; leave it at this point and continue up beside the river to a series of small cascades. This is a marvellous spot, especially when baked by the sun's rays reflecting off the corrie walls; in the heat of the day it may be difficult to get beyond here, for the next part of the ascent requires determination. Cross the burn and climb directly up steep slopes of grass and scree to the summit of Sgurr Thuilm, contouring left onto the west ridge if the going gets too wearisome.

The circuit of the corrie now begins, with a descent of the gentle south-east ridge to where it abuts sharply against the side of Sgurr a' Mhadaidh. The scramble up Sgurr a' Mhadaidh is hard and exposed, but if the route onward seems suicidal you have probably strayed too far to the left. If it all becomes too much, redescend to the foot of the scramble and traverse beneath the cliffs of Sgurr a' Mhadaidh to the prominent scree gully (An Dorus) between Sgurr a' Mhadaidh and Sgurr a' Ghreadaidh, and scramble to the summit from there.

Beyond An Dorus the ridge continues narrow and exciting, full of absorbing scrambling which never becomes exceptionally difficult although it is often exposed. Sgurr a' Ghreadaidh is reached, then Sgurr Thormaid with its three 'teeth', and finally Sgurr na Banachdich. Leave the main ridge here and descend stony slopes onto the long southern arm of Coire a' Ghreadaidh, where pleasant scrambling and ridge walking lead to the grass-topped sentinel of Sgurr nan Gobhar above Glen Brittle. There is no better place to end a day, especially late on a summer's evening when the views and the colours are hypnotic.

To regain the corrie, descend the steep gully between Sgurr nan Gobhar's two tops. This requires care at first, but soon develops into a good scree run that leads down towards the path beside the burn back to your starting point.

Route 96: **SGURR NAN GILLEAN (SKYE)**

OS MAP: 32
GR: 485298
Distance: 7 miles (11 km)
Ascent: 1,010 m (3,300 ft)
Time: 6½ hr

	1	2	3	4	5
Grade					●
Terrain				●	
Navigation					●
Seriousness					●

Assessment: a hard and exposed final scramble, but well worth the attempt for the fine situations of the approach route.
Seasonal notes: a major winter mountaineering expedition.

Sgurr nan Gillean (965 m, 3,165 ft)
    Skoor nan *Geel*-yan, Peak of the Gullies
Nead na h-Iolaire
    Nyed na *Hill*era, Eagle's Nest
Coire Riabhach*
    Corra *Ree*-ach, Brindled Corrie
Allt Dearg Mór (Beag)
    Owlt *Jerr*ak Moar (Bake), Big (Little) Red Stream

No one could fail to be thrilled by the first view of the Cuillin from Sligachan, the great rock peaks soaring above the moorland with the steep tapering cone of Sgurr nan Gillean prominent to the left. For the non-climber, the only feasible route to the summit of Sgurr nan Gillean is the misleadingly named Tourist Route, and even this is an exposed scramble in its final stages. The ascent has much to recommend it, however, even should you decide to leave the last few metres for another day.

Begin opposite Sligachan Hotel on the Allt Dearg Mór path. Cross the river (bridge) a few hundred metres upstream and take the path across the moor to the Allt Dearg Beag. At a bridge the path forks; the right branch continues up into Coire a' Bhasteir (route 92). Take the left branch that crosses the bridge, climbs over the small plateau to the right of the cliffs of Nead na h-Iolaire and descends slightly into Coire Riabhach, keeping well above the lochan. From the corrie, cairns mark the route up scree and boulders to the south-east ridge, and here the excitement begins as the airy crest is followed up to the summit platform. Should you decide, in your wisdom, that the summit rocks are for Munro baggers only, console yourself with the knowledge that Sgurr nan Gillean was considered unclimbable until its first ascent in 1836. There is but one route down—the way you came up.

212

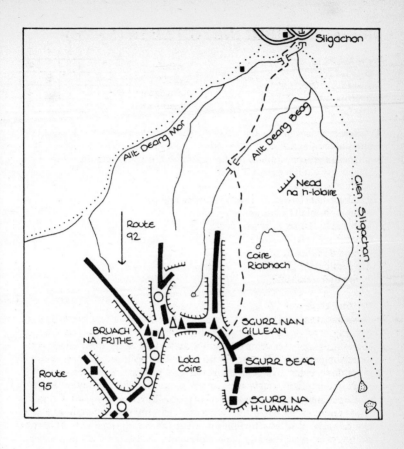

Route 97: **BLA BHEINN (SKYE)**

OS MAP: 32
GR: 545172
Distance: 8 miles (13 km)
Ascent: 1,100 m (3,600 ft)
Time: 6¹/₂ hr

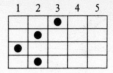

	1	2	3	4	5
Grade			●		
Terrain		●			
Navigation	●				
Seriousness		●			

Assessment: an untypically easy Cuillin ascent with typically superb views.
Seasonal notes: in rare winter conditions, this route remains probably the only easy Cuillin ascent.

Bla Bheinn (928 m, 3,044 ft) also written Blaven
    Blah-ven, Blue Mountain
Clach Glas★ (789 m, 2,588 ft)
    Clach Glass, Grey Stone
Strath na Creitheach
    Stra na *Cre*-hach, Valley of the Brushwood
Abhainn nan Leac
    *Av*in nan Lyechk, River of Slabs
Loch Coruisk
    Lock Coroosk, Loch of the Corrie of Water (from Gaelic Coir' Uisg)

Bla Bheinn is separated from the main Cuillin ridge by the deep troughs of Glen Sligachan and Strath na Creitheach. When climbed in conjunction with the main ridge it forms the Greater Cuillin Traverse, a major test of mountaineering skill and fitness involving over 4,000 m (13,000 ft) of ascent. It exhibits all the character of a typical Cuillin peak and in addition gains from its isolation, offering superb views of the main ridge. The complete traverse of Bla Bheinn and its neighbouring rock tower Clach Glas is Alpine in nature and is no place for walkers, but the south ridge provides a unique Cuillin ascent that is little more than a pleasant walk.

    Alexander Nicolson, that renowned pioneer explorer of the Cuillin, considered Bla Bheinn the finest mountain in Skye, and no finer case for this proposition could be made than the famous view of it across Loch Slapin from the A881 Broadford–Elgol road. The route to the foot of the south ridge, begins close to Loch Slapin, 400 m south of Kilmarie, where a Land Rover track leaves the road and crosses the shallow bealach of Am Mam (The Moor) south of Bla Bheinn to Camasunary on Loch Scavaig. This track, built by the army without consultation with the mountain rescue authorities to facilitate mountain rescue from Coruisk, was once a conservation *cause célèbre* as the existing path was perfectly adequate. Fortunately, the track got no further than Camasunary, and bridges built there and at Scavaig were soon washed away.

    Beyond Am Mam the gentle south ridge comes into view, rising evenly

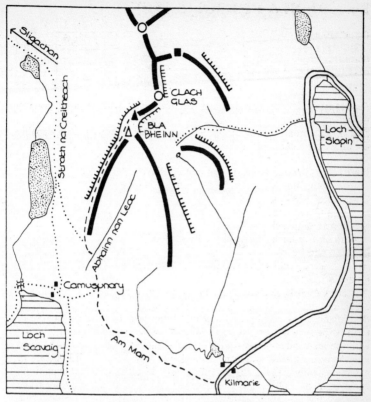

from seashore to mountain top. At a hairpin bend where the Land Rover track turns back on itself to descend to Camasunary the old path goes straight on, crossing the Abhainn nan Leac and continuing between Bla Bheinn and the main Cuillin ridge to Sligachan. Follow the path as far as the foot of the south ridge, then head directly up the ridge. It is no more than a long walk, described as 'delightfully easy' by an early guidebook, with interest maintained by the constantly expanding views. The summit has two tops of which that to the north is the higher; the traverse between the two involves some elementary handwork.

Descend by the same route. If time and fitness allow, it is worth following the coastal path round from Camasunary to the mountain fastness of Loch Coruisk, superbly situated in the middle of the Cuillin horseshoe. It was here that, among others, Sir Walter Scott found inspiration for his poetry and Turner for his painting. The path is straightforward, apart from the puzzling but ultimately easily negotiable Bad Step, and provides one of the most magnificent coastal walks in Britain.

215

Route 98: **THE STORR (SKYE)**

OS MAP: 23
GR: 509529
Distance: 3¹/₂ miles (6 km)
Ascent: 580 m (1,900 ft)
Time: 4 hr

	1	2	3	4	5
Grade		●			
Terrain			●		
Navigation			●		
Seriousness			●		

Assessment: a disturbing stroll among the weird rock pinnacles of The Sanctuary.
Seasonal notes: the steep ascent to and descent from the summit plateau require care under snow.

The Storr (719 m, 2,358 ft)
    from the Norse Staur, meaning Pillar or Stake
Corrie Faoin
    Corrie *Fœ*-in, Empty Corrie
Coire Scamadal
    Corrie of the Short Valley
Loch Leathan
    Loch *Lye*-han, Broad Loch

'Sign of life you perceive none; in all that wide landscape you might be the sole survivor; silence and immensity fill the soul, and the still small voice speaks and holds you spellbound.'

J.A. MACCULLOCH (*The Misty Isle of Skye*, 1905)

Note for lovers of weird pinnacles: the Quiraing and Leac nan Fionn, smaller hills to the north of the Storr, have collections of pinnacles rivalling those of The Sanctuary.

When the Cuillin are wrapped in mist, there is time to explore the many other delights of Skye, and high on this list must be The Storr, the highest hill in the Trotternish peninsula. The Storr's flat-topped summit and crumbling crags could not be in greater contrast to the Cuillin, yet an ascent via the remarkable Sanctuary is a fascinating experience.

Begin at the foot of The Storr, at the car park north of Loch Leathan on the A855 north of Portree. Take the forest path that climbs up boggy ground into the eerie Sanctuary, a basin containing a collection of weird and wonderful pinnacles. The shattered Needle and the teetering Old Man, 50 m (160 ft) high and undercut all around, are only two of the monoliths that give the place the aura of a prehistoric site.

Behind The Sanctuary rises 200 m (600 ft) of rotten crag. Gain the summit plateau by climbing the steep grass and scree slope left of the cliffs at the back of Coire Faoin, then wander along the cliff edge to the

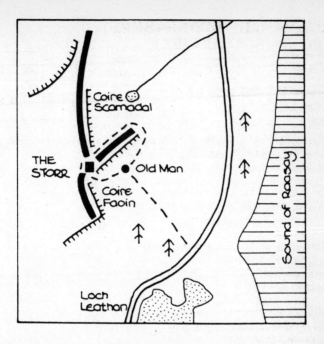

summit, with grand views of Raasay and south across Loch Leathan to the Cuillin. A short distance beyond the summit a cairn marks the start of the descent route, a grassy corridor through the small rock band that guards the plateau rim to the north. This leads down into a shallow basin above the cliffs of Coire Scamadal. At the low point of the basin, at the very edge of the cliffs, a path goes right, outflanking the cliffs of The Storr and leading back into The Sanctuary.

Route 99: **THE BEINN MHÓR GROUP (SOUTH UIST)**

OS MAP: 22
GR: 768346
Distance: 10¹/₂ miles (17 km)
Ascent: 1,170 m (3,850 ft)
Time: 8 hr

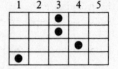

	1	2	3	4	5
Grade			●		
Terrain			●		
Navigation				●	
Seriousness	●				

Assessment: an enjoyable Hebridean stravaig with scrambling opportunities on a fine high-level ridge.
Seasonal notes: Beinn Mhór's summit ridge may provide some interesting, though rarely unavoidable, winter problems.

Beinn Mhór (620 m, 2,034 ft)
    Ben Voar, Big Mountain
Ben Corodale (527 m, 1,729 ft)
    Mountain of the Round Valley (poss)
Hecla (606 m, 1,988 ft)
    The Shroud
Maola Breac
    *Mæl*a Brechk, Speckled Hill
Abhainn Roag
    Avin Roe-ak, River of Roe Bay

South Uist is an island with two distinct sides, its flat east coast fringed by luxurious shell-sand beaches, its west coast dotted with peaks rising directly out of the sea. Only Beinn Mhór breaks 2,000 ft (610 m), but the round of the whole Beinn Mhór group, including Ben Corodale and Hecla,

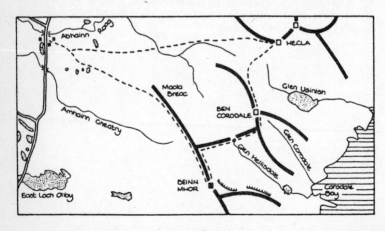

requires twice this amount of ascent and includes a sharp ridge walk above superlative seascapes.

Begin on the A865 at the first passing place south of the bridge over the Abhainn Roag. Follow a Land Rover track up onto the moor, then make for the shoulder of Maola Breac across surprisingly dry but tiring terrain. Continue up the shoulder of Beinn Mhór to reach the north-west top, beyond which an attractive narrow $1/2$ mile (1 km) long ridge, mainly grassy but with rocky bumps, which require handwork if the crest is adhered to, leads to the main summit. The traverse of the ridge gains from its setting; on your left is remote Corodale Bay where Prince Charlie found brief respite from his pursuers, and all around islands dot the horizon.

Returning to the north-west top, the completion of the round requires long descents and reascents, firstly over the Bealach Hellisdale to Ben Corodale, whose castellated summit sports a rim of crags that must be circumvented, then down to a low bealach before the final steep ascent of Hecla's south face. To return to your starting point, descend Hecla's west ridge and walk back across the moor. Care is required in adverse weather as the moor is featureless and the compass is unreliable, but note that all rivers drain into the Abhainn Roag.

Route 100: **CLISHAM (HARRIS)**

OS MAP: 13 or 14
GR: 183099
Distance: 8½ miles (14 km)
Ascent: 1,050 m (3,450 ft)
Time: 6½ hr

	1	2	3	4	5
Grade				●	
Terrain				●	
Navigation				●	
Seriousness			●		

Assessment: a magnificent ramble and scramble around a narrow ridge in Hebridean surroundings.

Seasonal notes: in winter, the ascent of Clisham's steep north-east face requires care. Several sections of the ridge around Glen Scaladale may give problems under snow, but all difficulties should be avoidable.

Clisham (799 m, 2,621 ft)
  obscure
Tomnaval (552 m, 1,811 ft)
  Knoll of the Hill (from Gaelic Tom na Mheall, pron Towm na Vyowl)
Mulla-fo-dheas (743 m, 2,437 ft)
  Mulla foe Yaiss, Summit to the South
Mulla-fo-thuath (c700 m, c2,300 ft)
  Mulla foe *Oo*-a, Summit to the North
Mullach an Langa (614 m, 2,014 ft)
  Summit of the Heather
Sgurr Scaladale
  Peak of the Valley of Shielings
Creag Mo
  Craig Maw, Bigger Crag (poss)

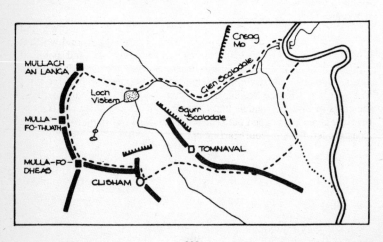

The island of Harris and Lewis is Scotland's largest island and appropriately contains the highest summit in the Outer Hebrides—Clisham, situated in the rugged mountain barrier that separates the rocky terrain of Harris from the peat moors of Lewis. It is rough, remote country with a distinctly un-Scottish flavour, for the landscape is barren and lonely and the hill names have a strong Norse influence.

In the long glens that penetrate the mountains there is much to explore, notably the tremendous overhangs of Strone Ulladale, the largest in Britain, and the many crags and lochans dotting the exotic-sounding mountains. Clisham, fittingly, provides the finest walking route; the traverse of the narrow ridges that connect it to its northern outliers around Glen Scaladale provides a pleasant scramble as well as a good introduction to Harris topography.

Begin at the bridge over the Scaladale River ½ mile (1 km) south of Ardvourlie Castle on the A859 Tarbert-Stornaway road. Walk south along the road for 500 m to pick up the obvious path crossing the hillside east of Tomnaval. Follow the path to its high point at the third of three lochans, then take to the gentle ridge rising to Tomnaval. In good weather it is best to contour left of Tomnaval's summit to avoid the 80 m (250 ft) descent to the saddle that separates it from Clisham. From the saddle a steep boulder-strewn ascent of Clisham's north-east face breaches a rim of broken crags and deposits you abruptly onto the narrow summit ridge.

The view is of Hebridean splendour, encompassing the whole of Harris and Lewis, Skye, the west coast of the mainland and, on a good day, the remote outpost of St Kilda 60 miles (100 km) to the west. Amidst this attractive panorama the skyline of Glen Scaladale beckons invitingly. From the north-west end of Clisham's summit ridge, boulder-hop down the broad western slopes to a bealach and climb the narrow east ridge of Mulla-fo-dheas. The first half of the ascent is on grass, then beyond a dip it becomes rocky and provides some easy scrambling.

At Mulla-fo-dheas the ridge turns north and descends narrowly and interestingly along a cliff edge towards Mulla-fo-thuath, beyond which it broadens over awkward boulders. Continue out to the end point of Mullach an Langa for the view northwards over the vast flatlands of Lewis, then descend easy-angled slopes to Glen Scaladale. Aim for Loch Vistem and follow the Scaladale river down over rough ground between the crags of Sgurr Scaladale and Creag Mo. When a loch on the right of the river is reached a good path (no longer marked on OS map) leads back along the left bank to your starting point.

Index of Mountains